J. B. (James Bowling) Mozley

The Theory of Development

A Criticism of Dr. Newman's Essay on the Development of Christian...

J. B. (James Bowling) Mozley

The Theory of Development
A Criticism of Dr. Newman's Essay on the Development of Christian...

ISBN/EAN: 9783337163778

Printed in Europe, USA, Canada, Australia, Japan

Cover: Foto ©Thomas Meinert / pixelio.de

More available books at **www.hansebooks.com**

THE
THEORY OF DEVELOPMENT

A CRITICISM OF DR. NEWMAN'S ESSAY ON THE DEVELOPMENT OF CHRISTIAN DOCTRINE

REPRINTED FROM 'THE CHRISTIAN REMEMBRANCER,'
JANUARY 1847

BY

J. B. MOZLEY, D.D.

LATE CANON OF CHRIST CHURCH, AND REGIUS PROFESSOR OF DIVINITY
IN THE UNIVERSITY OF OXFORD.

RIVINGTONS

London, Oxford, and Cambridge

MDCCCLXXVIII

ADVERTISEMENT.

THE following Article is reprinted at the call of persons well qualified to estimate its value as a contribution to the controversy of the present day.

The references to the work reviewed are necessarily made from the original edition; but the passages quoted do not stand in the same relative positions in the edition of 1878, in the preface to which the author explains that "various alterations have been made in the arrangement of its separate parts, and some, not indeed in its matter, but in its text."

SUMMARY OF CONTENTS.

RESPECTIVE replies of Dr. Moberly, Mr. Allies, and Mr. Palmer, 1; The author selects the argumentative part of the Essay under review, 2.

Lines of thought suggested by the idea of Development, 3; That of Growth, 4; That of Corruption, 5. Corruption acts by abuse as well as by extinction, 6; Examples of this abuse, 8; The gift of Illustration, 9; Excesses of the Imaginative Faculty, 10; Schools of Philosophy, 12; National characteristics, 13; Christian sects exhibit exaggerated forms of Development, 13; The Jesuits, 14. Examples of the corruption of exaggeration, 15; Aristotle; Practical Morality a complex balanced thing, 16; In Morals we cannot develop mathematically, 18; Sense in which Christianity was to develop, 19; Obvious forms of Development in its internal temper, 20; And in the department of Doctrine, 20; Doctrine of the Intermediate State, 21; Doctrine of Purgatory, 24; Relation of the living towards departed Saints, 26; Prayers to the Saints, 27; The honour of the Blessed Virgin, 27; Transubstantiation, 28. Our Church's charge against Rome is exaggeration, 30; Tendency of Protestantism is to decay, 30; Dr. Newman's definition of Corruption, 31; Analogies drawn from nature, 32; The fact of exaggerated Development admitted, but not recognised in his argument, 34; The hiatus illustrated from Bocardo, 39; Dr. Newman's tests of true Development, 40; The test of logical sequence, 41; The region of Logic a plain one where a thorough agreement as to premisses exists, but where it attempts discovery it loses this command, 41; In the first centuries each sect appealed to Logic, 42; To make Logic infallible, we must have infallible Logicians, 43; The Church's Creed kept a middle course, 44; Answer to the argument that the Doctrine of Purgatory is contained in that of Repentance, 45; And that Scripture represents the Day of Judgment as near, 49; Answer to the argument that Scripture contemplates Christians as sinless, 50; The New Testament throws a peaceful character on the state of good Christian souls departed; The Doctrine of Purgatory a contrary one, 52.

Summary of Contents.

The Cultus of the Virgin Mary, 53; Dr. Newman's argumentative position grounded on the Arian Controversy, 56; His use of the Arian Hypothesis, 65; His definition of Idolatry, 66; Idol worshipper of the Old Testament, 68; Idea of a Secondary Divinity, 73.

The Nicene Council; St. Athanasius's charge against the Arians, 74; St. Ambrose, St. Hilary, St. Cyril, Faustinus, 75; Distinction drawn by the Arians, 76; Summing up of the two views, 77; Athanasius's condemnation of the Arian position, 80; Dr. Newman's appeal to system, 81; Later Roman Doctrines, 82; Ultimate point of his argument the existence of an infallible guide; Papal Infallibility keystone of his argument, 83.

The claim of Infallibility more invidious than the mere assertion of the truth of certain Developments, 83; Where Revelation has left a blank the Mind naturally forms conjectures; Bishop Andrewes on Purgatory, 84; Dr. Newman's argument for Papal Infallibility, 85; Discussed, 87-95. The Argument of Analogy, 96; Bishop Butler claimed as a sympathiser with the Doctrine of Development, 96; This answered by Butler's argument against presumptions concerning Revelation; Extract given, 99; Reply to the distinction drawn between the hypothesis of a Revelation and an existing Revelation, 102; Supposed argument between a Sceptic and Bishop Butler, 106; Dr. Newman questions the Argument from Analogy on the point of anticipating a Revelation, 109; He draws a distinction between the facts of Revelation and its principles, 112; Butler's argument from our Ignorance, 113. Concluding remarks on Dr. Newman's whole mode of treating the Argument of Analogy, 114; The hypothesis of a standing Revelation cannot afford to make any large established idea in the earthly Church erroneous, 117; A Perfectionist view of the progress of Truth in the Christian world thus established, 119; The Argument of Analogy, on the other hand, gives a ground on which a more qualified system erects itself, 119. The popular Cultus of the Virgin, 121. Answer to the difficulty how God should permit holy men to think erroneously, 122; According to Analogy an original Creed is thrown into the world of human intelligence and exposed to the chance of human discolourment, the substantial Creed remaining throughout, 124.

M. de Maistre's argument of simple Church Government, 125. After drawing out his Theory for a standing Revelation, Dr. Newman joins on the subordinate one, the simple Monarchical Argument, 128; Answer; the idea of Unity does not imply a particular local centre of Unity, 129; Line of the *reductio ad absurdum* argument, 130;

The Eastern Church an answer to the assertion that whenever the Pope has been renounced, decay and division have been the consequence, 133; The line towards the Greek Church, 134; The Greek Church has produced great Spiritual deeds, 136; The dogmatic Creed of the Eastern Christian of this day the Creed of St. Basil and St. Chrysostom, 137; At the Council of Florence the Church of Rome was willing to receive the whole body of Eastern Canonised Saints, 139; Eastern sanctity presents some barbarian features to European eyes, 141; The Historical Argument for the Papacy regarded by Dr. Newman as secondary; not entered into here, 142.

Assertion that the Nicene Creed is a Development, 143; Different senses of Development, 144; Cases of explanatory Development; Of an arguer having to maintain a point against a circle of opponents, 145; Case of legal amplification, 145. Another form of Development positive increase of substance, as of the seed into a plant, 146; In growth it is the ultimate formation which is the substance of the thing growing, 147; All allow that Christian fundamental truth has been explained, 147; Example of explanation from Aquinas on the Doctrine of the Incarnation, 148. The parallel drawn between the Roman Doctrinal Developments and the Doctrinal Development at Nicæa, 150; The Vincentian rule, 152. "Christianity came into the world an idea," 153; Parallel between the Dogmatic Principle in the history of Christianity, and Conscience in the individual mind, 154; Answer to the analogy drawn between the Mosaic and the Christian Dispensation, 155; This view of Development has weight with a certain order of mind, 157.

A right side and a wrong to love of progress, 157. Abbot Joachim's opinion on the unity of God condemned by the Council of Lateran; Answer to the argument derived from it, 160. The word Homoousion, 163; The Fathers at the Nicene Council were taunted by the Arians for their appeal to the old doctrine, 166; The ante-Nicene Documents, 167; Bishop Bull's Answer to Petavius's doubts of their orthodoxy, 168; Dr. Newman's comments upon it, 169; The Negative ground of insufficiency, 173; On Discrepancies of Language, 174; St. Athanasius's vindication of the Antiochene Fathers in their rejection of the word Homoousion, 178; Paul of Samosata, 178; Particular phrases used in earlier times by St. Ignatius, St. Justin, St. Clement, etc.; Answers to objections, 181; View held by some early Fathers of the λόγος ἐνδιάθετος and λόγος προφορικὸς; Dr. Newman's explanation, 184; Supposed answer of the early Fathers to modern interpreters; Historical testimony, 188; Full belief of the Nicene Church that its belief had been the doctrine of the ante-Nicene up to the commencement of Christianity, 190 ; Extract from the Essay, with sayings of the Nicene Fathers, 192 ; Contradiction sharpens our logical view of truth, 195.

Summing up of the argument that Nicene truth was not a Development in the sense asserted, 196 ; Extract from Dr. Newman's Roman Catholic opponent, writing in Brownson's *Quarterly Review*, 200 ; Ambiguity in his meaning of the word Development, 203 ; His distinction between explicit and implicit knowledge, 204 ; In multitudes of cases implicit knowledge no knowledge at all, 204 ; The result of the argumentative parallel between Nicene Development and Roman, 207 ; Dr. Newman gives the Roman Church an hypothesis which is to account for her difficulties, 210 ; Extracts from Dr. Wiseman and Perrone counter to this hypothesis, 212 ; Again from Brownson's *Quarterly*, 215 ; In comparing the two hypotheses put forward by Rome, a member of the English Church has the same answer to them both, 218 ; What is Dr. Newman's theory? 222 ; Brownson's *Quarterly* on the words, "Christianity came into the world an idea," 223.

NEWMAN ON DEVELOPMENT.*

BEFORE entering upon an examination of this book we have to express our thanks, and to own our obligations, to the writers of various replies to it, the titles of which we have prefixed. To the replies of Dr. Moberly,

* 1. *An Essay on the Development of Christian Doctrine.* By JOHN HENRY NEWMAN, Author of Lectures on the Prophetical Office of the Church. London, 1845.

2. *The Sayings of the great Forty Days between the Resurrection and Ascension, regarded as the outlines of the kingdom of God; in Five Discourses; with an Examination of Mr. Newman's Theory of Development.* By GEORGE MOBERLY, D.C.L., Headmaster of Winchester College. Second Edition. London, 1846.

3. *The Doctrine of Development and Conscience, considered in relation to the Evidences of Christianity, and of the Catholic System.* By the Rev. WILLIAM PALMER, M.A., of Worcester College, Oxford. London, 1846.

4. *The Church of England cleared from the Charge of Schism, upon the Testimonies of Councils and Fathers of the first Six Centuries.* By THOMAS WILLIAM ALLIES, M.A., Rector of Launton, Oxon. London, 1846.

5. *The Epistle to the Hebrews; being the substance of Three Lectures, delivered in the Chapel of the Honourable Society of Lincoln's Inn, on the Foundation of Bishop Warburton; with a Preface, containing a Review of Mr. Newman's Theory of Development.* By FREDERICK DENISON MAURICE, M.A., Chaplain of Guy's Hospital. London, 1846.

6. *Remarks on certain Anglican Theories of Unity.* By EDWARD HEALY THOMPSON, M.A. London, 1846.

7. *The Fourfold Difficulty of Anglicanism: or, The Church of England tested by the Nicene Creed. In a Series of Letters.* By J. SPENCER NORTHCOTE, M.A., Late Scholar of Corpus Christi College, Oxford. London, 1846.

8. *The Theory of Development Examined, with reference especially to Mr. Newman's Essay, and to the Rule of St. Vincent of Lirins.* By W. J. IRONS, B.D., Vicar of Brompton. London, 1846.

9. *Mithridates: or, Mr. Newman's Essay on Development its own Confutation.* By a QUONDAM DISCIPLE. London, 1846.

10. *Romanism, as represented by the Rev. J. H. Newman, briefly considered.* By the Rev. A. IRVINE, B.D., Vicar of St. Margaret's, Leicester. London, 1846.

A

Mr. Allies, and Mr. Palmer, we would especially call attention. Dr. Moberly's essay has one fault, and that is its shortness. His clear and logical mind could easily have controlled a much wider region of theological and historical research; and the intellectual framework which he supplies would bear filling-up with large materials from the book-shelves. Mr. Allies's solid and able treatise we have already discussed. Mr. Palmer writes with the quiet, sustained circumspection, and even strength, which distinguish his regular theological works. He argues patiently, and in general closely. His style is clear and easy; and if it never carries the reader on by any overflow of impulse, never, at any rate, obstructs or entangles him. His extensive patristic and controversial reading gives him an ample command of passages, which he uses with singular judgment and discretion; not overloading his argument with the whole amount of the material bearing upon it, but selecting what is most applicable and to the purpose. We would point to the chapter on the "Argumentative foundation of the Theory of Development," as a favourable specimen of his mode of treating a question.

For ourselves, we must state at the outset that we cannot pretend to embrace, within that space which a review affords, the whole of that large field of matter which Mr. Newman's book presents to us. It is necessary to confine our scope; and, therefore, we shall select the argumentative part of the essay, in distinction to the historical, as the subject of this article.

A short acquaintance with the Essay on Development suggests to the reader such a division of the book as we mention. He sees some vividly drawn historical sketches, the object of which is to prove the identity of the present Church of Rome, in religious spirit and character, with the Church of the first centuries. This does not form a part of what we may call the strict logic of the Essay; because its truth is perfectly consistent with the truth of the identity, *e.g.* of the Greek Church also, in religious spirit and character, with the Church of the first centuries. An ethical similarity in one Church does not preclude an ethical similarity in another. And, therefore, such statements, as applied to the purpose of proving that the Church of Rome is the only Church of Christ upon earth, do not profess to be of the nature of logical arguments; though they produce their particular effect upon the mind as forcibly drawn pictures. On the other hand, there are arguments professing to prove, from the necessity of things, and the absolute wants of the Christian society, the full Roman developments and claims logically and conclusively. We shall confine ourselves, then, in this article to this latter part of the Essay, and shall devote some thoughts to Mr. Newman's argumentative proof of the doctrine of development in connection with the authoritative claims and the peculiar teaching of the Church of Rome. And we shall not scruple, in doing so, to avail ourselves of the assistance which some of the prefixed publications afford.

On the first opening, then, of this subject, two great lines of thought encounter us, each of them a true, natural, and legitimate line, and one of them tending to check and balance the other. One of these lines of thought takes up the idea of Development. We see unquestionably everywhere a law of development operating. It meets us in nature and art, in trade and politics, in life vegetable, animal, intellectual. The seed grows into the plant, the child into the man; the worm into the butterfly, the blossom into the fruit. Education develops the individual, civilisation the nation. The particular ideas we take up, grow. A simple thought, as soon as the mind has embraced it, ramifies in many directions, applies itself to many different cases, sees reflections of itself in nature and human life, gathers analogies around it, and illustrates and is illustrated in turn. Wealth and power both multiply themselves. The first round sum is the great difficulty to the rising merchant, which once made, a basis is gained, and money accumulates spontaneously. The nucleus of power, however small at first, once formed, enlarges, and absorbs material from all quarters. The jurisdiction of courts, boards, and committees grows; aggrandising cabinets get all the local interests of a country into their hands; and empires, from a union of two or three tribes, spread over half the globe. Our languages, our philosophies, our machinery and manufactures, our agriculture, our architecture, our legal codes, our political institutions, our systems of finance, our civil courts, our social distinctions, our rules of fashion, our amusements, our occupations, our whole worlds, domestic and public, are developments. We cannot walk, or sit, or stand, or think, or speak, without developing ourselves. We go into a room; we address somebody, or we listen to somebody addressing us; we act in some way or other under the situations in which successively we are; and are brought out by circumstances, acting upon us in connection with our own will, in one direction or another. This is the development of human character, which advances as life goes on. The whole constitution of the world physical and moral thus impresses development upon us, and points natural expectation in that direction. We find ourselves readily entertaining the probability that principles, sentiments, fashions, institutions, will expand. The change from the small to the large, and from the simple to the manifold, does not surprise us; and an image of that kind of alteration in things which is called growth, and takes them through different stages of magnitude and strength, is domesticated in our minds.

This is one great line of thought which encounters us, on a *primâ facie* view of the progress of any great political or religious institution. There is another equally genuine, natural, and true. If the idea of development has established itself as a natural and familiar one in our minds, the idea of corruption has done the same. If we see things grow larger, we also see things grow worse. History and experience have contrived to fix very deeply in us the apprehension of perversion, in some shape or other, and, in one or other degree, accompanying the progress of institutions, nations, schemes of life, and schools of thought. There is the maxim that the stream is purer at its source. It is observed that the intention with which a movement begins often insensibly declines, or becomes alloyed, in the progress. We attribute a mixed set of results to time, and welcome its operations in one aspect, and fear them in another. With all its functions of growth and enlargement, a general suspicion attaches to a class of slow, gentle, insinuating influences it betrays: the notion of the lapse of time suggests indefinite apprehensions, and the mind forms an instinctive augury of some change for the worse which it is to bring. Legislators, philosophers, and founders of institutions are haunted by the image of a progress destined for their creations, which they never designed for them; and portend some departure from original principles which would elicit their protest, by anticipation, could they foresee it accurately enough. That things are better at first, and then deteriorate; that freshness and purity wear off; that deflections arise, and that the inclination from the strict line, once made, widens with insensible but fatal steadiness; in a word, the tendency of things to degeneracy is one of those observed points which has naturalised itself in men's minds, and taken the position of an axiom. It is one of those large, broad, and fixed experiences which stand out in strong relief amid the mixed and shadowy world of minor and less settled ones. It cannot be passed over, or put aside, or touched on and left, as if it were a mere casual difficulty. It is one of those great settled judgments which we bring with us to the consideration of human questions; and it claims to be acknowledged as such.

Moreover, if we go a step farther, and fix upon one very important and prominent line which this general idea takes, we find that after establishing broadly and indefinitely this tendency in moral and physical nature, it next proceeds specially to remind us that this tendency acts by the perversion and abuse, as well as by the positive extinction of the good element which it accompanies. There is the corruption of exaggeration and excess, as well as that of decay. We see good tending to bad, without wholly losing its original type and character in the process. How this takes place, we are not at present concerned to inquire. Indeed, what the essential truth, the deep internal metaphysical reality in the case is,—what the thing is which really and at bottom takes place when we speak of good thus changing into bad,—is a question which perhaps lies below the reach of any limited powers of analysis. We are only concerned here with broad and practical truth, as the general sense of mankind has laid it down; and, practically speaking, we see corruption taking place constantly by some good principle's simple exaggeration and excess. Our fine moral qualities are proverbially subject to this change. Courage becomes rashness, and love becomes fondness, and liberality becomes profuseness, and self-respect becomes pride. In these and such like cases the original type of the virtue remains, but undergoes disproportion and disfigurement: the original disposition, which was good, does not evanesce and cease to be; but, continuing, is carried out beyond a certain limit, and transgresses some just standard. It would be absurd to say that the rashness of the soldier, whatever extravagances or madnesses it might commit, lost its type, and ceased to be courage. It retains the original element which we admire in the courageous character,—that species of indifference to self, and willingness to meet pain and death; but it retains it in a particular form, which we term exaggerated, and which is offensive to our moral taste. The rash man remains the courageous man; we cannot deny it: we feel ourselves compelled to preserve an under-current of admiration for him on this account; but we apply it to the simple original element itself of courage which we see in him, and not to its actual form and embodiment, as he exhibits it. A vast number of characters exist in the world, which we consider more or less faulty ones, of which the only account we have to give is, that they carry some natural principles of conduct, or some natural lines of feeling, too far. Men are over-busy, over-anxious, hasty, suspicious, thin-skinned, rigid, vehement, obstinate, passionate, yielding. In each fault we see the good element at the bottom, which it carries out unsoundly. How completely does the whole region of enthusiasm, when we look into it, present an essential similarity, as far as the fundamental quality itself is concerned! We see a certain wide-working mysterious mental characteristic, which we call by this name: all the enthusiasms which come before us in actual life and history, are of this stock; all the enthusiasts we see have this enthusiasm running in their veins; but, quite independently of the question of a good or a bad cause, we like one form of enthusiasm and dislike another. One man is a natural enthusiast, another an unnatural and extravagant one. In these instances, indeed, the continuity of development is even sometimes marked by the identity of the name. Jealousy is a virtue, and jealousy is a fault. We ought to be high-minded; we ought not to be. We ought, and we ought not, to be severe and stern, soft and tender. Such a person is so scrupulous, and another person also so scrupulous: we mean it favourably in one case, unfavourably in another. A fastidious taste is admired and is condemned. We extol zeal, and stigmatise the zealot. We use the word enthusiasm, in the same breath, in a good and a bad sense. The identity of the word in these cases, is symptomatic of some great intimacy in the two things; and often where we have not the same identical word bearing its cognate good and bad sense, an unfavourable sense hovers around the virtuous term, a favourable sense about the faulty one: each is capable of being used in its contiguous good or bad meaning, and viewed in the shade and the sunshine, which respectively haunt them. A particular look or half-formed smile in the speaker, who is describing a person's character, throws a dubiousness over the pleasing epithets of courteous, polite, agreeable, prudent. Even justice is rigid, and virtue is obstinate; and we call men determined, or vigorous, or simple, or strict, or pliant, or cautious, or sharp, when the context has to decide the favourable or unfavourable sense in which the epithets are used. A whole class of words, connected with character and action, are very neutral and ambiguous, capable of expressing bad or good, according as they are used. The look, the tone of the speaker, must give the bias which the term itself wants. And in exploring the region of verbal meanings and significances, we find ourselves wandering among unknown quantities and formless embryos, which wait in suspense for the decision of time, and place, and context, to give them definite and fixed being. That is to say, whereas one main idea runs through a whole series of characteristic epithets, it depends upon the stage and the measure of this idea whether it presents itself to us as right or wrong. Our verbal identities and verbal modifications, the defects and the pliabilities of language, point to some unity of element in the case of various virtues and faults, of which the former are the just, the latter the unjust developments, but in which it is the measure of development which makes the difference.

In the same way, the intellectual character of a man's mind is often unfavourably affected by the over-expansion of an intellectual gift. A talent, however noble and useful in itself, requires reining in. Eloquence, versatility, richness of thought, power of illustration, are mighty gifts, and great snares at the same time. The mind of the writer or speaker is barren and feeble without them; and if it has them, we see it carried away by them. How does the impoverished mind long for the power of illustration; the author seems to be able to do nothing without it; every truth falls dead, and every thought comes out hard and attenuated: but give it him, and it instantly begins to clog his course; its impertinent fertility interrupts his argument; it interferes where it is not wanted; it goes on where it ought to stop; it cheats and fascinates his eye, and leads him off his road in the pursuit of far-fetched analogies and superfluous parallelisms and juxta-positions. Some intellects, again, are too accurate, and narrow themselves by their own over-definiteness; they refuse to see anything vaguely, and consequently see nothing grandly; they leave the picturesque masses and groupings of a view, and always put their minds too close to each part to see the form and outline of the whole. Thus argumentative subtlety is a real gift, and at the same time a most dangerous one. We see it at first dividing acutely and truly, cutting a clear course through perplexing statements, and winding through a circuitous argument with self-possessed flexibility. But how easily does its fineness become too fine, and its nicety minute and trivial. Thus, men of the world are not rare who would often judge much better, if they were less shrewd; their shrewdness carries them away, and they are always seeing deeper and further than the fact before them, and never rest in an ordinary natural view of a man's character and actions.

It is in particulars, however, that is, in insulated processes of the intellect and movements of the feelings, that the truth perhaps comes nearest home to us. In such cases, however fairly we may start, we often feel ourselves under the influence of some active though hidden force, some spring of motion in our minds, which impels and expands us with a strength greater than that of constitutional nature; and carries the internal movement, seeming all the time simply to advance and go farther and add one degree of force and depth to another, by that very accumulation and continuous increasing intensity, to an exaggerative issue and a plain corruption. Thus, in movements of the imagination, we observe the poet's mind too often starting with the natural, and ending with the morbid. The sentiment which in its first stage was healthy and sound, becomes, as his fancy works more and more upon it, as he draws it out and carries it on and on, sickly and artificial. We may be able to fix on no exact line where poetical rectitude ended and deterioration commenced, yet there is the result. By fine imperceptible steps, and a continuity which seemed actually to forbid the developing operation a pause, simplicity has become puerility, and sweetness mawkishness. While the poet has been fondly dwelling upon his own idea, and caressing it, and contemplating himself in it, he has spoiled it by his own weak idolatry; till, spun out, exhausted, attenuated, and frittered away, the mind of the healthy reader rejects it in disgust. A like process has spoiled real grandeur and sublimity. How difficult does the poet seem to find it to prevent himself, in unfolding ideas of that character, from becoming bombastic. Even Shakespeare does not always succeed. In truth, real and deep poetry of a certain class, and not a weak and hollow one only, has a strong tendency to bombast; and the bombastic development need not rise upon a false basis, but only exaggerate upon a true one. A poet expands a grand idea, and is only bent on expanding it; he attends to that too exclusively; he does not check or balance himself by other points of view. The thought swells, in the very act of simply expressing and unfolding itself, into rude and gigantic dimensions, and seeks unsuitable and excessive height. And an expansion, going upon the basis of the original thought, and only seeming at the time its essential elevation and full poetical career, in the result spoils its subject-matter, and does the work of an enemy, while it acts as pure exponent and promoter. Thus many an emotion of heart can appeal confidently to a line of continuity which it has maintained from its very commencement to its very last stage and extreme vent; and yet, from a sound natural impulse, it has become an extravagant and morbid one. "Be ye angry, and sin not," the Apostle says; that is to say, anger is a natural and proper feeling at a certain point in its duration. "Let not the sun go down upon your wrath," he adds; that is to say, anger beyond that point is wrong. There is no change of type or essence in the feeling contemplated; it becomes wrong by the act of simply going on beyond a limit assigned for it. It is the same with other affections. The genuine moral affection of love becomes, before persons are aware of it, partiality and favouritism, and proceeds to idolise an object. Yet it only seems to itself to follow in the process, step by step, that tenderness which is its natural character and very constitution. Indeed, in the mind's daily and hourly history, every feeling and thought, as it arises, seems to go through a like course, and the process of corruption seems to go on in miniature, with respect to every creation of taste, and every stir of heart within us. Nature herself is sound; the thought, immediately as it arises, is true, the impulse clear; just the very first dawn of a sentiment, when the mind is half unconscious of it, its primordia and earliest infancy are pure. But the perfect healthy stage is an evanescent one; it is gone before it can be caught. Follow the impression for any time, and it glides out of our control; it swells, and unfolds itself too freely and boldly, and we are conscious it has passed out of its stage of simplicity into a more or less unsound state.

The characters of great systems, schools of philosophy, religions, nations, instance the same excessive stamp. The Spartan character was an exaggeration; the Cynic was; the Stoic was; the fatalist temper of the Mahometan religionist, the fortitude of the American savage, the self-denial of the Hindoo saint, are exaggerations. The idea at the bottom of these characters we admire, but there is something painful about them; we shrink from the boldness of the moral development, as from something out of measure, unnatural, and prodigious. National characters are exaggerations. Anglo-Saxon stubbornness, French vivacity, Italian subtlety, Spanish pride, German speculativeness, Irish warmth, Scotch shrewdness, are excessive developments of good national elements of character. Nations gradually alter, and show, in the course of a century or two, that a particular character has grown upon them. The Anglo-Saxon becomes stiff-necked, the Frenchman revolutionary. The Greek, of the age of Pericles, was the Græculus of the Augustan era. Philosophical schools exhibit the same history; they exaggerate the mystical, or the argumentative character, whichever it may be, of the original philosophy. The tempered mysticism of Plato is extravagantly reflected in the wild obscurities of Alexandrian Platonism; and Aristotelian logic became disputatious and rationalistic in the hands of the sophistical schools.

The history of Christianity presents us with like phenomena; and particular schools or sects have carried out particular gospel precepts immoderately, and exhibited an exaggerated and deformed development of the Christian ἦθος. The peculiar meekness inculcated in the precepts, "Resist not evil," "Unto him that smiteth thee on the one cheek offer also the other, and him that taketh away thy cloak, forbid not to take thy coat also," and other similar texts, has been carried out into Quietism and Quakerism. The temper of reserve has been exaggerated in the same way, and developed into a tortuous and underhand spirit. There can be no doubt that Christianity does very significantly recommend, and very naturally produce, a temper of reserve; the temper is a feature in Christian morals, and other religions have not paid such attention to it. Christianity has done this because it is so essentially practical a religion; it does not stand aloof from the human throng, it enters boldly and familiarly into it, and deals with human nature as it finds it. It therefore thinks much of the quality of considerateness, and it tells its disciples to be watchful and gentle to people's feelings and prejudices. Violence defeats itself. This quality, on the other hand, sees difficulties, looks beforehand, and suits itself to the state of mind it addresses; mixes tenderness and prudence, forbearance and penetration, love and good sense. Such texts as "Be ye wise as serpents, and harmless as doves," "Give not that which is holy unto the dogs, neither cast ye your pearls before swine," and such declarations as that of St. Paul's, that he "became all things to all men," evidently suggest some modification or other of the politic type of mind, as one intended to exist under the Gospel. Now, whether or not the Jesuitical order as a whole has exaggerated this type, at any rate it seems certain that some members of it have, and that many who have not been Jesuits also have. Indeed, it is one easily exaggerated: there is an indefiniteness as to what it allows and what it does not; as to where its prudential character ends, and deceitful begins. A sort of cowardice soon couples itself with it, and a man uses reserve as a shelter and fortress to himself, instead of a charity to another. In time, the principle of accommodation becomes relished for its own sake. The machinery of management pleases. The undermining position flatters the mind with sensations of its own depth and power. The relation of watcher and schemer with respect to others, which makes one side the material upon which the other exercises his skill and tact, feeds a subtle vanity, and stimulates an earthly activity. A keen professional spirit grows upon the mind, like the love of some trade or occupation. The fineness of natural conscience with respect to sincerity is dullened,—a technical standard obtains; and, step by step, without transgressing any absolute law at any one point, the principle of Christian reserve has developed into that policy which is often conventionally called Jesuitism; though we want to lay our stress not on the name, but on the thing. That which people mean to censure under the name, is the abuse of a good and a specially Christian principle. There is a legitimate principle of economy, which simple forbearance and charity in dealing with other minds involve; and this has received an inordinate and excessive development.

A general view of things thus impresses strongly a form of corruption upon us, which is the corruption of exaggeration, and not that of failure; the perversion, and not the destruction, of an original type: we see in a multitude of cases principles, in themselves true, overacted, good feelings over-wrought, fine perceptions over-cultivated. Our moral nature tends to indignation, enthusiasm, tenderness, determination, self-respect in excess. The intellect may be too rich, too accurate, too subtle, too shrewd; and poetry can develop into bombast and sentimentalism, philosophy into sophistry, national character into caricature. Whether any particular illustrations are right or wrong, and apply to the case or not, that form of corruption which consists in excess, and not failure, is too clearly marked, too broad, too common and palpable a one, to admit of any doubt. We may add, that though the word corruption suggests etymologically the latter rather than the former, and puts the image of decay primarily before us, yet the strong habitual observation amongst us of corruption exaggerative, has turned it the other way; and in calling the excess of a virtue, rather than its failure, its corruption, made the word suggestive of excess. This form of corruption Aristotle saw as a fact, and gave it a place in his philosophy. He said a thing can become worse by excess; the good principle need not cease, and an evil one be substituted in its place, in order to have deterioration; it may continue to exist, but exist inordinately. The measure, as well as the substance, is part of the virtue. *Est modus in rebus:* there is symmetry and form in moral nature; there is a standard of growth in the constitution of things. It is not enough that the good principle simply exists; it should exist in a certain way. True, indeed, good is good, and evil evil, and there is nothing between; but this settles nothing as to the mode by which good and by which evil become such. In forming a correct image in our minds of what makes good and makes evil, we must not only have the image of two separate principles, as it were two points or atoms, and say that one of these is good and the other is evil. Practical morality is a more complex and balanced thing; and the principle of form, as well as that of substance, should enter into the idea of good. If good refuses to exist according to a certain standard or measure, it gets wrong by excess, just as, if it declines, it gets wrong by ceasing altogether. Without diving, however, into the metaphysical part of the subject, or attempting to get at the bottom of the relation of good and evil, it is enough to appeal to a plain and practical truth. All phenomena, natural or moral, are more or less inexplicable when we come to analyse them; but the difficulty of the analysis does not interfere at all with the certainty of the fact. And the matter of common sense, the practical phenomenon, is plain, that things become worse upon their original basis, and that good becomes evil by exaggeration.

Thus early, indeed, and in the moral department, before coming to theology at all, we find ourselves in collision with a certain idea of development. There is a philosophy of development, which regards it in its progressive aspect exclusively, and puts its form and measure in the background. Such a view has the advantage of simplicity; it makes the question of truth a question of quantity, and the biggest development, whatever it be, the truest. Development, simply as such,—as so much continuous swelling and pushing forward of an original idea,—is the more perfect the farther it goes, up to the very extremest conceptions of size and extension which the mind can entertain. A pure, progressive, illimitable, mathematical movement hangs argumentatively *in terrorem* over us, with the assertion of a logical necessity and impossibility of stopping short of consequences. But such a rationale of development is inapplicable to the subject-matter to which it is applied. In morals we cannot develop mathematically, because we have not a basis which will bear it. In mathematics we have fixed and defined principles to start from,—we have them by hypothesis; we know, therefore, exactly what we are about, and have a pledge, in a known and ascertained premiss, for the truth of all the results. But in morals we have no ascertained premiss to begin with. We do not know what we have; we have to wait for a development before we do know. Here is the point. In mathematics the principle is known prior to its results. In morals it is only known in its results. Take the principle of love and fear in religion and morals. We call them two principles conventionally, and imagine them, for convenience sake, existing as two definite entities, prior to any concrete manifestations or developments of them. But the truth is, we do not know them or their character, except in their manifestations and developments. We see moral principles, as we see the laws of material motion, not prior to, but in their external and cognisable action; and the dramatic or practical developments of love and fear alone declare what love and fear are. The developments thus, in morals, explaining the principle, to argue from the principle to the developments is to argue in a circle. And, therefore, to any mathematical veto forbidding us to form a distinct judgment of any moral development, on the ground that we have already committed ourselves to the principle from which it proceeds, the answer is obvious :—we could not have committed ourselves in such a sense to the principle, because we never committed ourselves to this development. In other words, in the department of morals, as distinguished from that of mathematics, we go by the eye; and the moral taste necessarily forms its judgment of a moral exhibition, as a present object before it. The general principle being allowed, the phenomenon has still to be judged of: the mode of development is a separate question when development arrives; and the undefined moral substance has to receive its form and measure before it becomes that final reality about which we judge.

To go back to the point at which we started.

We have, then, two great lines of thought encountering us *in limine*, in entering upon the question which the Essay before us raises. We have the natural idea of development, and we have the natural idea of a tendency to exaggeration and abuse in development. In giving an account of the progress of any great institution, political or religious, either of these ideas is admissible; and one party may put forward the rationale of development, and another the rationale of abuse. One may fasten singly on the former idea, may illustrate it copiously, and by filling the imagination with the idea of development exclusively, preclude all other aspects in which any given progressive changes can be viewed; another may carry to the consideration of such changes the idea of development, and the idea of abuse too.

Under the contending claims, then, of these two ideas,

the history of Christianity comes before us; and the question is how to decide between the pretensions of the two. The principle of development is of course admitted, to begin with, in this case. There can be no doubt that Christianity was intended to develop itself. It was intended to do so on the same general law on which great principles and institutions, we may say all things, great or small, do. If a man cannot enter a room full of fellow-creatures without developing himself, still less could Christianity enter into this world without developing itself. It had precepts, it had doctrines; those precepts must be practised, those doctrines must be entertained in the mind. Human life and human thought were the receptacles of the gospel. People who became Christians would have to act upon, and to think of, what Christianity imparted to them. The peculiar Christian temper, in the first place, would be brought out more prominently, as different relations, religious or secular, social or civil, had to be sustained and responded to. While the apostles lived, Christians showed their obedience to apostles; when the apostolic office descended to bishops, Christians showed their obedience to bishops, and the hierarchical spirit of Christianity appeared in more regular form. Christians found themselves, as a matter of fact, under civil governments; and they had to act *as* Christians in this relation. They had a general principle inculcating meekness; that meekness became in this relation the temper of non-resistance. The charity enjoined in the Gospel developed itself, under the particular circumstances of the Church after the day of Pentecost, in community of goods. It afterwards developed itself in Sunday collections for the poor, and all the charitable rules and institutions of the early Church. Thus there could not be martyrs before there were persecutions; the latter developed the martyr spirit in the Christian mind :—that generosity which made the individual ready wholly to sacrifice himself for the Truth and for the brethren. Heresies developed the dogmatic temper of Christianity; it could not show its fidelity to the Truth so forcibly before as it could after the Truth was assailed. The self-denying temper of Christianity developed itself in stated fasts, voluntary poverty, retirement from society, celibacy, and monasticism. It was necessary that the Christian temper, when it found itself in the world, should act in some way or other; it could not act without developing itself: action is itself development. The simple fact of Christianity being in the world—being there just as other things are—being among governments, the poor, persecutions, heretics, made a Christian development. The question whether that peculiar temper has always developed itself properly in the world—one which we incidentally alluded to above—is one which we need not pursue.

Besides this internal temper of Christianity, a department of doctrine, or rather a mixed department of doctrine and feeling, was brought into existence by the New Dispensation, which, when once existing, could not but expand, and lead to farther ideas. And though those ideas might at first be strictly apostolical in their origin, and have the rank of an unwritten revelation, yet a time would come when inspiration would cease, and the uninspired operations of human feeling and reason begin. We will instance three or four important departments in which original doctrine has received development from the thought and feeling of the general Christian mind to which it was communicated; not disguising, as we proceed, our preference of some to other stages of that development, though we are only giving at present its whole course as a fact. And we shall take development upon its broad and practical ground, not confining ourselves to public verbal statements only, but looking to their actual interpretation and mode of reception in the Church.

The doctrine of an intermediate state, with the relations of Christians to the departed accompanying it, presents, in the successive stages it has gone through, an instance of this development. The Gospel revealed, with a clearness with which it had not been before, the doctrine of the immortality of the soul. The dead were, to the Christian believer, real persons, living in another state; that he did not see them was nothing to the purpose—they existed: the same personal beings whom he had known upon earth were alive in some invisible portion of the universe. But the dead could not exist without some relation between him and them ensuing. The first duty of a being to all other beings, is to wish them well. The Christian could not, on the first principles of religion, help wishing the dead well. If he wished them well, he implicitly prayed for them; for the wish of a religious mind is itself a prayer. Every one's eternal lot, indeed, is decided at his death; and that lot in the case of all for whom we can pray is a happy one. But we can pray for a benefit which is already certain, where that certainty is only the certainty of faith, and not of sight. The certainty of faith as to any event, can never of its own nature be so certain as not to leave room for a wish or prayer for it. We believe, but do not see; we look upon the dark; there is a veil before us, and we pray that something, which we believe to take place behind it, may take place. We pray in the baptismal service that the water may regenerate the infant, though we believe, in accordance with Catholic doctrine, that it certainly will; and in the same way the early Church prayed that the righteous dead might receive their eternal reward, though it believed, for certain, that they would. The doctrine of the intermediate state and prayers for the dead was thus a natural development of the revelation of the soul's immortality, specially made in the Gospel. The dead existed now ; the day of judgment was yet to come ; an intermediate state of existence therefore between death and judgment there must be : the righteous souls waited for their eternal reward, the wicked for their eternal doom. The primitive doctrine of the intermediate state reflected simply the original Christian truths, of the departed soul's present existence and future judgment. For the righteous it was thus a state of pure rest ; their earthly labours over, their final bliss gradually approaching. "Blessed are the dead which die in the Lord, even so saith the Spirit, for they rest from their labours." "Verily, I say unto thee, To-day shalt thou be with me in Paradise." Nature was a type of grace :—" Man went forth to his work and to his labour until the evening ;" in the evening he rested. From the whole idea of life as a scene of labour, followed naturally the idea of death as a state of peace ; and the life after was not the continuation, but correlative, of the life before. The busy day, the still night, the journey and the rest, waking and sleeping, life and death, corresponded to each other in the Divine dispensation of things. "Them that sleep in Jesus, will God bring with him." "We which are alive shall not prevent them which are asleep." The language of the New Testament ascribes a character of peace and rest to the state of true believers after death ; the idea pervades it remarkably, and lays strong hold of a reader. It is impossible for one careful and anxious about a true belief in this subject, not to regard with awe that sentence which, in its obvious meaning, seems so clearly to intimate what was in our Lord's own mind on this subject. The Liturgies of the early Church followed up this tone in their prayers for the righteous dead. " Return, my soul, into thy rest." —" I will fear no evil because Thou art with me."—" Be mindful, O Lord God of the spirits of all flesh, of such as we have remembered, and such as we have not remembered, being of right belief, from Abel the just unto this present day. Do Thou cause them to rest in the land of the living, in Thy kingdom, in the delight of Paradise, in the bosom of Abraham, Isaac, and Jacob, our holy fathers."—" Remember, O Lord, Thy servants and handmaids, which have gone before us with the ensign of faith, and sleep in the sleep of peace. To them, O Lord, and to all that are in rest in Christ, we beseech Thee that Thou wouldst grant a place of refreshing, light, and peace."—" Vouchsafe to place in the bosom of Abraham the souls of those that be at rest."—" Place in rest the spirits of those which are gone before us, in the Lord's peace, and raise them in the part of the first resurrection."

So stood the doctrine of the intermediate state for some centuries. It then gradually altered, till the simply waiting expectant state at last issued in a painful and troubled one, and the interval between earth and heaven, in which the righteous had rested, was occupied with pain and torture. A purgatorial doctrine had existed from the first in the Church. It was piously and naturally held that the soul did not enter heaven without some purifying process at some point of time intervening, to take away the vestiges of its earthly stains. The day of judgment was fixed for this process by some, others did not fix a time. This belief long went on harmonising with the primitive peaceful idea of the intermediate state; and an intervening purification of some kind, and at some time, supposed, left the general idea of the intermediate rest still whole and entire. By degrees, however, the purgatorial idea attached to this state grew and expanded; it grew, till it at last completely drove out the idea of rest. The purgatorial idea absorbed the whole state, and placing at once some highest saints in heaven, the obstinately wicked in hell, made the intermediate state one scene of fiery punishment for the great body of the faithful; the souls of the righteous suffering in flames equal to those of hell in intensity. As to the length of their continuance in such torture, nothing was certified; but nothing also was certified as to their deliverance. That they had gone there, the believer upon earth knew; when they would come out, he knew not. They would come out when they were perfected; but when would that be? The chantry was founded to pray and offer masses, throughout all time, for righteous human souls, not quite perfected, and suffering this pain so long as they remained so. The difference between a process and a place was great. The idea of a purifying process, even though it be by fire, suggested a vague, transient, and merciful purification, and did not destroy the general image of the intermediate rest of the righteous; a purgatorial place, on the other hand, suggests the idea of punishment always going on in it, and makes the idea of punishment the standing, lasting, prominent one. The primitive purgatorial process having now become the fixed purgatorial place, the purgatory and prison of human souls, while that fixed place existed, the departed soul could not, in the idea of the believers upon earth, be quite separated from it; and that place existed till the end of the world. Thus a whole different impression from the primitive one, as to the intermediate state, spread and became dominant. The state of rest was changed into a temporary hell. A whole growth of popular theology filled it with horrible, minute, circumstantial details and particulars. The image was fastened on the popular mind, and a complete legendary creation arose. The system of indulgences made a constant appeal to it. Days, weeks, years, hundreds of years of purgatory were commuted, in the popular divinity, for penances upon earth; a second commutation turned those penances into alms. So much money bought off so many years of purgatorial suffering. The expenses of wars were defrayed, the necessities of the Papal see supplied, churches built and ornamented, out of the appeal to purgatory. The doctrine of purgatory was wielded as an established ecclesiastical engine, became a regular source of revenue, and could be counted on. It was eagerly applied, and warmly responded to; and a whole mixed practical system, carrying with it good and evil, much real devotion and charity, with much trickery, profaneness, and profligacy, completed the development.

Again, in the feelings and regards of Christians towards saints and holy men, development was natural and necessary. When Christians died, Christians began to feel relations to the dead. When saints departed, left a name and memory behind them, Christians began to feel relations to saints. The new relation followed from the fact, and honour to the saints arose on the same law as prayers for the dead did. It was natural to reverence their memories, and take care to transmit them. Any memorials of them would be tenderly preserved; their tombs would be especially sacred; the martyrdom would be celebrated; the saint's day would be kept. The mind would image to itself their present state, as resting from their labours and waiting for their crowns. Thoughts upon thoughts, in this natural line of meditation, would follow. It is unnatural to suppose that souls departed cannot pray. The prayers of saintly souls were intercessory in life : why may they not be so afterwards? We do not *know*, indeed, that in their present state they remember us, or think of us, or know anything about us upon earth; but neither do we know that they do not. All we know is, that saints, once intimately connected with us, are now personally existing in some portion of the universe of God, having the same essential disposition to intercede for us that they ever had. Upon this knowledge, when realised in a certain strong way, a farther step might not unnaturally follow in some minds; and supposing departed saints could intercede for them, the wish might arise that they should. The wish again that they should, might, in some minds, lead to a kind of apostrophe or an hypothetical address to them to do so, only as a mode of expressing that wish. "If you hear me and I do not know that you do not, do what I ask you; if I *can* address you I do." If even some very ardent religious imagination, annihilating the interval between what may be and what is, hardly felt the hypothetical chain, and sent its address straight and unconditional into the spiritual world, the liberty might only be a mode of expressing the lively and realising impressions which such an imagination creates. A whole line of indefinite feeling to, thought of, mental reference of some kind to departed saints, extending from the most ordinary popular honour to their memories to the most internal supposition of individual piety and imaginative meditation about them, would thus not unnaturally follow from the fact of their existence, and would express itself in ways open or secret, public or private.

This is a development. But development being necessary to some extent, development goes on farther. The pious inward wish of the journeyer upon earth that the saints might intercede for him; the inward apostrophe and address which arose in individual minds, in moments of deep and imaginative meditation, when the spiritual eye seemed to see the invisible world actually open, and the saints in their own regions above taking part with the prayers of the Church upon earth; all which pious individual impulse might just allow of or sanction in its own inward sphere was brought into regular public usage, and made part of the established worship of the Church. The indefiniteness which inspiration had left over the fact of such intercourse between us and the saints departed, that veil of uncertainty which unsuited it for the Church's whole public ground removed,—that the saints heard prayers became a simple popular fact. The prayer to the saint was offered up publicly, side by side with the prayer to God. By degrees, the language of the prayer itself became bolder. The *ora pro nobis* had to be understood, and the earthly supplicant, as far as language went, asked of the saint the same things which he did of the Almighty, in the same form. Other and other developments followed, which it is unnecessary here to go through; the result was the present recognised worship of the saints established over so large a part of Christendom.

The honour of the blessed Virgin has been developed still more boldly, largely, unflinchingly, with a boldness and a largeness, indeed, which serve to throw all other developments into the background. But as we shall have to enter upon this more at length farther on in this article, we shall content ourselves for the present with a simple allusion, and leave the reader to recall to his own mind the general features of it; the style adopted in the "Litanies of the Blessed Virgin," and such books as St. Bonaventure's Psalter, the Gloires de Marie, and innumerable others; and the whole position given to St. Mary in the Roman Church.

The doctrine of transubstantiation is another bold development in another department. The doctrine of the early Church on the subject of the Lord's Supper declared that the bread and wine were changed into the Body and Blood of Christ. Nevertheless, it regarded the bread and wine as continuing to be bread and wine, the same in all material respects as what they were before. Bread and wine were material substances before their conversion; they were material substances after. Looking upon consecrated and looking upon unconsecrated bread and wine, it regarded the former as being all that the latter was, however much more it might be; there was no idea of matter which the human mind could entertain, which it did not entertain of the material bread and wine in the Eucharist. How the material substance, continuing such, was at the same time changed into a spiritual one, it did not profess to say; it asserted the truth, and maintaining a thoroughly natural view as to the material bread and wine, such a view in all respects as any ordinary human intellect would take, on the one side, and the truth that they were become our Lord's body and blood, on the other, left the two truths to stand together. A simple, absolute, mysterious idea of a change; not analysed or pushed out, but stopping at its first conception; practically intelligible, intellectually unintelligible, combined both. Our ideas on mysterious subjects are necessarily superficial; they are intellectually paper ideas, they will not stand examination; they vanish into darkness if we try to analyse them. A child, on reading in fairy tales about magical conversions and metamorphoses, has most simple definite *ideas* instantly of things, of which the *reality* is purely unintelligible. His ideas are paper ones; a philosopher may tell him that he cannot have them really, because they issue when pursued in something self-contradictory and absurd; that he is mistaken, and only thinks he has them; but the child has them such as they are, and they are powerful ones, and mean something real at the bottom. Our ideas, in the region of religious mystery, have this childish character; the early Church had such. It held a simple, superficial, childlike idea of an absolute conversion of the bread and wine into the body and blood; and with this idea, as with an hieroglyphic emblem of some mysterious and awful reality, it stopped short. But the time came when the idea of conversion was analysed and pushed; it was inferred that if the bread and wine were changed into the body and blood, they must cease to be the substances of bread and wine; and comparing consecrated with other bread, the Roman Church pronounced this difference between them,—that whereas all other pieces of bread in the world were material substances, this particular bread was not. The bread upon the altar was not a material thing, it only had the appearance and not the reality of it. We look on matter as a substance. We take up a piece of wood, or piece of stone: the wood is grainy, fibrous, igneous, and has all ligneous qualities; the stone is gritty and frangible, and has all lapideous qualities: but no assemblage of ligneous or lapideous qualities is to us the wood or the stone; we regard the latter not as those qualities, but as the substances which have those qualities, the qualities essentially implying to our minds the substance which has them: and the idea of wood or stone is utterly void and hollow while the substance is withdrawn, and is satisfied only when that comes in. Thus bread means substantial bread, and wine substantial wine, and they are not in idea bread and wine unless they are this. And this the doctrine of transubstantiation, unsubstantiating the bread and wine upon the altar as it does, denies the bread and wine upon the altar to be. The doctrine of their conversion has been pushed out into a denial of their continued existence, and the idea of change has gained a forced intensity at the expense of ordinary truth and reasonableness.

Taking these, then, as samples of a general development which has gone on in the Christian Church, here is a course of development before us, and the question is, Is all of it right, or is only some of it right? Has development simply brought out truth, or has it exceeded a limit, and become, beyond that limit, erroneous? One general view taken of this course of development holds it to have exceeded. Of the later and more extreme developments, what is ordinarily asserted by writers of our Church is, that they are exaggerations; that they push certain feelings or ideas to excess, and corrupt them by doing so; that they go beyond the authorised boundary, and overlay the truth. The general form of charge against Rome is this, as distinguished from the charge of having extinguished truth: it points to the faults of an adding, not a diminishing system; to error in the line of growth and not that of decay. The tendency of Protestantism is to decay: it diminishes, dilutes, speculates away Christian truth: it dislikes mystery, distrusts awe; and therefore the Christian religion, as an essentially mysterious and essentially devotional one, would gradually lose its fundamental characteristics and original type under the sway of unchecked Protestantism. Upon the Roman system, on the other hand, the special charge made is, that in various doctrines, keeping the original type, it has introduced an exaggerative corruption of it. The care for the dead, the veneration of saints, the peculiar reverence to the Mother of God, the acknowledgment of the change in the Eucharist, the sense of punishment due to sin, are all Christian feelings and doctrines, and they all exist in the

Roman system; but they are asserted to exist in an immoderate and disproportionate way. The system which intensifies the spiritual by denying the material substance in the Eucharist; which gives the Mother of our Lord, because great honour is due to her, the place which it does give her; which makes, because it was natural to imagine some purification of the soul before its entrance into heaven, the whole intermediate state a simple penal fiery purgatory; which pushes out doctrines and expands feeling towards particular objects to the extent to which it does, has had one general fault very prominently charged to it, viz., that of exaggeration, including in that term all that, commonly called, extravagance, all that abuse and perversion of the exaggerative kind, which it practically means.

Such is the view which one side takes of certain large developments of Christian doctrine, which took place over the world after the first centuries, viz., as deteriorations or corruptions; let us now see how Mr. Newman, as the advocate of the other side, proves them not to be corruptions, but true and sound developments.

Mr. Newman's argument on this point proceeds on a certain definition of corruption; a certain view which he lays down of what corruption is. His definition of corruption is "the destruction of the norm or type." "The corruption of philosophical or political ideas is a process ending in dissolution of the body of thought and usage, which was bound up, as it were, into one system; in the destruction of the norm or type, whatever it may be considered, which made it one; in its disorganisation; in its loss of the principle of life and growth; in its resolution into other distinct lives, that is into other ideas which take the place of it."[1] He adds:—"That development,

[1] Development of Christian Doctrine, first Edition, p. 62.

then, is to be considered a corruption which obscures or prejudices its essential idea, or which disturbs the laws of development which constitute its organisation, or which reverses its course of development; that is not a corruption which is both a chronic and an active state, or which is capable of holding together the component parts of a system."[1] Again, "The corruption of an idea is that state of a development which undoes its previous advances."[2] He goes to the analogy of nature: " Corruption, as seen in the physical world, not only immediately precedes dissolution, but immediately follows upon development. It is the turning-point or transition-state in that continuous process, by which the birth of a living thing is mysteriously connected with its death. In this it differs from a reaction, innovation, or reform, that it is a state to which a development tends from the first, at which sooner or later it arrives, and which is its reversal, while it is its continuation. Animated natures live on till they die; they grow in order to decrease; and every hour which brings them nearer to perfection, brings them nearer to their end. Hence the resemblance and the difference between a development and corruption are brought into close juxtaposition."[3] He introduces the existence of a falling state: "Thus, as to nations, when we talk of the spirit of a people being lost, we do not mean that this or that act has been committed, or measure carried, but that certain lines of thought or conduct, by which it has grown great, are abandoned."[4] In all these passages, with the exception of that slight ambiguity occasionally, which in argumentative writing fulfils the purpose rather of guarding and securing a bold position than really modifying it, one bold assertion runs throughout, viz., that corruption

---

[1] Development of Christian Doctrine, first Edition, p. 63.
[2] *Ibid.*   [3] *Ibid.*   [4] Page 69.

can only take place by positive failure and decay. Corruption is the "abandonment of a line of thought." Corruption is that which "reverses its course of development."[1] Corruption is "that state of an idea which undoes its previous advances;"[2] that is to say, so long as an idea goes onward at all, it is sure not to be wrong, the onwardness of the movement constituting its truth. "Where then was the opportunity of corruption," he argues in another place, "in the three hundred years between St. Ignatius and St. Augustine? or between St. Augustine and St. Bede? or between St. Bede and St. Peter Damiani? . . . The tradition of eighteen centuries becomes a chain of indefinitely many links, one crossing the other; and each year as it comes is guaranteed with various degrees of cogency by every year which has gone before it."[3] That is to say, corruption is excluded by the simple continuity of progress on the part of the idea : there is no interval by which it can slip in : the steps lap over one another like scales : " one is so near to another that no air can come between them : they are joined one to another, they stick together that they cannot be sundered."[4] The definition of true development and of corruption is thus,—of development, simple advance; of corruption, simple retrogression : of true development, that which pushes out an idea ; and of corruption, that which extinguishes it. A philosophical theory of development makes all development true, so long as it is such in kind,—so long as there is progression as distinguished from retreat, and enlargement as distinguished from reduction. The fact is its own evidence, the mathematical pledge and certificate of its own correctness. So long as an idea is simply pushed out, extended, added to ; so long as one step has naturally led

[1] Page 63.
[2] Ibid.
[3] Page 367.
[4] Job xli. 16, 17.

to another, and the movement has been continuous, and course onward; so long as it can appeal to a naturally gliding career, to a process in which the end of one advance has fitted on to the beginning of the next, to a line of arithmetical consistency and material succession, so long its career is *ipso facto* right. "The *destruction* of the special laws or principles of a development is the corruption of an idea,"[1] and that only.

Now this definition simply omits the whole notice of corruption by excess. Corruption being defined to be loss of type, it follows that exaggeration, which is not this, is not corruption. The latter has no head for it to come under, and is not taken cognisance of. If indeed it be asked whether Mr. Newman wholly denies that there can be such a thing as exaggeration, the answer is that he does not, but that he does not admit and recognise it argumentatively. The value of a truth lies in its recognition in the argument. If the argument does not recognise it, an incidental allusion to such a truth in some other connection is nothing to the purpose. In those two or three places where he appears to allude to this truth, the allusion stops with itself, and nothing comes of it. To take the following passage:—

"It is the rule of creation, or rather of the phenomena which it presents, that life passes on to its termination by a gradual imperceptible course of change. There is ever a maximum in earthly excellence, and the operation of the same causes which made things great makes them small again. Weakness is but the resulting product of power. Events move in cycles; all things come round, 'the sun ariseth and goeth down, and hasteth to his place where he arose.' Flowers first bloom and then fade; fruit ripens and decays. The fermenting process, unless stopped at the due point, corrupts the liquor which it has created. The grace

[1] Development of Christian Doctrine, first Edition, page 69.

of spring, the richness of autumn, are but for a moment, and worldly moralists bid us *carpe diem*, for we shall have no second opportunity. Virtue seems to lie in a mean between vice and vice, and, as it grew out of imperfection, so to grow into enormity. There is a limit to human knowledge, and both sacred and profane writers witness that overwisdom is folly. And in the political world states rise and fall, instruments of their aggrandisement becoming the weapons of their destruction. And hence the frequent ethical maxims, such as 'Ne quid nimis,' 'Medio tutissimus,' 'Vaulting ambition,' which seem to imply that too much of what is good is evil."[1]

Here allusion is made to the idea of exaggeration, and it is implied that the idea is true, and that there may be such a thing. Various time-honoured maxims, "Ne quid nimis!" "Medio tutissimus," are alluded to. The "virtue which grows into enormity," and that "too much of good which is evil," are alluded to. A whole side of truth, as seen in " the appearance of things and popular language,"[2] the phenomenon of good becoming evil by excess (though with the protest against the paradox that good leads "*literally*" to evil,—a metaphysical part of the subject which we have already shown not to interfere with the phenomenon), are alluded to. The chapter is on the subject of "Preservative additions," and therefore the idea of exaggeration almost necessarily must be alluded to in it. And accordingly we do find an allusion to it. But when it has been alluded to, it is alluded to no more. The subject drops. The idea of excess in growth becomes mixed with quite a different idea, that of a climax or end of growth, the consummation which precedes decay, the bloom of flowers before they fade, the maturity of fruits before they rot; and after coming up to the top once or twice, vanishes altogether, leaving

[1] Page 87.   [2] *Ibid.*

that of a "corroborative," "adding," "illustrating" development to proceed without a check.

Whereas then the ordinary charge maintained by English divines against the Roman system is, as we have said, that of exaggeration, and abuse in exaggeration, we have here a definition of corruption which excludes exaggeration from its meaning. With such a definition, an arguer of course proceeds with considerable advantage to vindicate the Roman system from all corruption. He has only to say that Roman doctrines have not destroyed or reversed the ideas and feelings in which they arose; that in distinction to being departures from original truths altogether, they have been expansions, growths, developments; and immediately no absence whatever of measure in extent of expansion, growth, development, can make corruptions of them. They are secure by the definition, and have a pledge of faultlessness which no controversialist can touch.

Such is Mr. Newman's general argument; and we need not say there is an obvious form of reply to it. It is open to any one to deny the correctness and completeness of Mr. Newman's definition, and to assert that there is a kind of corruption which is not a whole departure from an original type, but which carries out that type excessively and extravagantly; that such a kind is seen in life and morals; and that it may take place in religious systems too. Mr. Newman asks, indeed, what room there is for error to slip in in a course of absolutely continuous advance; but is not this just the question which any one in any case of the most ordinary exaggeration may ask? A man carries out some natural feeling or habit to an obvious excess. If fault is found with him, he can of course demand to know the exact point at which the action of the feeling ceased to be right and began to be wrong. He can say that the feeling was certainly good in him to begin with; that being good to begin with, it has been carried on continuously, each advance in it naturally leading to a further one; and that at last he finds himself in the state of feeling in which he is. An ultra-fastidious taste, a morbid delicacy, a lavish liberality, a haughty self-respect, a venturesome, a hasty, an obstinate, a garrulous, a taciturn temper, may each give this account of itself. And our answer in each case would be, that we were not obliged to fix accurately on the particular line which separated good from bad, sound from unsound; that we observed the feeling or habit had made the advance which it had, and that we judged of it as we did. It is characteristic of the process of exaggeration to be thus continuous, subtle, and gradual. But this is no difficulty with us. We look to the result, which is plain and large, and not to the steps, which are subtle and small. And therefore, when Mr. Newman, in the case of the Roman development, sends us back from the result to the process, and with a phenomenon before us, will not let us judge of it till we have accurately accounted for its rise; when he says, "Where was the opportunity between St. Augustine and St. Bede, and between St. Bede and St. Peter Damiani?" and requires us to pick some definite hole in the process as such, before we hesitate at the result, we can only say that the request is not a reasonable one; that we do not judge in moral and religious subjects as we do in mathematical, in which the process is everything, and the result mechanically forced upon us by it, but judge of the result independently, and seeing an exaggeration for a result, can pronounce that the process has been in some way or other, however gradually and insensibly, an exaggerating process.

Indeed, Mr. Newman's own reason, incidentally given

in one place, for his taking no notice of this great department of error, is a sufficiently self-convicting one. He mentions excess in one place, and mentions it as something wrong; but says he is not concerned with it, because excess is not "corruption," and he is only concerned with the question whether Roman doctrines are corruptions or not. "We predicate corruption not of the *extreme* (meaning something wrong by the extreme), which preserves, but that which destroys a type."[1] That is to say, he excludes the idea of excess, because he has limited the idea of corruption so as to exclude it. But surely this is no legitimate reason, for the question is easily asked, Why did he so limit his idea of corruption? He has, by the nature of his argument, to clear the Roman developments of all that is wrong, of whatever kind and by whatever name called. Well, here is something wrong, and something, therefore, from which he has to clear the Roman developments. He does not relieve himself of this task by saying that he does not admit this particular wrong thing into his definition of corruption; it exists all the same whether admitted into that definition or not, and whether outside or inside of the meaning of that word; and, existing, has to be disproved. The arguer in the present case may take corruption in any sense he likes, as far as the word is concerned, and may take it exclusively in its etymological sense of decay or dissolution. But in that sense, if there is anything else wrong which is not corruption, he cannot put it aside, because he has not made it corruption. He has adopted a defective and partial type of evil, and therefore must admit other types to his argumentative notice when they present themselves. At present the hiatus in the argument before us is a large one. We wonder, while

---

[1] Page 64.

we read, at the ease with which the conclusion is arrived at, and feel an argumentative power drawing us along without a tendency to convince us, or relieve the perpetual undefined consciousness of something wanting. As Mr. Newman's argument stands at present, he first excludes that form of error which is charged upon the Roman system from the field of existence, and then securely determines on that system's perfection. He defines, and then proceeds on his own definition. The scholar, in the old illustration of logic, who was locked up in the Bodleian after four o'clock, and from the window asked the beadle in the quadrangle to let him out, was refuted out of Bocardo: no man is in the Bodleian after four o'clock; therefore you are not in the Bodleian. The arguer first limited the capacity of the Bodleian for holding human beings to the part of the day before four o'clock, and then irresistibly inferred that there were none in it after. Mr. Newman limits deterioration to that form in which it does not apply to the Roman system, and then confidently determines that there has been no deterioration.

Having noticed the substantial argument, we shall not follow the detail and division through which Mr. Newman subsequently takes it. The Christian "Tests of true development" which he gives, only profess to be, and only are, an expansion of the one and leading argument. They all successively go on the supposition that there is no kind of corruption but that of the departure from, and destruction of an idea. In a development he says there should be, first, the "preservation of the idea;"[1] secondly, "continuity of principles;" thirdly, "power of assimilation;" fourthly, "early anticipation;" fifthly, "logical sequence;" sixthly, "preservative additions;" seventhly,

[1] Page 64.

"chronic continuance." Of such a series of tests we can only say, that in any sense—and we presume this is not intended—in which they do not beg the question at issue every one of them may be responded to, and the result may still be an exaggeration,—an enormity. An evident exaggeration may "preserve the idea," may "continue the principles," *i.e.* go on in the same direction, as distinguished from a totally contrary one, with the original idea; it may make its additions preservative of, as distinguished from destructive of, the idea. Of logical sequence, we have something to say shortly. How "power of assimilation," "early anticipation,"[1] and "chronic continuance," can prove a doctrine in a Church, any more than a disposition in an individual, to be correct, we do not see. The latter test is proved thus:— "Dissolution is the state to which corruption tends: corruption, therefore, cannot be of long standing."[2] "Corruption is a transition state, leading to a crisis,"[3] the crisis, viz., of extinction. It follows that "that which is both a chronic and an active state is not a corruption," and that "duration is a test of a faithful development."[4] But this proof rests entirely on the one prevailing assumption, viz., that there is no other kind of corruption or deterioration but that of failure. The idea of exaggeration does not enter. We see no reason for our part why failure may not be a long as well as a short process. But to say that doctrinal exaggerations may not get strong hold of large portions of the world, and gain a chronic continuance, would certainly be, in our opinion, as purely arbitrary an assumption as any reasoner could make. The tests as a whole, in short, following the general argument of which they are the ramifications, just refuse to touch the point for which their testing virtue is most solicited; and allow

[1] Pages 73, 77. [2] Page 90. [3] *Ibid.* [4] Page 91.

the most common fault charged upon the system they are to test, to slip through them.

Of one of these tests, however, we must speak, inasmuch as it is one which, if truly answered to, entirely settles the question of truth or falsehood in a development. We mean the test of logical sequence. There can be no doubt that what is logically derived from any acknowledged truth is as true as that from which it is derived. But then the question comes, How are we to insure the right application of this test, and how prove, in any given case, to other minds, that such and such inferences are logically drawn? We have heard much lately of the necessity of accepting all the consequences of the truths we hold, to the utmost bounds of logical exhaustion. Perfectly acknowledging the necessity, we want to know how the acknowledgment is to facilitate the argument, and how certain conclusions are proved to be logical.

The region of logic is a very plain and very unanimous one, up to a certain line. Where a thorough agreement and understanding as to any premisses exist, all competent men will draw the same conclusions from them; and the inference will command acceptance, and carry self-evident truth with it. All mankind infer from the facts before them, that sunshine ripens, that rain makes things grow, that food nourishes, that fire warms. All men who knew what a watch was, would infer that it had a maker. We may go into moral nature,—and so far as people understand, and are agreed upon their moral ground, they will raise the same inferences upon it; all people, *e.g.*, who appreciate the fact of a conscience, will infer from it future reward or punishment. We may come to theology, and so far as men have a fair agreement and understanding as to any idea, they will draw the same inference from it. In all these cases the inferences will be the same, because the premisses being the same in people's minds, the inferences are actually contained in the premisses, and go along with them. But what explains the commanding irresistibleness of the inferential process at the same time limits its range. When the inferential process enters upon a ground where there is not this good understanding, or when it slides out of its own simply inferential functions into conjectural ones and attempts discovery, it loses this command; and the appeal to simple logic to force unaccepted premisses, or subtle conjectures, will not answer. On this latter sort of ground, one man's logic will differ from another man's logic; and one will draw one inference and another another; and one will draw more and another less in the same direction of inference. In this way the logical controversy proceeded on the great doctrines of Christianity in the first centuries: different sects developed them in their own way; and each sect appealed triumphantly to the logical irresistibleness of its development. The Arian, the Nestorian, the Apollinarian, the Eutychian, the Monothelite developments, each began with a great truth, and each professed to demand one, and only one, treatment for it. All successively had one watchword, and that was, Be logical. Be logical, said the Arian: Jesus Christ is the son of God; a son cannot be coeval with his father. Be logical, said the Nestorian: Jesus Christ was man and was God; he was therefore two persons. Be logical, said the Apollinarian: Jesus Christ was not two persons; he was not, therefore, perfect God and perfect man too. Be logical, said the Eutychian: Jesus Christ was only one person; he could therefore only have one nature. Be logical, said the Monothelite: Jesus Christ was only one person; he could therefore only have one will. Be logical, said the Macedonian: the Holy Ghost is the Spirit of the Father, and therefore cannot be a person distinct from the Father. Be logical, said the Sabellian : God is one, and therefore cannot be three. Be logical, said the Manichean : evil is not derived from God, and therefore must be an original substance independent of Him. Be logical, said the Gnostic : an infinite Deity cannot really assume a finite body. Be logical, said the Novatian : there is only one baptism for the remission of sins; there is therefore no remission for sin after baptism. Be logical, to come to later times, said the Calvinist : God predestinates, and therefore man has not free will. Be logical, said the Anabaptist : the Gospel bids us to communicate our goods, and therefore does not sanction property in them. Be logical, says the Quaker : the Gospel enjoins meekness, and therefore forbids war. Be logical, says every sect and school: you admit our premisses; you do not admit our conclusions. You are inconsistent. You go a certain way, and then arbitrarily stop. You admit a truth, but do not push it to its legitimate consequences. You are superficial; you want depth. Thus on every kind of question in religion has human logic from the first imposed imperially its own conclusions; and encountered equally imperial counter ones. The truth is, that human reason is liable to error; and to make logic infallible, we must have an infallible logician. Whenever such infallibility speaks to us, if ancient proved tradition be such, or if the contemporary voice of the universal Church be such, we are bound to obey; but the mere apparent consecutiveness itself, which carries on an idea from one stage to another, is no sort of guarantee, except to the mind of the individual thinker himself. The whole dogmatic creed of the Church has been formed in direct contradiction to such apparent lines of consecutiveness. The Nestorian saw as clearly as his logic could tell him, that two persons must follow from two natures. The Monophysite saw as clearly as his logic could tell him, that one nature must follow from one person. The Arian, the Monothelite, the Manichean, saw as clearly as their logic could tell them on their respective questions, and argued inevitably and convincingly to themselves. To the intellectual imagination of the great heresiarchs of the early ages, the doctrine of our Lord's nature took boldly some one line, and developed continuously and straightforwardly some one idea; it demanded unity and consistency. The creed of the Church, steering between extremes and uniting opposites was a timid artificial creation, a work of diplomacy. In a sense they were right. The explanatory creed of the Church was a diplomatic work; it was diplomatic, because it was faithful. With a shrewdness and nicety like that of some ablest and most sustained course of state-craft and cabinet policy, it went on adhering to a complex original idea, and balancing one tendency in it by another. One heresiarch after another would have infused boldness into it; they appealed to one element and another in it, which they wanted to be developed indefinitely. The creed kept its middle course, rigidly combining opposites; and a mixed and balanced erection of dogmatic language arose. One can conceive the view which a great heretical mind, like that of Nestorius, *e.g.*, would take of such a course; the keen, bitter, and almost lofty contempt which —with his logical view of our Lord inevitably deduced and clearly drawn out in his own mind,—he would cast upon that creed which obstinately shrank from the call, and seemed to prefer inconsistency, and refuse to carry out truth.

Let us examine how this logical process acts, in one or two instances, in the department of doctrine before us.

In the case of Purgatory, for example. The doctrine

of Purgatory, we are told, is a corollary from the doctrine of Repentance.[1] The one is contained in the other. Admit the doctrine of Repentance, in its genuine meaning, and you cannot stop short: it carries you, by necessary reasoning, to a Purgatory.

It is not easy, indeed, to see at first what this logical claim means. The principle of Repentance is a general Gospel principle. Taken in a satisfactional sense, it still remains a general principle,—the principle that sin should be atoned for by pain. Purgatory, on the other hand, is a particular fact. A general principle cannot involve, logically, a particular fact. Charity is a general principle —the principle that we should love and do good to others. The general principle of Charity cannot, without an absurdity, be said logically to involve a given instance of it at a given time; as that we should give, on such a day, such a sum to such a person. If such a fact takes place, indeed, it is a consequence of the principle, but the fact cannot be inferred from the principle. Purgatory is a particular place, entered into at a particular time, viz., between death and the Day of Judgment, for the endurance of pain for sin. That particular endurance of pain is no more to be inferred from the general principle that pain should be endured for sin, than the particular act of charity is to be inferred from the general principle that we should act charitably. We draw from an approving and disapproving conscience, indeed, the inference of reward or punishment for actions. True; but that the sentence will be awarded on a particular day, that that day will be at a particular time, viz., at the end of the world, and that all the world will be judged together, are not contained in the principle of conscience, but are matters of simple revelation. We believe in a Day of Judgment, because

[1] Page 417.

the fact is revealed to us; and why are we to believe in a Purgatory, but for a similar reason?

There is an obvious hiatus in such an argument, and Mr. Newman fills it up in the following way. If the pain endured for sin, he says, is necessary, not only as a sign of contrition for, but as an absolute satisfaction for sin, then whatever amount of it ought to be endured cannot be diminished from. Consequently, if it is not endured in this world, it must be endured in another. The early Church, by their rigorous penances, inflicted it in this world: those penances have since been softened: it follows that the difference must be suffered in purgatory. "How," he asks, "is the complement of that satisfaction to be wrought out, which on just grounds of expedience has been suspended in the Church now?"[1] ... If in consequence of death or the exercise of the Church's discretion, the '*plena penitentia*' is not accomplished in its ecclesiastical shape, how or when will the residue be exacted?"[2] We will explain the particular assumption on which the force of this reasoning depends:—

Minds properly alive to the nature of sin, will admit the doctrine of satisfactional pain in every practical and ethical sense. It is a doctrine not peculiar to Christianity, but part of natural religion, and does not apply to post-baptismal sin only, but to all sin whatever. Every one who genuinely feels that he has committed a sin, will feel something of an impulse to punish himself for it. A heathen will feel it. It is an original instinct in our nature, though post-baptismal sin comes peculiarly under its operation, as being the much greater sin of a fall from special grace. The mere necessary pain contained in the sense of guilt tends to lead us to some action similar and cognate to itself. Even the mere additional internal self-

[1] Page 414.   [2] Page 415.

mortification which the increase of care and vigilance to avoid a repetition of the sin will cause, will be regarded by the mind as in some way satisfactional, and atoning for the past; and that aspect of such discipline will be reposed in with a natural accompanying sense of relief to the mind, side by side with, but distinct from, the other aspect of self-amendment and improvement. The idea has laid irrevocable hold of common language, and we talk about a person "atoning for his conduct," "making satisfaction," and so on, not confining the meaning of such expressions, though we use them vaguely enough, to effects of such atoning conduct in the way of compensation to others, but including the person himself also under its benefit and grace. As a practical truth, then, we believe in satisfactional pain ; we believe, *i.e.* that we ought to be willing to undergo pain as a punishment for sin, and that to do so is beneficial to us and pleasing to God.

But as soon as we leave the practical ground, and enter on the metaphysical,—as soon as we have to do with the intrinsic value of such pain itself, and its real effect, as so much pain, upon our eternal condition, we enter upon a subject on which we are wholly ignorant, and on which we have no means of forming a conclusion. Mr. Newman's argument proceeds on the assumption that equal sinners must suffer equal amounts of pain, in punishment for their sin. But this is an assumption and nothing more. We know what the sinner's disposition should be, on his side : we do not know what God's dispensation is, on the the other. We do not fully know upon what laws, or for what reasons, He inflicts, in the course of His Providence, various degrees and forms of suffering upon those moral beings whom He is training for a future life. The improvements in the art of medicine, and the greater security of civil government, have relieved Christians of a later age from much pain which Christians of an earlier underwent. There are all shades of difference in suffering among Christians of the same age; and some of the same apparent goodness have much less bodily illness than others. We do not know why all these differences take place; and therefore to proceed to calculate them, and infer from them that complement to come in each case, which is to give the balance, would be to argue in the dark. The Christian penances were less rigorous at first, became more rigorous after, became less rigorous after that: to say that a Christian, who repented with the same sustained care and self-denying disposition in a less severe age of the Church, would have to go, after death, into Purgatory, because he had not suffered so much pain as a brother Christian in another age, is one of those forced pieces of reasoning which show their arbitrary basis. The great difficulties connected with the visible course of Providence, as regards our preparation for a final state, every one grants. The difference we see in persons' situations, educations, spiritual opportunities here; the premature death, which seems to cut the formation of a character in the middle; the existence of those vast masses we see, of whose character we cannot pronounce decidedly either way, suggest undefined and involuntary conjectures to our minds with respect to the intermediate state. But we are not concerned here with conjecture but with logic.

Such is the main argument for the doctrine of Purgatory itself. A defensive one, to account for the fact of its late introduction, is skilfully turned into the same channel, and made to tell positively for it. "Considering," says Mr. Newman, "the length of time which separates Christ's first and second coming, the millions of faithful souls who are exhausting it, and the intimate concern which every Christian has in the determination of its character, it might have been expected that Scripture would have spoken explicitly concerning it, whereas, in fact, its notices are but brief and obscure. We might indeed have argued that this silence was intentional, with a view of discouraging speculations upon the subject, except for the circumstance that, as in the question of our post-baptismal state, its teaching seems to proceed upon an hypothesis inapplicable to the state of the Church since the time it was delivered. As Scripture contemplates Christians, not as backsliders, but as saints, so does it apparently represent the Day of Judgment as immediate, and the interval of expectation as evanescent. It leaves on our minds the general impression that Christ was returning on earth at once, 'the time short,' worldly engagements superseded by 'the present distress,' persecutors urgent, Christians sinless and expectant, without home, without plan for the future, looking up to heaven. But outward circumstances have changed; and with the change of necessity a different application of the revealed word became necessary."[1] The argument here accounts for the difference of doctrine in the primitive and in a later age, by the fact of there being a totally different state of things before the Christian mind at these two periods; it asserts that, Christians being contemplated as sinless, and the Day of Judgment as immediate in the first, and both of these views being reversed in the second, Purgatory, which was superfluous in the former of the two periods, obtained a legitimate existence in the latter. Now with respect to one of these two assertions,—without at all denying the existence of such an expectation as Mr. Newman mentions in the early Church, viz., that the

[1] Page 100.

world was coming immediately to an end—it is surely not true to say that "Scripture leaves on the mind the general impression" that that expectation was right. The prophecies of St. Paul, pointing forward to the "fulness of the Gentiles," *i.e.* the spread of the Gospel over the world, and the restoration of the Jews (whatever that is) to take place when that epoch had arrived, convey a first impression certainly of a very opposite kind. Those prophecies of St. John, which look onward to the rise of great events and large changes and commotions over the political surface of the world, to the career of empires and to their fall, and to the time "when the kingdoms of this world are become the kingdoms of our Lord and of his Christ," leave a like impression. We do not naturally imagine St. Paul or St. John thinking that the world was going to end immediately; and St. Paul in one place specially corrects that notion.

With respect to the other point, that Scripture "contemplates Christians as sinless," if it be meant by this that it contemplates them as sinless so far as they are Christians, it certainly does; and so has the Church done always. But if it be meant—and the distinction in the matter-of-fact state of things at the two periods is the one wanted for the argument—that Scripture contemplates Christians as sinless in fact, this it certainly does not do, for there is no ordinary vice, bodily or mental, which the New Testament does not allude to as more or less prevailing in the Christian society of that day. They are Christians of the days of the Apostles who are described as "unruly and vain talkers and deceivers,"[1] acting from the love of "filthy lucre;" "having their mind and conscience defiled," professing that they know God, but in works denying him, "being abominable and disobedient,

[1] Titus i. 10.

and unto every good work reprobate." Those Christians could hardly be contemplated as sinless about whom the memento was given, "the Cretians are alway liars, evil beasts, slow bellies," with the addition, "this witness is true, therefore rebuke them sharply." The existence of "rioters," "drunkards," "brawlers," "strikers," "self-willed" and passionate persons in the Church of that day was certainly distinctly contemplated in that direction which provided that a bishop should not be chosen out of such a class. A very far from perfect state of the Christian temper was certainly contemplated in those Christians who, according to their condition or sex, were to be specially exhorted "not to purloin" from their masters, not to be "false accusers and slanderers," not to be "gadders about," not to be "disobedient to their husbands." The men of the Church described in the New Testament appear to have exhibited amongst them very obviously and definitely the common faults of men; intemperance in eating and drinking, violence, covetousness, envy, pride and boastfulness, over-respect to worldly rank and station: the women to have exhibited among them the common faults of women, those "of being idle, wandering about from house to house, tattlers, busy-bodies, speaking things which they ought not." The Christian Church of that day, as the Christian Church of a later age, had "spots in its feasts of charity," and displayed as coarse a mixture of bad and good, in the very sanctuary of religious fellowship, as it ever did afterwards. "Filthy dreamers among them despised dominion, defiled the flesh, turned grace into lasciviousness, spoke evil of the things which they knew not, and what they knew naturally as brute beasts, in those things corrupted themselves."[1] Men externally Christians "went after the way of Cain, ran greedily

[1] Jude 8.

after the error of Balaam, perished in the gainsaying of Core." They were "murmurers, complainers, walking after their own lusts, speaking great swelling words, having men's persons in admiration because of advantage." External Christians were "mockers," "sensual" men, "feeding themselves without fear;" were "clouds without water carried about of winds; trees whose fruit withereth, without fruit, twice dead, plucked up by the roots; raging waves of the sea foaming out their own shame, wandering stars to whom is reserved the blackness of darkness for ever." It was in days in which all the above descriptions had their application, that Mr. Newman says, "Christians were contemplated as sinless;" and that the actual state of the Church, small and holy, did not suggest a purgatory, whereas afterwards, "when the nations were converted and offences abounded," it did. "Christians did not recognise a purgatory as a part of the dispensation till the world had flowed into the Church, and a habit of corruption had been superinduced." We see no essential distinction in the actual moral condition of the Christian society at the former and in the latter period; none to suggest to Christian minds at one age a purgatory as necessary, while it precludes it at the other as not wanted. And the facts of the case appear simply to refute the view taken of them, and the argument which is built upon it.

We will add that it is not the omission in Scripture with which we are concerned, so much as a positive counter-tone. With the Christian Church, a mixed body around them, and containing all the moral shades and inconsistencies, all the unformed, half-formed characters, all the alloy and general imperfection which it did afterward, Apostles preached the doctrine that "the dead which die in the Lord rest from their labours." An arguer may doubtless insist on being told accurately who were "the dead which died in the Lord," and assert that it meant some true believers, and not others; but we do not see how any fair mind can deny that the New Testament, as a whole, throws a peaceful and tranquil character over the collective state of good Christian souls departed, and that the established doctrine of Purgatory throws a directly contrary one; and that, without insisting on the universally traditionary meaning given to the "Paradise" and "Abraham's bosom" of the Gospels, the intermediate state to which good souls went after death has a paradisal character in inspired and primitive, and an infernal one in later theology.

We come to another and much more formidable instance of the asserted "logical sequency" in development.

The whole extreme cultus of the Virgin Mary,—involving all the prerogatives, distinctions, powers, and attributes assigned to her in the practical Roman system, and in the works of those Divines who have gone the greatest lengths on this subject,—is made the logical result of the fact that she was, in His human nature, the mother of our Lord. We are referred to the word Theotocos as the voucher and proof of the whole. The relationship of mother to God as man, so mysteriously and awfully near to Him as man, although infinitely distant from Him as God, has appeared to include, by logical sequence, ratifying itself step by step, to some minds, as they dwelt in long speculative contemplation on that one idea, the whole formal and distinct "place of St. Mary in the economy of Grace," which we see assigned to her. The idea—mother of God—was entered into, pursued, brought out; it seemed mathematically to contain, to the religious reasoner, such further truths about her. Far be it from us, as members of the English Church, to deny the incommunicable dignity bestowed upon the Blessed Virgin in that mysterious relationship. We write now under the painful conviction that she has been, in our popular theology, abridged of that honour which is due to her, though how far the known principles of reaction may operate or not, as our excuse, we do not now inquire. But nevertheless when such inferences as we are speaking of are said to be logically drawn from the simple original fact of the relationship, the question must be asked how we can argue certainly from data so mysterious and incomprehensible. We can express the truth indeed that the blessed Mary was the Mother of God, as we can express the doctrine of the Trinity, in all modes and forms which amount but to the expression of that truth; and the truth itself invests her with an incommunicable dignity. But when the reasoner goes further and says— She was the mother of our Lord; therefore she was born without original sin, in the first place; therefore she was the "created idea in the making of the world,"[1] in the second place; therefore she is the one channel through which all grace flows, in the third place; it is right to ask, Why? How do these second truths follow necessarily from the first? Show, for example, that it inevitably follows, from her being the Theotocos, that her own conception was immaculate? "Can a clean thing come from an unclean," we are told. But it is evident that on such an application of Scripture as this, the mother of the Virgin must be immaculate, for the same reason that the Virgin herself was; and so the stream of original sin is driven backward till no place is left where it ever could have existed. The truth is, we are not sufficiently acquainted with the nature of the mystery of the Incarnation to be drawing such conclusions from it. Show us indeed, as we said before, an infallible logician, and we

[1] Quoted from Segneri, p.444.

will accept whatever his logic extracts. But it is absurd to suppose that the mere consecutiveness which human logic sees in this or that line of thought and process of evolution, can be appealed to as proof of a doctrine.

Without dwelling, however, further on such general lines of argument, we will proceed at once to the examination of the particular argumentative position which Mr. Newman has put forward on this subject. Mr. Newman has discovered,—discovered we say, because we are not aware that any one has maintained it before him,—a new argumentative position for the extreme cultus of the Virgin;—a position, moreover, which does not stop at a simple defence of the existing doctrine, but aims distinctly at heightening it, and giving new and indefinite space for it to expand in. Exerting the privilege of genius, Mr. Newman does not enter the Roman Church as a simple pupil and follower. He enters magisterially. He surveys her with the eye of a teacher. He tells her new truth. He commences a doctrinal rise in her; he takes her by the hand, and lifts her up a whole step, in system and idea, on her very boldest ground of development. He will not allow her to stand still even there, and rest contented with her advances. "Catholicity," he says emphatically, "does not sleep; it is not stationary *even now*."[1] He points out, and institutes accordingly, a new doctrinal movement within the Roman pale, before he is himself in it; and he does not permit her to "be stationary even now," but gives her a distinct move forward in what occupies so bold and extreme a place in her system as her view of the Virgin Mary.

It is unnecessary for us here to transcribe all the authorised titles of the Blessed Virgin in the Roman Church, or describe again what has been so often described, the whole practical and authorised idea of the Virgin's

[1] Page 446.

position, with the *cultus* attached to it, and all the ramifications of the *cultus*, the nature of the litanies and prayers addressed to her, and other expressions of the general idea. The reader may easily recall them, and suppose them put down here.

Now Mr. Newman seems to himself to see that if the Church of Rome goes so far as this in her view of the Virgin, she ought to go farther; and that all those prerogatives and powers assigned to her want some one comprehensive basis to stand on, some one hypothesis to systematise and consolidate them. He accordingly provides one, and takes care that it is sufficiently ample. The early controversies on the subject of the Divinity of our Lord led, as an inevitable result, the opposers of that doctrine into a very difficult position. Overwhelmed by the force of universal testimony and tradition, which spoke to the fact of the revelation of that doctrine, and affirmed it to have been distinctly and uninterruptedly handed down from the days of the Apostles, the Arians wanted to deny the doctrine, if we may so speak, as little as they could,—as little, that is, as was consistent with their own logical hypothesis on the subject. They would not acknowledge our Lord to be God; but, that provided against, they made His being, with an anxious and emulous subtlety, as near that of absolute Godhead as it was possible for the speculative faculty to conceive. They raised Him to the very highest and farthest point of secondary divinity;—"they did all but confess," says Mr. Newman, "that He was the Almighty."[1] First of all they said He *was* God: He was πλήρης Θεός, full and perfect God; that is to say, they tried to make secondary Divinity more than secondary, and lift it above itself in the instance of our Lord. They proceeded: He existed

[1] Page 405.

before all worlds; He was the actual Creator of the universe; the God of the Evangelical Covenant; the Mediator between God and man. He was, as such, a legitimate object of Christian worship. This position the Arians gave our Lord. This position Mr. Newman claims for the Virgin Mary. "The Arian controversy," he says, "opened a question which it did not settle. It discovered a new sphere, if we may so speak, in the realms of light, to which the Church had not yet assigned its inhabitant. Arianism had admitted that our Lord was both the God of the Evangelical Covenant and the actual Creator of the universe; but even this was not enough, because it did not confess Him to be the One, Everlasting, Infinite, Supreme Being, but to be made by Him. It was not enough, with that heresy, to proclaim Him to be begotten ineffably[1] before all worlds; not enough to place Him high above all creatures as the type of all the works of God's hands; not enough to make Him the Lord of His saints, the Mediator between God and man, the Object of worship, the Image of the Father: not enough, because it was not all, and between all, and anything short of all, —there was an infinite interval. The highest of creatures is levelled with the lowest, in comparison of the One Creator Himself. That is, the Nicene Council recognised the eventful principle, that while we believe and profess anything to be a creature, such a being is really no God to us, though honoured by us with whatever high titles, and with whatever homage. Arius, or Asterius, did all but confess that Christ was the Almighty; they said much more than St. Bernard or St. Alphonso have since said of St. Mary; yet they left Him a creature, and were

[1] In the edition of 1878, for the words "begotten ineffably," we read "having an ineffable origin;" for "Lord of His saints," "King of all saints;" for "Mediator between God and Man," "the Intercessor for man with God."—Page 143.

found wanting. Thus there was 'a wonder in heaven:' a throne was seen, far above all created powers, mediatorial, intercessory; a title archetypal; a crown bright as the morning star; a glory issuing from the Eternal Throne; robes pure as the heavens; and a sceptre over all; and who was the predestined heir of that Majesty? Who was that Wisdom, and what was her name, 'the Mother of fair love, and fear, and holy hope'—'exalted like a palm-tree in Engaddi, and a rose plant in Jericho;' 'created from the beginning before the world,' in God's counsels, and 'in Jerusalem was her power?' The vision is found in the Apocalypse,—'a Woman clothed with the sun, and the moon under her feet, and upon her head a crown of twelve stars.'"[1] The conclusion of the argument is that St. Mary is truly that being which the Arians falsely maintained our Lord to be. She "supplies the subject of that august proposition of which Arianism provided the predicate:"[2]—"As containing all created perfection, she has all those attributes, which, as noticed above, the Arians and other heretics applied to our Lord."[3]

Now, in the first place, what does Mr. Newman mean here? The attributes which he noticed above as those which the Arians applied to our Lord, were, that He was "begotten before the world;" that He was "the actual Creator of the universe;" that He was "the Mediator between God and man;" and others. Does he mean to say that the Virgin Mary was "begotten before the worlds;" that the Virgin Mary was "the actual Creator of the universe?" Without a wish to attribute to him such ideas, we must at any rate be permitted to say, that if he does not mean these, his language is loose, and is not what language should be on such an awful subject. We are told, generally, that the Virgin supplies the sub-

[1] First Edition, p. 405.   [2] *Ibid.* p. 407.   [3] Page 444.

ject of that august proposition of which "Arianism provided the predicate." We are told, particularly, that "as containing all created perfection, she has all those attributes which the Arians applied to our Lord." And the attributes here referred to are those of "being begotten before the worlds," being "the actual Creator of the universe," being "the Mediator between God and man." Nor does "as containing all created perfection" qualify, but only explain the application of them. Interpreting Mr. Newman grammatically here, we cannot understand him but as asserting that the Virgin Mary was "begotten before the worlds," was "the actual Creator of the universe," was "the Mediator between God and man."[1] If Mr. Newman uses the terms "mere child of Adam," and "mere human being," of the Virgin, in one part of his book, we will not charge him with the full grammatical meaning of another. But the question still remains, and is not answered—What is his meaning? Does he confine himself to the general animus of the Arian proposition, which was to make our Lord simply and shortly all but God? The general proposition, however, does not omit the fact of, but only the mention of, the particulars. Does he mean that the position of the Virgin Mary is equal, and tantamount in dignity, to the position of the Arian "perfect God," without being the same? But this would be a vague difference; and, moreover, the whole position of the Arian Demiurge was expressed with the view to quantity—greatest imaginable quantity of dignity not Divine: if it is to be adequately represented then, it must be represented as it was expressed, and with those attributes by which it was. To express an equal position to it there must be the same means used to express it. We are not, however, strictly speaking, concerned with

[1] See *ante*, p. 57, note.

the process by which Mr. Newman enables himself to hold such a view. It is enough that, as a matter of fact, he does hold it; that, whatever he may do with obstacles to it, he holds, and holds directly and categorically, the view that the Virgin Mary "supplies the subject of that august proposition of which Arianism provided the predicate;" that she is what the Arians affirmed. the Second Person in the Trinity to be.

To proceed then : what is the proof which Mr. Newman gives of the Arian idea being thus fulfilled in the person of the Virgin ? The answer is, none at all, except the facts that Arianism existed, and that the cultus of the Virgin does. The rest is supplied by assumption. Let us follow him. First in order there is the fact that the Arians, in depriving our Lord of His divinity, made Him as divine as they could, consistent with so depriving Him; and that thus a certain idea was arrived at, viz., the Arian idea of secondary Divinity. He then proceeds : "Thus there was a wonder in heaven ; a throne was seen far above all created powers, mediatorial, intercessory ; a title archetypal; a crown bright as the morning star; a glory issuing from the eternal throne; robes pure as the heavens; and a sceptre over all. And who was the predestined heir of this great Majesty ? " He proceeds, that is, to say that this Arian idea demanded fulfilment ; and asks, Who was to fulfil it ? To which the answer follows, no one but the Virgin. The Arians imagined a position. It was necessary that that position should be impersonated. As our Lord was not the impersonator of it, some one else must be ; and no one comes before us so suited for it as the Virgin Mary.

We must be allowed to pause, in some degree of wonder, at a train of reasoning like this, exhibiting such largeness, we must even say, wildness of assumption.

It is assumed that the Arian idea must be realised, must be fulfilled, must be verified in some personage or other. Why? Are all conceptions, as such, true ones? Are all ideas, as such, verified by facts? If not, why must the Arian idea of our Lord needs be verified? What reason is there to be on the look-out for any personage at all to substantiate it? Why trouble ourselves to find a subject for an Arian predicate? What is there to prevent us from considering the whole idea of those heretics, subject, predicate, and all, as a falsehood and a nullity, *their* idea, and nothing more? Certainly, there may be such a case as an idea strongly suggesting its own fulfilment; but in such a case the idea must show some peculiar tokens of truth, genuineness, authoritativeness, and even then the argument is a hazardous one. But to say that because a profane heresy raises an idea, that therefore orthodox Christians are bound to discover a verification of it, and that if Arianism conceives a predicate, the Church must supply the subject—How can this be reasonable? Let those who conceived the one discover the other if they can, and let them verify their own conception; but they are responsible for it, and not others. If the Arian conception remain the Arian conception, and nothing more; if an idea in this case has no fulfilment, a predicate no subject; if a whole speculation issues in hollowness, vacancy, and delusion, it is no more than what has happened to the conceptions of a hundred other sects, and is happening to ten thousand creations of the human brain every day.

We must add, that if anything can increase the strangeness of such an assumption, it is the absolutely matter-of-course way in which it is made. It is not mentioned, it does not appear; it simply lies underneath the argument, is simply supposed, and gone upon, as any self-evident principle is in ordinary reasoning. "The Arian controversy opened a question which it did not settle." He means that the Arians put forth a position, and that the Church did not decide who occupied it. Observe the implied assumption, as if it was self-evidently necessary that it should be occupied. "Arianism discovered a new sphere in the realms of light, to which the Church had not yet assigned its inhabitant." The same implied assumption again, as if it were self-evidently necessary that it should have its inhabitant. Arianism gave its "throne and sceptre over all; and who was the predestined heir of that Majesty?" The same implied assumption again, as if it were self-evidently necessary that there should be an heir.

The historical view is drawn up in a somewhat similar style to the argumentative. The drawer-up describes an easy, a natural, an inevitable succession of ideas on the subject. He exhibits the Church as going on in one continuous line of thought, and forming in two grand successive stages a doctrinal creation; first, embracing an ideal position, and then proceeding in due course to impersonate it. "There was in the first ages no public or ecclesiastical recognition of the place which St. Mary holds in the economy of grace; this was reserved for the fifth century, as the definition of our Lord's proper Divinity had been the work of the fourth. There was a controversy contemporary with those I have already mentioned, I mean the Nestorian, which brought out the complement of the development. . . . In order to do honour to Christ, in order to defend the true doctrine of the Incarnation, in order to secure a right faith in the manhood of the Eternal Son, the Council of Ephesus determined the Blessed Virgin to be the Mother of God. Thus all the heresies of that day, though opposite to each other, tended in a most wonderful way to her exaltation; and the School of Antioch, the fountain of primitive rationalism, led the Church to lay down, first, the conceivable greatness of a creature, and then the incommunicable dignity of St. Mary."[1] We have here an illustration of what may be effected by the instrumentality of partial aspects and points of view. The writer fixes an aspect on the Arian controversy;—the Church took cognisance then of the idea of a secondary Divinity. He fixes an aspect on the Nestorian controversy;—the Church decided then that a certain high title was due to the Virgin Mary; and these two put together are the Church's successive steps of predicate and subject. Now what are the facts of the case on which these aspects are fixed? The Church condemned the Arians for attributing to our Lord only a secondary Divinity: the Church condemned the Nestorians for making God and man in the Incarnation two persons. On this latter point we will speak more at length.

It is true then that the Virgin was declared to be the Theotocos at the Council of Ephesus; but that title had final reference in its bestowal, not to her, but to our Lord. The Council of Ephesus pronounced our Lord to be One Person. It necessarily followed hence that the Virgin Mary, being the mother of that One Person, was the mother of God; but the assertion of our Lord's one personality was the end for which the Council of Ephesus met; and the term Theotocos was introduced subordinately, as the sign of that one personality. The Council had not the rank of the Virgin Mary, but the truth of the Incarnation as its object; and the word Theotocos comes down to us with this distinctly subordinated character and significance stamped upon it by

[1] Page 407.

its early use. It may be said, indeed, that it makes no difference whether the Church used the word primarily or subordinately, so long as the word was used as a fact; and that the rank of the Virgin is a result from the word itself, with whatever view employed. But it is undeniable that the original motive for the word necessarily presents it to the mind, with a certain connection, direction, and meaning attached to it. Between being used for one purpose, and being used for another, there is unquestionably a difference; and that difference has an inevitable bearing upon the word itself. Mr. Newman, at any rate, seems to acknowledge this; for he studiously moulds his whole historical statement so as to leave an impression on the reader of the rank, as such, of the Virgin being the subject of the Church's deliberations. Even the construction of a sentence, aiding as it does a general bias in this direction, is symptomatic. "In order to do honour to Christ, in order to defend the true doctrine of the Incarnation, in order to secure a right faith in the manhood of the Eternal Son, the Council of Ephesus determined the Blessed Virgin to be the Mother of God." The reader will observe that the sentence leads up to the Virgin's title as to a climax; and at the very time that a statement recognises its subordinateness, a certain form and arrangement makes it a principal. A simple transposition would considerably alter the effect:—"The Council of Ephesus determined the Blessed Virgin to be the Mother of God in order to do honour to Christ, in order to," etc. etc. We instance this to show what a very little tells in this way. The whole statement of the case is moulded with the same view; in order to produce, viz., a general impression different from what the facts of the case themselves give, an impression of the Virgin's personal rank as the primary subject of, her personal elevation as the crowning work of, the Ephesian Council.

Such are the two proceedings of the Church on which Mr. Newman has to build. And he builds thus. Out of the Arian idea of our Lord, and its condemnation, he chooses the idea itself apart from our Lord, and apart from its condemnation, and so gets an idea of secondary Divinity simply taken cognisance of by the Church. Out of the Nestorian controversy again he selects the Virgin's title apart from the doctrine to which it was subordinated. Thus, on his view, the Church first takes cognisance of a position of secondary Divinity, and then provides formally an occupant for it. But of this argumentative proof by a succession of aspects, it must be remarked that that whole mode of arguing cannot be considered conclusive which goes upon arbitrarily selected abstractions from facts, and not from the actual facts themselves. An arguer may abstract one aspect, but all the others which he does not abstract still remain; and it will continually happen that one aspect of the selfsame fact will wholly negative another for a given argumentative purpose. Mr. Newman holds up the Arian idea, in its aspect as taken cognisance of by the Church: it certainly has that aspect; but it was taken cognisance of only as the idea of an heretical party; and that is another aspect. Mr. Newman takes the former and omits the latter; and the Arian hypothesis accordingly appears, in his view, as the sacred and awful property of the Church from the first, insisted upon, pursued, and in time furnished with its occupant.

Such is Mr. Newman's positive use of the Arian hypothesis, as brought to bear on the cultus of the Virgin: but he also uses it negatively, and as a defensive argument, for that cultus. The Arians were denounced by the

Church as disbelievers in our Lord's divinity, notwithstanding their high and *quasi*-deifying hypothesis concerning Him. Upon that fact the general principle is raised, that no one who regards any being as at all short of the One and Supreme God, can be charged with regarding that being as God, or be charged, therefore, with idolatry with respect to such a being. "Between all and anything short of all there is an infinite interval." "The highest of creatures is levelled with the lowest in comparison of the One Creator Himself. The Nicene Council recognised the eventful principle, that while we believe and profess any being to be a creature, such a being is really no God to us, though honoured by us with whatever high titles, and with whatever homage. Arius, or Asterius, did all but confess that Christ was the Almighty; they said much more than St. Bernard or St. Alphonso have since said of St. Mary, yet they left Him a creature, and were found wanting." He concludes— "The votaries of St. Mary do not exceed the true faith, unless the blasphemers of her Son come up to it. The Church of Rome is not idolatrous, unless Arianism is orthodoxy."[1]

Now, without at all professing to be of that number who throw a whole-length charge of idolatry upon the Roman Church, we see an argument here before us, and we would deal with it as an argument. The argument, then, is based on a particular implied definition of idolatry; idolatry being considered to mean the regarding of a being as the One and Supreme God who is not such, and nothing short of such regard being considered to be idolatry. This definition, we must next remark, the writer gets from his own mind, and not from the Nicene Council. The Nicene Council asserts that a being who

[1] Page 406.

is not the One Supreme God, *is not God*,—God being the One and Supreme God. Mr. Newman turns this assertion into the assertion that "such a being can be really *no God to us.*" Now, if by the latter phrase Mr. Newman means simply, "not regarded as the One and Supreme God by us," in that sense his assertion is coincident with that of the Nicene Council; but it is not the assertion which he wants, because it does not declare that such a being may not be idolatrously regarded by us. If, on the other hand, he intends his phrase positively to express the meaning wanted, viz., "not regarded idolatrously by us," in that sense it is only coincident with the assertion of the Nicene Council on the supposition that the two meanings, "not regarded as Supreme God," and "not regarded idolatrously," are the same; that is to say, on the supposition that his definition of idolatry is true. He argues in a circle, and has to assert the definition on his own authority to begin with, in order to prove it to be of Nicene.

Of the definition of idolatry, then, thus assumed in Mr. Newman's argument, we must observe that it appears to us a wholly inadequate and a practically futile one. There is a look indeed of irresistible logic about a train of reasoning which runs:—Idolatry implies regarding as God: no being is regarded as God who is regarded as anything short of the One and Supreme God; therefore the attribution of no kind of secondary divinity to a being, even up to the point of making it "all but" the One and Supreme God, is idolatry. Such an argument may appear at first sight to bring the matter to an immediate point, and to the test of mathematical demonstration. But an argument is too irresistible, if one may say so, and defeats itself, if it refutes demonstrably a plain and obvious fact. The plain and obvious fact, in the present instance, is that there has been all along, for ages and ages in the world, an idolatry which has not answered to this definition. It is well known—and the fact is largely dwelt on in the first volume of Cudworth—that the ancient Polytheisms, expressly condemned as idolatrous in the Bible, acknowledged a subordination in the sphere of deity, and placed over all the minor and secondary divinities, notwithstanding their temples and worship, one God supreme, the Creator of all things.[1] Scripture takes the broad and practical view here, viz., that such divinities were gods, and that they received divine worship; and that, however persons might intellectually deify, in a peculiarly deifying

[1] "Let it be granted, as you assert," says Arnobius, "that your Jupiter and the Eternal Omnipotent God are one and the same. Are not almost all your gods such as were taken out from the rank of men, and placed among the stars? Have you not advanced into the number of your Divi, Bacchus or Liber for inventing the use of the wine, Ceres of corn, Æsculapius of herbs, Minerva of the olive, Triptolemus of the plough, and Hercules for subduing beasts, thieves, and monsters?" "The one and only God," says Clemens, "is worshipped by the Greeks paganically." "It is unquestionable," says Cudworth, "that the more intelligent of the Greekish Pagans did frequently understand by Zeus, the supreme unmade Deity, who was the Maker of the world, and all the inferior gods." "That there is one supreme Deity," says Lactantius, "both philosophers and poets, and even the vulgar worshippers of the gods themselves, frequently confess." "The Pagans," says St. Augustine, "had not so far degenerated as to have lost the knowledge of one supreme God, from whom is all nature whatsoever; and they derived all their gods from one." "The Maker of the universe," says Proclus, "is celebrated both by Plato and Orpheus, and the Oracles, as the father of gods and men, who produceth multitudes of gods, and sends down souls for the generation of men. We have the Orphic verses—

>   . . . Διὸς πάλιν ἐντὸς ἐτύχθη
> Αἰθέρος εὐρείης ἠδ' οὐρανοῦ ἀγλαον ὕψος
> Πάντες τ' ἀθάνατοι μάκαρες θεοὶ ἠδὲ θέαιναι,

and the celebrated—

> Ζεὺς πρῶτος γένετο, Ζεὺς ὕστατος,

and Homer's—

> Τόσσον ἐγὼ περί τ' εἰμὶ θεῶν, περί τ' εἰμ' ἀνθρώπων.

sense, some Highest Being distinct from them all, they practically treated the latter as divine, and put themselves in their whole feelings and ideas in a certain practical position to them, to which the term idolatry was due. But upon Mr. Newman's definition, how Scripture will prove its charge against the Polytheist, it is not easy to see. The latter will immediately present his belief in the One and Supreme God, as the infallible security against the idolatrous regard of the subordinate ones, and will say, "Between all and anything short of all there is an infinite interval; the highest of creatures is levelled with the lowest in comparison with the One Creator himself."

Or put such a summary mode of reasoning as Mr. Newman's into the hands of the idol-worshipper of the Old Testament. It appears to be quite certain that if such logic as this is to be allowed to settle the question, the idol-worshipper has a ground positively irresistible, to fall back upon against the charge of the prophet. The prophet charges him with regarding an idol which he has himself made as God. He enters into the most vivid and accurate detail in describing the entire and unqualified way in which this worshipped god is a creature, known to be a creature, actually made by the hands of the worshipper. The worshipper does not worship the matter as such,—he worships the form; that form is the actual workmanship of the person who worships it. "The smith with the tongs both worketh in the coals, and fashioneth it with hammers, and worketh it with the strength of his arms: yea, he is hungry, and his strength faileth: he drinketh no water, and is faint. The carpenter stretcheth out his rule; he marketh it out with a line; he fitteth it with planes, and he marketh it out with the compass, and maketh it after the figure of a man, according to the beauty of a man, that it may remain in the house. He heweth him down cedars, and taketh the cypress and the oak, which he strengtheneth for himself among the trees of the forest: he planteth an ash, and the rain doth nourish it. Then shall it be for a man to burn: for he will take thereof, and warm himself; yea, he kindleth it, and baketh bread; yea, he maketh a god, and worshippeth it; he maketh it a graven image, and falleth down thereto. He burneth part thereof in the fire; with part thereof he eateth flesh; he roasteth roast, and is satisfied: yea, he warmeth himself, and saith, Aha, I am warm, I have seen the fire: and the residue thereof he maketh a god, even his graven image; he falleth down unto it, and worshippeth it, and prayeth unto it, and saith, Deliver me; for thou art my god. They have not known nor understood: for He hath shut their eyes, that they cannot see; and their hearts, that they cannot understand. And none considereth in his heart, neither is there knowledge nor understanding to say, I have burned part of it in the fire; yea, also I have baked bread upon the coals thereof; I have roasted flesh, and eaten it: and shall I make the residue thereof an abomination? shall I fall down to the stock of a tree?"[1] Now the idol-worshipper of the old world, because he was spiritually hardened, was not therefore intellectually stupified. We are expressly told of such, that "professing themselves wise, they became fools." He was, in regard to intellectual power, fully as profound a philosopher, as deep a thinker, as subtle a reasoner, as the worshipper of the One Invisible God. Let us at any rate suppose him so, for it is all the same for the argument. Is it possible to imagine that an intellectual idolater would not have had the wit to urge in his defence that he did not worship

[1] Is. xliv. 12.

the idol itself, and that the prophet misapprehended him. Could he not confront his accuser *in limine*, and before he troubled himself with a single step in the line of apology, with the self-evident proposition that it was simply impossible, an absurdity in terms, that he should regard a piece of matter as God? And could he not retort, with irresistible effect upon the prophet, those very details of image-making which had been urged against him? Could he not say that that very description only proved the more vividly that the idol was, because it *must* be, looked upon by the worshipper as a creature? that if the latter made the image with his own hand, he had an *ipso facto* proof, which it was not in his power as a rational being to deny, that it was a creature? that if he knew it to be a creature, he must think it to be one? and that if he thought it to be a creature, he could not at the same time think it to be God? What logical contradiction could be given to such a defence? Undoubtedly it is impossible that any human being should think the material substance of a stone or a log to be God. The prophet would, of course, proceeding upon his own substantial meaning in his charge, treat such a reply to it as an evasion and not an answer. If there be a species of regard to, a feeling to, a whole internal attitude of the mind toward an image which is idolatrous, while it does not absolutely deify it, such idolatry is not refuted by this reply. But take away this species of idolatry from the field of existence, as Mr. Newman does, and we do not see how the prophet can make good a charge of idolatry in the case. He must yield to irresistible logic; the thing charged is simply impossible. Mr. Newman's reasoning makes the plain assertions of Scripture inexplicable, and empties the whole arguments of the whole line of prophets on the subject of idolatry of validity. The Bible is made to talk what is in truth nonsense; and the refinement of later speculative analysis throws over its holy scorn and confident denunciation, a character of little more than—to use the expression—a high fanaticism.

Such logic, then, as that before us is refuted by the fact. And this is only another form of stating that it is not sound logic. The principle of *summum jus summa injuria* in justice has its counterpart in reasoning. There is an extreme, a purist species of logic, which marches through a question like a phantom, and leaves it just where it was. The present is an attempt to decide a practical question by the test of an abstract truth. Idolatry is a practical thing; it exists, where it does exist, in the shape of a certain actual state of feeling and sentiment in an individual mind toward a particular object; and it must be tested by being compared with the same individual's actual state of feeling toward another object, viz., God. If the former, on comparison, exhibits a sufficient distinction from the latter, it avoids the idolatrous character; if it does not, it assumes it; but the distinction lies between two practical states of feeling. Mr. Newman's test, on the other hand, is a belief in the abstract truth that one being is God and the other not. Now the reception of the abstract distinction does not necessarily carry with it that amount of the practical one. It might seem, indeed, at first sight, that the simple idea of a Supreme Being implied in the holder of it a corresponding supreme and inapproachable standard in his idea of that Being's dignity, as compared with his idea of any other's. Because we form the idea of an infinite Being, we seem to have an infinite idea, and therefore to be *ipso facto* secured from the possibility of an approach to it in our idea of any other being. But that is not true.

In the present case the Being is infinite, our idea of Him is finite. We have from the imperfection of our nature a necessarily limited idea of God; the consequence is that that idea is not incapable of being approached in the case of forming a conception of some other being, and that such a thing is possible as raising the dignity of some other being too near to His to leave room for that difference which should exist between them. "Between all, and anything short of all, there is an infinite interval;" certainly, in the region of abstract truth, but not in the region of human idea and conception. The human idea of "all" is a finite one, and therefore the interval between that "all" and something just short of it is not infinite in the human mind. Were we infinite beings, indeed, and had an infinite idea of God to begin with, we could afford to erect any finite conception of any magnitude whatever, and run no risk of approach to the infinite one. But such a liberty cannot be conceded to circumscribed minds without an interference with their finite idea of that Being. And to throw open the whole world of human conception to them, and allow them to raise their idea of secondary divinity as high as they please, only with the abstract salvo that it is short of supreme, is to be secure in the finiteness of the idea approaching, while we forget the finiteness of the idea approached. The image which our limited faculties can form of the Supreme Being is one to which daring ascents in the scale of secondary divinity can, if pursued, make an approach, and attain an improper vicinity. And although it may be argued that if our idea of the Supreme Being is finite, we have the evil, anyhow, of a less interval than there ought to be between our idea of Him and other beings; still we may have quite a sufficiently large and awful idea of Him to make the practical distinction we want: and an interval may be wide enough, if properly preserved, though it may not be if rudely invaded.

Moreover, this whole argument is just not the one which, as a matter of fact, the Fathers of Nice took with respect to the Arian hypothesis. Mr. Newman says, "The Nicene Council recognised the eventful principle, that while we believe and profess any being to be a creature, such a being is really no God to us, though honoured by us with whatever high titles, and with whatever homage." If this, as we said before, means only that the Nicene Council asserted of the created God of the Arians, that such a being could not be regarded as the One and Supreme God by them, that is, indeed, as true as it is irrelevant. But if it means that the Council asserted that such a being could not be "God to them,"—be regarded idolatrously by them,—because they professed Him to be a creature, then, so far from asserting such a thing, the Nicene Council, in the person of her principal Father and expositor, most clearly, positively, and literally asserted the contrary. "If," says Athanasius, "the Word is a creature, either He is not true God, or they must of necessity say that there are two Gods—one Creator, and the other creature; and must serve two Lords—one ingenerate, and the other generate and a creature. Wherefore, when the Arians have these speculations and views, do they not rank themselves with the Gentiles? For they, like the Gentiles, *worship the creature."* St. Athanasius here clearly asserts, that the titles and homage with which the Arians honoured our Lord made our Lord a God to them, notwithstanding His being pronounced by them a creature: he clearly asserts that they paid divine worship to this creature, believing Him to be such. He charges them with idolatry, as the immediate and necessary result of their position. St. Ambrose repeats the charge, and attacks their worship of a created god: "If the Son is posterior to the Father," he says, "He is a new god: if He is not one with the Father, He is a strange god: why do they worship a strange god?" It is obvious that he could not imagine the Arian paying such divine worship in the first instance, on the principle that the bare acknowledgment of creatureship in the being honoured precluded the possibility of such worship in the honourer. St. Hilary has the same argument. "Knowest thou not, O heretic, who callest Christ a creature, that cursed are they who serve the creature? Thou confessest Christ to be a creature: know what this confession makes of thee: know that cursed is the worship of a creature." St. Hilary, that is to say, recognises the fact of divine worship being paid to a creature, confessed by the worshipper to be such. "Why," says St. Cyril, "do they believe the Son to be a creature, and yet worship him?" the same fact recognised. "God forbids us," says St. Cyril again, "to think any new god to be God, or to adore a strange god;" and he proceeds to enlarge on the sin of paying divine worship to a being confessed not to be the Supreme and Eternal God. "If thou believest in," says Faustinus, "and worshippest and servest the only begotten Son of God, calling Him a creature, expect the punishment due to those who turn the truth of God into a lie." "Very many of the ancient Fathers," says Petavius, "were accustomed to call the Arians idolaters, because they adored one whom they confessed to be a creature; and they assert that they did not differ from the heathen. . . . So says Cyril, in his fourth dialogue on the Trinity. He shows the dogma of these heretics to be that the Son was not true God, and was yet to be adored and worshipped; from Christians, he thus argues, they had become Gentiles again, for that they adored and served creatures, and confessed a plurality of gods, just as the Gentiles did. Inasmuch as even the Gentiles served the creature, and worshipped gods, who are no gods, with the understanding that they gave, while they did so, the first place to some One and Supreme God, the Maker of the universe."[1]

The Fathers, then, certainly considered the Arian position an idolatrous one. If it be said that this was a mistake as to a fact; that they misapprehended the Arian worship; that if they had asked the Arians, the latter would have told them that they could only, from the very nature of their hypothesis, pay a relative and not a divine worship to their Demiurge, the plain answer, in the first place, is, that the Fathers knew that the Arians *could* say this—it is so obvious a defence—and that they charged them with such worship, notwithstanding. And the answer, in the second place, is, that the Arians *did* say this, and that the Fathers did not listen to them. The Arians made this very distinction; they asserted that they worshipped Christ, σχετικῶς, with a relative worship. They said, what the early Socinians have said since, that they paid a relative worship to Christ as to a created God. "Is honour and worship," stands the question in the Racovian Catechism, "paid to Christ in such a way as for there to be no distinction between Christ and God in this respect?" And the answer is: "No: there is a great distinction. For we adore and worship God as the primary cause of our salvation; Christ as the secondary: God as Him from whom, Christ as Him through whom, are all things." Such a defence had the Arians, and it did not avail them. The judgment of the Fathers was decided. Nay, we have Mr. Newman's own authority for the fact of, and Mr. Newman's own concurrence in, the truth of this judgment. "The Arians," he says, "were

[1] Petavius, de Trinitate, lib. ii. cap. xii. sect. vi.

under the dilemma of holding two gods, or worshipping the creature." "The reason," he says again, "for the title ungodliness (ἀθεότης) as applied to the Arians, seems to have lain in the idolatrous character of the Arian worship, on its own showing, viz., as worshipping One whom they yet maintained to be a creature."[1] What? the Arian worship idolatrous on its own showing? A creature worshipped as God, by those who maintained Him to be a creature? But this is exactly the thing of which we have just heard Mr. Newman denying the possibility. Let us put the two sentences side by side: "That while we believe and profess any being to be a creature, such a being is really no God to us," is what we heard asserted just now as the view of the Fathers, and of the writer: that Arian "worship is idolatrous on its own showing, as being the worship of one, who is maintained to be a creature," is what we next hear asserted as also the view of the Fathers and of the writer. On the same self-evident ground, of "its own showing," in both cases, the same worship is pronounced to be essentially idolatrous in the latter sentence; essentially *not* idolatrous in the former.[2]

The truth is—for it is time that the distinction between the two views should be summed up—the Fathers plainly condemned the whole Arian hypothesis, application, substance and all. Mr. Newman does not do this, and does not allow that the Fathers did. He views the Arian hypothesis as consisting of two parts: the hypothesis itself, as we may call it, and the subject of it. To make the subject of it our Lord was erroneous. But the hypothesis itself involved no idolatry, and was sound.

[1] St. Athanasius against Arianism, Part I. p. 3.
[2] We have to acknowledge many obligations here and throughout this article to Mr. Palmer's able and learned treatise.

He separates, by an ingenious process, the application of the Arian idea from its substance, and applies the censures of the Fathers to the former, and not to the latter. But the Fathers censured the latter. They condemned the application of the idea of a created divinity to our Lord: they also condemned that idea of created divinity. They charged the Arians with idolatry. But idolatry could not attach to the Arian idea in its application; for so far as our Lord was the object of their worship, they were not idolatrous. It attached to it in its substance. The position was in itself an idolatrous one. It supposed a being, who was not to be supposed,—a being who demanded worship on account of his greatness, and could not receive it on account of his creatureship,—endowed with a *quasi-*eternity and creatorial attributes which overwhelmed the imagination with the look of, while they did not touch the abstract notion of, Deity: a being, virtually a god to human minds, and yet an idol the instant he was a god. The conception produced idolatrous relations from within itself, and made its disciples and believers, necessarily, worshippers of what they ought not to worship. The ideas of heretics are perpetually inconsistencies and obliquities, and this was one. The hypothesis was internally unsound. The Fathers, as a matter of fact, did not view the Arian created godhead as "a wonder in heaven, a throne mediatorial, a title archetypal, a crown bright as the morning-star, a glory issuing from the eternal throne, robes pure as the heavens, and a sceptre over all." They did not look upon the conception as a noble, grand, and inspired one. They regarded it with simple detestation and abhorrence; and the Arian Demiurgus,—not simply as a misrepresentation of another, but also as being what he was,—was a theological monster in their eyes, unlawfully, profanely, and falsely imagined. It was a principle with them to dislike proximities to Deity. They feared and suspected, as such, ambiguities and borderings in this department; and a scrupulous and jealous eye was ever on the watch to preserve, in its proper broadness, not merely by abstract definition, but in actual image and idea to the mind, the interval between the Creator and all created beings. Let creatures be creatures, and let God be God, their theology said: the halfway and mixed being, who was a god to the imagination and not to the reason, the nature which trembled on the very verge of godhead, just "all but" divine, and yet not divine, were not legitimate existences in their eyes. They dreaded the confusion which vicinity caused; the shading off of the keen distinction between what was God and what was not; the dilution of the idea of Deity. The heathens, with their gradual ascent of being up to the Supreme, and system of approximation, had diluted the idea of Deity: the work of the chosen people, on the other hand, was to preserve that idea keen and pure. The Fathers showed, on this subject, much of what a modern philosophical developist will perhaps think a Judaic spirit, and the $\eta\theta o\varsigma$ of the law; mental vestiges of the old dispensation still surviving, but intended to disappear with the progress of truth. "It pleased God," says Athanasius, "to show in man His own Lordship, and so to draw all men to Himself. But to do this by a mere man beseemed not, lest having man for our Lord, we should become worshippers of man. Therefore the Word Himself became flesh, and the Father called His name Jesus; and so made Him Lord and Christ, as much as to say, 'He made Him to rule and reign.'" The idea is, evidently, that a human, a created Redeemer, would have been an ensnaring object to us, on this ground, as seeming to claim worship, while he was after all only a creature. It is the midway being, the secondary god which is objected to. "Consistently," says the same writer again, in mentioning some of the features of the Incarnation, "were such ascribed not to another, but to the Lord, that the grace also may be from Him, and that we may become not worshippers of any other, but truly devout towards God; because we pray to no creature, no ordinary man, but to the natural and true Son from God, who has become man, yet is not less Lord and God and Saviour." The drift is clear, and pointedly against the idea of secondary godhead. Again, "It was right that the redemption should take place through none other than Him who is the Lord by nature, lest we should name another Lord, and fall into the Arian and Greek folly, serving the creature." Again, "If the Son was worshipped by the angels, as excelling them in glory, each of things subservient ought to worship what excels itself. But this is not the case, for creature does not worship creature, but servant Lord, and creature God. Thus Peter the Apostle hinders Cornelius, who would worship him, saying, I myself also am a man. And an angel, when John would worship him, in the Apocalypse, hinders him, saying, See thou do it not: for I am thy fellow-servant: worship God. Therefore to God alone appertains worship; and this the very angels know, that though they excel other beings in glory, yet they are all creatures and not to be worshipped, but worship the Lord." Again, "Since He is not a creature, but the proper offspring of the substance of God, therefore is He worshipped." Certainly Athanasius's condemnation of the Arian position is no "vindication" of a theology that would profess to verify and impersonate it. The whole tone of mind, line of thought, implied principles, on which the Fathers' condemnation of the Arians proceeds, and which runs through their arguments, is repugnant to the fundamental idea of the Arian Demiurge. The modern theologian may say, that it is an open question whether they were right or wrong; but that the Fathers had their theological line, and that that was not one of sympathy with secondary divinity, is a matter of fact; and the advocate of that idea must go to other ages than that of Athanasius for its defence.

To return now to the main line of argument with which we commenced.

We gave at an early point in this article, a statement of the question of development; that the mind has a natural idea of development, and has a natural idea of the tendency to exaggeration and abuse in development; that if, in any given case, the former supplied a rationale on one side, the latter supplied a rationale on another; that the history of Christianity comes before us under the contending claims of these two rationales; and that the question is how to decide between the pretensions of the two. We now observe that Mr. Newman has not hitherto decided this question. He has given a series of tests, to distinguish a true from a false development, which,—in the way we explained,—entirely omit one very large, important, and common kind of false development, viz., exaggeration, and suppose abuse upon the same type to be impossible. And one of these tests, which seemed to demand peculiar attention, from its summary and conclusive pretensions, viz., that of logical sequence, has appeared to possess no force whatever (in any sense which does not make it assume the question at issue), inasmuch as persons differ very much in their views of what is logic;—in particular, some arguments which appeared very conclusive to Mr. Newman having appeared quite inconclusive to ourselves. The appeal to "system" is only another form of this appeal to logic, and fails for the same reasons. And such challenges as the following, which almost pervade, in one or other shape, the whole essay, fall dead. To say that "we must accept the whole, or reject the whole; that reduction does but enfeeble, and amputation mutilate; that it is trifling to receive all but something, which is as integral as any other portion; and that on the other hand it is a solemn thing to receive a part, for before you know where you are, you may be carried on by a stern logical necessity to accept the whole;"[1]—to say of later Roman doctrines "that they include in their own unity even those primary articles of faith, such as that of the Incarnation, which many an impugner of the system of doctrine, as a system, professes to accept, and which, do what he will, he cannot intelligibly separate, whether in point of evidence or of internal form, from others which he disavows"[2]—to say this again and again is throughout one appeal of the writer to the certainty of his own logic; that is to say, one act of begging the question. Indeed Mr. Newman himself admits the incompetency of his arguments, in any practical sense, for deciding the question. "Tests," he says, "it is true, for ascertaining the correctness of developments in general, have been drawn out in a former chapter, and shall presently be used; but they are insufficient for the guidance of individuals in the case of so large and complicated a problem as Christianity, though they may aid our inquiries and support our conclusions in particular points. They are of a scientific and controversial, not of a practical character, and are instruments rather than warrants of right decisions. While, then, on the one hand, it is probable that some means will be granted for ascertaining the legitimate and true developments of Revelation, it appears, on the other, that these means must of necessity be external to the developments themselves."[3]

[1] Page 154.   [2] Page 146.   [3] Page 115.

Here, then, one division of our subject ends, and another begins. We enter on another and a further field of argument, and perceive that, in distinction to taking any representation, however large, ingenious, and exuberant of the simple notion of development,—any explanation, however full, of its naturalness, probability, commonness in ordinary life, and the career of nations and schools, as a single step towards settling the question of the rightness or wrongness, the justness or immoderateness of any given development,—we are referred, as the ultimate point on which the whole argument turns, to the asserted existence of an infallible guide, who is able to, and does in each case, decide the question by that simple gift of infallibility; and pronounces with certainty the fact of a development being right or wrong. The doctrine of the Papal Infallibility comes out as the keystone of Mr. Newman's whole argument, and according as he proves, or fails to prove, that doctrine, that argument stands or falls.

The argumentative ground here for the opponent of Mr. Newman has a very different general character from the one he has hitherto had to maintain. He has hitherto had to argue against the faultlessness of certain developments themselves, and to give his rationale of them, as opposed to Mr. Newman's. The general direction of his argument now is, not so much against those developments as against the necessity of imposing them. For though the argument against the Papal Infallibility comes on in the present discussion as an argument against a professed conclusive proof of the faultlessness of these developments, still what it directly proceeds against is that claim itself of infallibly sanctioning and enforcing them. The assertion of this claim is of course a much more invidious one than the mere assertion of the truth of the developments themselves. Where Revelation has left a blank, the human mind, if it dwells at all upon the unknown contents of it, will naturally form some sort of conjecture about them. To take the example already referred to, of the state of departed souls: Scripture has, to a great extent, left a veil upon it; and we are not told what will happen after death to a great number of imperfect Christians, who seem to go out of this life with good dispositions, and often generous hearts in the main, but who have lived carelessly. It is better, doubtless, to form no conjecture about them; at the same time we are not positively forbidden to form conjectures within our own minds, as to the unknown and unseen world. If any one from a religiously amiable repugnance, on the one hand, to supposing that such persons as the above are necessarily reserved for eternal damnation, and from a strong idea, on the other, that they must require some searching purification to fit them for a heavenly state, attaches some accompaniment specially purgatorial to the intermediate state in their case, it would be hard to condemn him for doing so. The formal doctrine itself of Purgatory, Bishop Andrewes would allow as an opinion of the schools. But it is a different thing when the pious conjecture is made a fixed doctrine, an article of faith, and people are not allowed a neutral state of mind on a subject which Revelation has left veiled.

Before examining Mr. Newman's argument for the Papal Infallibility, there is one preliminary remark we will make about it, and that is the exceedingly small space that it occupies in the book. Certainly quantity is no test of strength in such a matter, and yet where a particular hypothesis is the turning-point of the whole argument of a book, we expect to see its establishment occupy some proportion of the book, and to see some legitimate prominence given to it. But amidst large, expansive, and detailed representations of development itself, the argument for the only position which can decide that development in his favour comes in, in the book, as a kind of subordinate point. No reader would find out, from the way in which it comes in, the absolutely fundamental place which it holds in the discussion. Of this argument for infallibility again, a very large proportion is taken up in the statement and refutation of certain arguments against it, and is of no positive force whatever for it. After such reductions, the solid positive argument for the Papal Infallibility is found to occupy but a small space in the essay. It hangs and hovers over the reader throughout as a thing supposed to be proved, making good, *if* true, the whole of the rest of the argument as it goes on, supporting, *if* solid, all that wants supporting; but the actual proof of it hardly catches his eye as he turns over the pages. We are not saying that this is difficult to be accounted for, or that Mr. Newman does not know best his own line of argument; and that the fact of developments is not, in his view, itself the substantial proof of the existence of an infallible decider upon them; it is, however, worth noticing such a feature as this.

Mr. Newman states then the positive argument for infallibility as follows :—

" Let the state of the case be carefully considered. If the Christian doctrine, as originally taught, admits of true and important developments, as was argued in the foregoing Section, this is a strong antecedent argument in favour of a provision in the Dispensation for putting a seal of authority upon those developments. The probability of their being known to be true varies with their truth. The two ideas are certainly quite distinct of revealing and guaranteeing a truth, and they are often distinct in fact. There are various revelations all over the earth which do not carry with them the evidence of their divinity. Such are the inward suggestions and secret illuminations granted to so many individuals; such are the traditionary doctrines which are found among the heathen, that 'vague and unconnected family of religious truths, originally from God, but sojourning, without the sanction of miracle, or a definite home, as pilgrims up and down the world, and discernible and separable from the corrupt legends with which they are mixed by the spiritual mind alone.' There is nothing impossible in the notion of a revelation occurring without evidences that it is a revelation; just as human sciences are a divine gift, yet are reached by our ordinary powers, and have no claim on our faith. But Christianity is not of this nature; it is a revelation which comes to us as a revelation, as a whole, objectively, and with a profession of infallibility; and the only question to be determined relates to the matter of the revelation. If, then, there are certain great truths, or proprieties, or observances, naturally and legitimately resulting from the doctrines originally professed, it is but reasonable to include these new results in the idea of the revelation, to consider them parts of it, and if the revelation be not only true, but guaranteed as true, to anticipate that they will be guaranteed inclusively. Christianity, unlike other revelations of God's will, except the Jewish, of which it is a continuation, is an objective religion, or a revelation with credentials; it is natural to view it wholly as such, and not partly *sui generis*, partly like others. Such as it begins, such let it be considered to continue; if certain large developments of it are true, they must surely be accredited as true."—Pages 117-119.

Now, the proof of the Papal Infallibility is made here to rest on the necessity of the continuance of a revelation if once given. The argument is that so long as nature is our basis of knowledge, we have no reason to look for certainty of knowledge; but that when a revelation has been once made, we have: that a Divine act of communicating truth has thus taken place, different from the ordinary one by natural means, and having once taken place, must be expected to go on. This granted, it follows, of course, that there must be some person or tribunal always to keep this communication, this revelation, going: and that tribunal is then pronounced to be the Papal one.

But it is to be observed that this argument is put in a peculiar form in the passage before us; and this form deserves some examination in the first instance. "Christianity is a revelation which comes to us as a revelation, as a whole, objectively, and with a profession of infallibility; and the only question to be determined relates to the matter of the revelation. If, then, there are certain great truths, or proprieties, or observances, naturally and legitimately resulting from the doctrines originally professed, it is but reasonable to include these true results in the idea of the revelation, to consider them parts of it; and if the revelation be not only true, but guaranteed as true, to anticipate that they will be guaranteed inclusively."[1] We will examine, then, this form of putting the argument for a standing revelation before we proceed to the argument itself, and attend to the subtler dress before we go to the simpler substance.

We have then here supposed, to begin with, an original revelation, and various unrevealed results and developments from it. The arguer for a continuing revelation has to convert this unrevealed truth into revealed; and he does it by an argument which runs thus:—A revelation must have consequences and developments of some kind or other beyond its own original substance. Of these developments some must be true, though others may be false. The true ones, whatever they are, being real results of the original revelation, are a part of that revelation; and being a part of it, must be revealed with the rest.— Now if Mr. Newman means here that there exist in the

[1] Page 118.

abstract universe of truth such absolutely true ulterior results of the original revealed truth as he describes; fully admitting this, we ask, Why must such results be a part of the original revelation? Because they exist in the universe of abstract truth, it does not follow that they are even known to a single human being, much less known for certain, and revealed. Undoubtedly, if they were revealed, they would be a part of the original revelation, but their abstract existence does not go one step to making them revealed. It is almost a truism, indeed, to say that there must be, at this moment, an infinite number of results from the Christian revelation existing in the universe of truth, which have not so much as entered the mere threshold of human thought, and which never will enter it so long as the world lasts. Again, if Mr. Newman means that a certain number of such true results must, in the progress of Christianity, have entered into the human mind; that it is unreasonable to suppose that the whole mass of actual Christian developments is every bit of it false, and therefore but reasonable to allow that there have been and now are actually in the world some or other existing really true developments, we do not see, even if we admit this, what he has gained in the way of proof that we have such developments revealed to us, in the ordinary sense of the word revelation. Because such developments are somewhere, we do not therefore know where they are; and if we see them, we do not know them as true. We may make a guess, and that is all. Mr. Newman starts with uncertainty; he has a mass of developments from an original revelation before him, of which, by the supposition, he does not know which are true and which are false ones. He professes to convert this uncertainty into certainty, by simply saying that some are really true, and others really false. He divides uncertainty to us into absolute truth and absolute error in themselves; and to any one asking where certain developed truths are, and what they are, simply answers, Never mind, they are somewhere; and if they are somewhere, that proves that you must know them. But, surely, uncertainty to us is not removed by being viewed as certainty in the abstract; and truth is not a bit the more ascertained and revealed because one side or another must be true.

It will be seen that the whole point of this argument lies in viewing the truths, for the additional revelation of which it contends, as *resulting* truths, instead of truths simply. But this is not a relevant difference. It makes no difference if the uncertain truths in question *are*, supposing we knew them, results and developments of some truth which we know. If they are uncertain, the fact of their coming from something else which is certain does not the least repair or undo their uncertainty. All truth is connected together, we believe, and forms one whole; and yet that does not prevent part of it being ascertained, and part of it not being. "Christianity," says Mr. Newman, "is a revelation which comes to us *as a whole;*" and he specially argues, therefore, that its results and developments being included in that whole, are revealed to us. But if he means by the "revelation coming as a whole," that the whole of what is revealed to us is revealed as a whole, such a truism does not help him the least to his inference that a variety of indefinite resulting truths are in that whole : if he means that that revelation, from the fact of revealing certain fundamental truths, pledges itself to reveal these other indefinite resulting ones, in that case we entirely deny the assumption. And, therefore, the particular point on which so much stress is laid, that the uncertain truths in the present case are developments from an original truth, and not independent and isolated truths, does not seem to us to add anything to the argument. Mr. Newman lays out, as it were, a general substratum of truth *in se* before us, part of this truth being in the revealed world, and part of it out of it. On the view, then, of all of it, whether revealed or not, having one common existence as truth *in se*, he calls upon us to infer that it has all one common revelation. But this is to ask us simply to contradict ourselves. We suppose all this further existence of truth *in se* when we talk of any given part of truth being revealed, and cannot undo this limitation of revealed truth by simply resupposing that further existence of abstract truth.

Nor is it anything to the purpose, again, to call Christianity a "guaranteed revelation,"[1] a "revelation" that comes to us with a profession of "infallibility;" as if such phrases amounted to anything more than saying that Christianity was a revelation, as everybody believes it to be. What we *mean* by a revelation is a guaranteed revelation: we use the word, in contradistinction to natural religion, in that sense. Mr. Newman separates, indeed, in his use of the word, the guarantee from the revelation, the truth *in* revelation from the guarantee for that truth. Recurring, that is, to the simply etymological meaning, he makes the word revelation mean whatever is disclosed—whatever has been made to enter into any human mind—being also true: in which latter sense all true thought in the world whatever may be called revelation ; and, with it, these true results from the original revelation, in whosesoever mind entertained, may be called revelation. But though, as a mere verbal transposition, this makes certain indefinite unascertained results of the

[1] Page 118.

original revelation *look* more like revelation themselves, because, if they have *de facto* occurred to any minds, they are, by this verbal process, raised to the rank of unguaranteed revelation :—yet the reality remains exactly the same as before. And when Mr. Newman asks whether the *guarantee* for the original revelation does not include these (in his sense) revealed results from it, he only asks, in another form, the question, whether the *revelation*, because it reveals some truth, does not reveal a variety of other resulting truths. The original absence of revelation in the developments it deals with, which the argument found at starting, and which it undertook to remove from them, never is removed : the defect adheres to its subject-matter, through every stage that the arguer takes it, and confronts him at the end, the same as it was at the beginning.

Let us see : If an original revelation is guaranteed, its resulting truths will be. Apply this formula to a common case. A powerful medicine is discovered, and attested or guaranteed beyond a question by actual experiment : but some properties remain unguaranteed and conjectural, and medical men dispute about them : there is a revelation certain, that is to say, with some resulting truths uncertain, but existing in the world of truth somewhere, could they be ascertained. Apply the formula : the original discovery is guaranteed, therefore the ulterior results are : therefore they are known and ascertained, and medical men need not dispute about them. A great chemical law is guaranteed to a certain point by actual discovery ; ulterior and finer results from the same law are uncertain, but there are some, could they be hit on. Apply the formula : the law is guaranteed ; therefore the results are : therefore you are wrong in supposing that you do not know them, because you do.

The fact is, this whole mode of arguing from the mere supposition of truth abstract beforehand, before we know *what* is true, to the fact that we know the latter, is a simple anticipation and forestalment,—an antedating of the known before its real existence. Mr. Newman professes to perform a feat of logical magic, and to get something out of something else which has nothing at all to do with it. He converts the known into the unknown, as a conjuror changes one thing into another before our eyes: we know that the change does not really take place. With the formula, "Some uncertain truths are results of certain truth: if they are, they are certain themselves," he gets something out of nothing, converts uncertainty into certainty without a medium; and transmutes the known into the unknown by a stroke of legerdemain. The case is like trying to make a number more than it is by transposition, and to produce additional length by a rapid shifting from the bottom to the top. Impress the addition at the top on the eye, before it has realised the shortening at the bottom, and the line seems longer. Make the mind put unknown truth before itself, as truth, and it will imagine it as *known* truth.

We must add—besides what we have said about this form of argument itself—that Mr. Newman states it in a way in which he has no right to state it, and assumes in connection with it what he cannot possibly by the supposition know. For he says, "If certain *large* developments of it are true, they must surely be accredited as true."[1] Now if he is referring here to the world of abstract truth, there certainly are in that world large, nay, infinite true developments of this original revealed truth; but with which, as we said, human knowledge has nothing to do. But if he is speaking of the true *actual*

[1] Page 119.

developments existing in this concrete world, what does he know of these developments by the supposition as to whether they are large or small? He is stating the case of actual truth in the Christian developments in the world, and he states it exactly to coincide with the desiderated truth of the Roman developments. He assumes that there are large existing developments of the original revelation *absolutely true;* and he appeals to us to know whether, there being these large existing developments which are purely and absolutely true, it is not reasonable just to crown their truth with the guarantee. But this is to lay out the state of Christian truth in the world upon a mere assumption. Of the existing true developments of Christian truth in the world, he does not know whether they are large; of the existing large ones, he does not know whether they are true. The general state of development may be, for anything he knows, neither wholly true nor wholly false, but a mixture of both. And if his anticipatory picture of it describes his view of the Roman developments, another anticipatory picture may describe another.

With this preliminary notice on the form of putting the argument, we proceed to the substance of the argument itself. Divested of its particular form, that argument stands thus :—That because God guarantees some truth, he must necessarily guarantee more : that because there is certainty to some extent, there must be certainty to a greater : that because an original act of revelation took place, it must be continued. To this we answer, Why? We see no reason for thinking so; no presumption for the expectation. If the argument is then stated with greater point, and revealed religion is exhibited in its special distinction to natural, to remind us that God has confessedly done something different in the latter from what he did in the former, and that having done differently, He must be expected to continue to do so, we answer again, as we did at first, Why? Why should He go on acting differently? Why should He not cease acting differently? Why should He not, after acting differently, recur to acting as He did before? Is it impossible to look upon the act of revelation as an exception to a general rule, which, having taken place, the general rule operates again? Are there no such things as general rules with exceptions to, or particular interruptions of them in the ordinary government of the world? And is an act of revelation, therefore, because it takes place, necessarily not an exception to a general rule, but a new general rule itself? Whence do you get that latter view of it but from pure hypothesis? You may say, indeed, that you have as much right to an hypothesis of continuation as another has to an hypothesis of cessation. But who forms an hypothesis of cessation? We do not. We form no hypothesis at all; but taking the fact of a revelation simply, of which fact we are certain, ask you for your ground for more than that fact, viz., for that revelation's continuation. We stop with the fact: you go beyond the fact, and must, therefore, give a reason why you do so. And the only reason you can have is a simple hypothesis of your own. You say a particular kind of communication must be continuously repeated, because it has been made. We say we see the fact in the case, but do not see at all why it should be a reason for that conclusion. Let us consider.—Revelation is a new course of proceeding entered on by God: if it begins, it must be expected to continue—"The circumstance that a work has begun makes it more probable than not that it will proceed."[1] But what does this mean? Beginning is not

---
[1] Page 123.

an idea we have got from the fact, because beginning implies continuance: we do not get the fact of a revelation *beginning* in the mere fact of it being given. If by putting revelation before our minds as a new *course* of Divine action, in this way the arguer makes revelation a continuous thing to begin with; he is begging the question. If he means that a Divine *act* of revelation took place, the question is then simply whether that act must be continuously repeated; and to that we say again, Why? Let Mr. Newman put the question in his own peculiar or any other way, the same substantial argument has the same answer ready for it. "If a revelation be guaranteed as true, its true results will be guaranteed inclusively."[1] Why? "Such as a revelation begins, such let it be considered to continue." Why? "If certain developments of it are true, they must surely be accredited as true."[2] Why? We cannot possibly know what the whole of God's purpose was in making at a particular time a revelation: we cannot possibly therefore have the ground necessary for asserting that he must "surely" make other revelations in continuous succession after it. On the contrary, if we are to go at all by the actual course of Providence before us, it is most natural to suppose that God would after such a revelation leave men, with the additional light of truth, and all the other advantages of every kind which may be part of it, in their possession, to carry it out with more or less of abuse or perversion if they will. To whatever extent we have positive evidence for His not doing so, we must believe that He does not do so. But the facts of Providence before our eye would lead us to expect that course rather than the other, and tend to discourage the idea of a revelation always going on.

[1] Page 118.   [2] Page 119.

We are approaching here that whole line of argument called the argument of analogy. The argument of analogy takes the course which has just now been taken, and maintains the valuelessness of simple presumptions respecting revelation. The argument of analogy brings us at once upon Butler's great treatise. Mr. Newman here comes into collision (we have not a right as yet to call it more than a *primâ facie* one, but that it certainly is) with the argument of a writer for whom he has necessarily a great respect, and with whom he has many reasons for wishing to be in harmony. To guard his Essay from the disadvantage of having so great an authority in opposition to it, he has to explain Butler. One or two instances, before we come to the main one with which we are concerned, will serve to show the character of the explanation which goes on, and the way in which particular meanings are extracted. The writer presents Butler to us as a sympathiser at bottom with the doctrine of development advocated in the Essay; as holding and teaching principles which necessarily lead to that doctrine.

The medium of such an interpretation is the fact of Butler holding *a* principle of development; speaking of some truth as involved in other truth; of natural inference; of necessary result. For example: The divinity of the Second and Third Persons in the Trinity being granted, Butler says the duty of worshipping them necessarily follows. "The duty of religious regards to both those Divine Persons immediately arises to the view of reason out of the very nature of the relations in which they stand to us. . . . The relations being known, the obligations to internal worship are obligations of reason, arising out of those relations themselves." "Here," says Mr. Newman, "is the development of doctrine into worship."[1] Butler is teaching development. It is true he is. But he is only, by the very nature of the argument, teaching a development which is necessarily contained in the original truth. Mr. Newman cannot apply this reasoning to the support of the "hyperdulia" paid to St. Mary, except he first assumes the existence of certain relations to St. Mary which oblige to such worship of her. Grant these relations, and the cultus will follow, on Butler's principles; but Butler's principles have no kind of tendency to establish those relations.

Again, Butler in a remarkable passage speaks of the meaning of Scripture being brought out more and more in the course of ages by study and reflection on the part of thoughtful minds. He says, " Practical Christianity, or that faith and behaviour which renders a man a Christian, is a plain and obvious thing; like the common rules of conduct, with respect to our ordinary temporal affairs. The more distinct and particular knowledge of those things, the study of which the apostle calls *going on unto perfection*, and of the prophetic parts of revelation, like many parts of natural and even civil knowledge, may require very exact thought and careful consideration. The hindrances, too, of natural and of supernatural light and knowledge, have been of the same kind. And as it is owned the whole scheme of Scripture is not yet understood, so, if it ever comes to be understood before the *restitution of all things*, and without miraculous interpositions, it must be in the same way as natural knowledge is come at,—by the continuance and progress of learning and of liberty, and by particular persons attending to, comparing, and pursuing intimations scattered up and down it, which are overlooked and disregarded by the generality of the world. For this is the way in which all

[1] Page 50.

improvements are made, by thoughtful men tracing out obscure hints, as it were, dropped us by nature accidentally, or which seem to come into our minds by chance. Nor is it at all incredible that a book, which has been so long in the possession of mankind, should contain many truths as yet undiscovered. For all the same phenomena, and the same faculties of investigation, from which such great discoveries in natural knowledge have been made in the present and last age, were equally in possession of mankind several thousand years before. And possibly it might be intended that events, as they come to pass, should open and ascertain the meaning of several parts of Scripture."

Of this passage Mr. Newman says, "Butler, as a well-known passage of his work shows, is far from denying the principle of progressive development."[1] "Butler is bearing witness to the probability of developments in Christian doctrine." If by "doctrine" he means anything that is taught, truth of any kind connected with Christianity, in that sense Butler is certainly "witnessing to the probability of development in Christian doctrine." But if "doctrine" is at all intended to mean necessary doctrine, or the faith, in that sense the passage does not throughout give the least sanction to a development of doctrine. Mr. Newman allows this, but he seems to allow it only as the absence of a conclusion, a stopping short in a line of reasoning which intrinsically proceeded further. "Butler of course was not contemplating the case of new articles of faith, or developments imperative on our acceptance."[2] It ought rather to be said that it is quite obvious from the whole passage that he was contemplating something totally different from it. Indeed the very first sentence in it happens to show the fact not only that he "did not contemplate," but that he expressly

[1] Page 102. [2] Page 111.

disavowed any reference to the Christian creed, for he there carefully prefixes the mention of "that *faith* and behaviour which makes a man a Christian" as being specially that which he is *not* going to talk about, and to which the passage he is about to write will not refer.

To return to the subject. The argument of Butler with respect to presumptions concerning revelation, and our incompetency to form them, is as follows :—

"As God governs the world, and instructs His creatures, according to certain laws or rules, in the known course of nature known by reason together with experience, so the Scripture informs us of a scheme of Divine providence additional to this. It relates that God has, by revelation, instructed men in things concerning His government, which they could not otherwise have known, and reminded them of things which they might otherwise know; and attested the truth of the whole by miracles. Now, if the natural and the revealed dispensation of things are both from God, if they coincide with each other, and together make up one scheme of Providence, our being incompetent judges of one must render it credible that we may be incompetent judges also of the other. Since, upon experience, the acknowledged constitution and course of nature is found to be greatly different from what, before experience, would have been expected, and such as, men fancy, there lie great objections against, this renders it beforehand highly credible, that they may find the revealed dispensation likewise, if they judge of it as they do of the constitution of nature, very different from expectations formed beforehand, and liable, in appearance, to great objections,—objections against the scheme itself, and against the degrees and manners of the miraculous interpositions, by which it was attested and carried on. Thus, suppose a prince to govern his dominions in the wisest manner possible, by common known laws; and that upon some exigencies he should suspend these laws, and govern, in several instances, in a different manner; if one of his subjects were not a competent judge beforehand, by what common rules the government should or would be carried on ; it could not be expected that the same person would be a competent judge, in what exigencies, or in what manner, or to what degree, those laws commonly observed would be suspended or deviated from. If he were not a judge of the wisdom of the ordinary administration, there is no reason to think he would be a judge of the wisdom of the extraordinary. If he thought he had objections against the former, doubtless, it is highly supposable, he might think also that he had objections against the latter. And thus, as we fall into infinite follies and mistakes whenever we pretend, otherwise than from experience and analogy, to judge of the constitution and course of nature, it is evidently supposable beforehand that we should fall into as great, in pretending to judge, in like manner, concerning revelation. Nor is there any more ground to expect that this latter should appear to us clear of objections than that the former should.

"These observations, relating to the whole of Christianity, are applicable to inspiration in particular. As we are in no sort judges beforehand, by what laws or rules, in what degree, or by what means, it were to have been expected that God would naturally instruct us; so, upon supposition of His affording us light and instruction by revelation, additional to what He has afforded us by reason and experience, we are in no sort judges, by what methods, and in what proportion, it were to be expected that this supernatural light and instruction would be afforded us. We know not beforehand what degree or kind of natural information it were to be expected God would afford men, each by his own reason and experience ; nor how far He would enable, and effectually dispose them to communicate it, whatever it should be, to each other ; nor whether the evidence of it would be certain, highly probable, or doubtful ; nor whether it would be given with equal clearness and conviction to all. Nor could we guess, upon any good ground, I mean, whether natural knowledge, or even the faculty itself by which we are capable of attaining it, reason, would be given us at once, or gradually. In like manner, we are wholly ignorant what degree of new knowledge, it were to be expected, God would give mankind by revelation, upon supposition of his affording one ; or how far, or in what way, He would interpose miraculously, to qualify them, to whom He should originally make the revelation, for communicating the knowledge given by it; and to secure their doing it to the age in which they should live; and to secure its being transmitted to posterity. We are equally ignorant whether the evidence of it would be certain, or highly probable, or doubtful; or whether all who should have any degree of instruction from it, and any degree of evidence of its truth, would have the same ; or whether the scheme would be revealed at once, or unfolded gradually. Nay, we are not in any sort able to judge whether it were to have been expected that the revelation should have been committed to writing, or left to be handed down, and consequently corrupted by verbal tradition, and at length sunk under it, if mankind so pleased, and during such time as they are permitted, in the degree they evidently are, to act as they will.

"But it may be said, 'that a revelation in some of the above-mentioned circumstances, one, for instance, which was not committed to writing, and thus secured against danger of corruption, would not have answered its purpose.' I ask, what purpose ? It would not have answered all the purposes which it has now answered, and in the same degree ; but it would have answered others, or the same in different degrees. And which of these were the purposes of God, and best fell in with His general government, we could not at all have determined beforehand."[1]

Now such a passage as this, supported as it is by, and forming part of, one whole line of reasoning which runs through the "Analogy," appears to decide beyond a doubt what Butler's view was. He asserts generally in the first place, that, the existence of a revelation supposed, we are in no way whatever judges à *priori* as to the whole plan on which it is conducted ; that we are quite ignorant, and that our presumptions on the whole subject are

[1] *Analogy*, Part II. Chap. III.

valueless. Then, in particular, among the items mentioned, about which we are totally ignorant, and about which our presumptions are valueless, is that of "degree." He says plainly we "are not competent judges of the *degree* to which God's ordinary laws should be suspended," supposing a suspension of them: that we "are in no sort judges in what proportion supernatural light should be afforded us," supposing it afforded us; "*what* supernatural instruction were to have been expected" supposing any given. Now supposing a revelation made, the question of its going on or stopping at a certain point is one as to its degree: Butler therefore plainly asserts that we are no judges whether a revelation, supposed to be made, will go on indefinitely, or stop at a certain point; will be given once for all, or be a standing revelation.

To this Mr. Newman says: "This reasoning does not here apply: it contemplates only the abstract *hypothesis* of a revelation, not the fact of an existing revelation of a particular kind, which may of course in various ways modify our state of knowledge by settling some of those very points on which, before it was given, we had no means of deciding."[1] Again: "He (Butler) is speaking of our judging *before* a revelation is given. He observes that 'we have no principles of reason upon which to judge beforehand how it were to be expected revelation should have been left, or what was most suitable to the Divine plan of government,' in various respects; but the case is altogether altered when a revelation is vouchsafed, for then a new precedent, or what he calls 'principle of reason,' is there introduced, and from what is actually put into our hand we can form a judgment whether more is to be expected."[2] The conclusion is that there is an essential distinction between the presumption Mr.

[1] Page 122. [2] Page 102.

Newman contends for and that which Butler's reasoning invalidates. But is such a distinction shown?

First of all we have the distinction between "the hypothesis of a revelation and the fact of an existing revelation,"—between judging beforehand and judging after; that if a revelation actually exists, we can argue that it will go on, whereas, in Butler's reasoning, it was only hypothetical, and therefore he could not so argue. This is absolutely a distinction without a difference. True it is that Butler is *supposing* a revelation with his opponent; and true it is that Mr. Newman can take for granted a revelation with us. But what is the difference between a fact and a supposed fact, as to the argumentative erection upon it? In supposing a fact, you make it a fact as far as reasoning is concerned; a real fact is, as far as reasoning is concerned, no more. Its hypothetical, as distinguished from its actual existence, makes all the difference to it *as* a fact, but can make none whatever to it as a premiss. In the present case, agreeing with Mr. Newman in the fact of a revelation, we are solely concerned with that fact as the premiss of a conclusion which he fastens upon it. Bishop Butler says, on the supposition of a revelation we are no judges beforehand to what extent it ought to go on. In supposing a revelation Butler supposed the fact of it; he supposed it being made. He might have presumed with Mr. Newman from that supposed existence, that once existing it would go on *in perpetuum* revealing; but he does not presume so. He had the self-same argumentative ground in an hypothetical fact which Mr. Newman has in an actual one, and he argues differently from it. Mr. Newman's fact is the *idea* of the fact, the same as Butler's was: *if* a revelation takes place it must go on : a revelation *does* take place, and therefore goes on : it is the same thing : Butler, in denying the former, denies the latter. Indeed, for a person to form a certain inference (or absence of one) from a supposed fact, and then to form a totally different one from the same fact afterwards because it is a real one,—to say, I judged thus beforehand before it did take place, but I judge differently afterwards because it does take place,—is simply self-contradictory. If we abstain from presuming beforehand the continuation of a revelation from its original bestowal, we must abstain from presuming it after. "Before" and "after" are nothing in the case; we do not argue from the fact as before, or from the fact as after, but from the nature of the fact itself. Mr. Newman thinks that from the fact of a revelation taking place, we must presume that it will continue; Butler had that very fact before him, and he forbade such a presumption.

We mean to say that Butler only differed from Mr. Newman in the persons he was arguing with, not at all in what he was arguing from. He had the actual fact of a revelation before him, as far as he himself was concerned, just as Mr. Newman has; and of that actual revelation he argued that it need not, because it was a revelation, be such and such a kind of one, which persons presume it ought to be. Mr. Newman, on the other hand, argues that because it is a revelation it *ought* to be a certain kind of one, viz., a standing and continuing one.

Mr. Newman next urges that Butler contemplated indeed a revelation, but did not contemplate a revelation "of a particular kind:" of the kind, viz., which Mr. Newman is contemplating. And to this it is enough to answer, that it is not necessary that Butler should particularise all the kinds of revelation in the case of which he does not allow presumption, for that would be endless; it is sufficient if he lays down a general head of what he considers groundless presumptions, and if Mr. Newman's comes under it. His argument asserts generally that we are not judges of what a revelation should be; and therefore any particular judgment formed on this subject comes, by the nature of the case, within his argument's operation. However, he does happen to go very near to mentioning the very particular which Mr. Newman's presumption concerns. Mr. Newman's argument on this latter head proceeds thus:—"The developments of Christianity are proved to have been in the contemplation of its Divine Author, by an argument parallel to that by which we infer intelligence in the system of the physical world. In whatever sense the need and its supply are a proof of design in the visible creation, in the same do the gaps, if the word may be used, which occur in the structure of the original creed of the Church, make it probable that those developments which grow out of the truths which lie around them, were intended to complete it."[1] Hence he concludes, that when we have a revelation before us "of a particular kind," *then*, "from what is actually put into our hands, we can form a judgment whether more is to be expected." Now the "particular kind" of revelation, described above, is a revelation which reveals some truths, and does not reveal others; which guarantees some ground, and does not guarantee more. The creed is what is revealed; the gaps are what are not revealed. So far as the word "gap" means anything more than this, so far, *e.g.*, as it is intended to insinuate in the word that the original revelation is inconsistent without the additions to it, so far its meaning, as begging the whole question at issue, is irrelevant and is to be excluded. The fact before us is a revelation, which tells us some things, which does not tell us others. However much we may desire to know those other things, however much we may be led by that

[1] Page 101.

part of truth which is revealed to us to desire to know them, however well, supposing them to be known, they would join on to and complete an original revelation, such a revelation comes, with all those accompaniments, under the head of a revelation which tells us some truth and does not tell us more. Now this kind of revelation Butler distinctly contemplates. He contemplates many kinds of revelations. He contemplates a revelation with "certain evidence," one with "highly probable" evidence, one with "doubtful evidence;" a "revelation revealed at once," a revelation "unfolded gradually," a revelation "committed to writing," a revelation "handed down by verbal tradition" only. He contemplates other kinds of revelations. Among these various kinds of revelation thus contemplated, he contemplates a revelation which revealed to a certain "degree" and not further; a "supernatural light afforded" in a certain "proportion," and not a larger one. He contemplates, that is, a revelation incomplete in its communication of truth. And of such a revelation he distinctly asserts that there is no presumption whatever against it. That is to say, in other words, there is no presumption from the fact of its incompleteness that it will go on to fill that incompleteness up. Let us take one of Mr. Newman's instances of the argument. The original revelation does not tell us what the divine dispensation is with respect to a large mass of imperfect human souls on their departure from this life: this is a gap; purgatory fills up this gap; therefore purgatory is a revealed doctrine. Can Mr. Newman seriously think that Butler would have admitted such a mode of arguing (we mean the mode simply without reference to the subject of it) as this? Suppose a sceptic coming to him, and saying that he could not believe in the Christian revelation because it had so many gaps in it. Would he have set to work to prove one by one that these different gaps were in reality filled up? or would he have told him that it did not become a person of his imperfect knowledge to be bringing gaps at all as any objection; that he could not know what God's whole purpose was in a revelation, and therefore could not know that such gaps were inconsistent with His purpose? And if the sceptic replied that these gaps were of more than intellectual importance, inasmuch as if they were filled up some practical duties would ensue, which do not exist now, or would at any rate have a clear positive ground, instead of an hypothetical one, would the line and tone of the "Analogy" compel us to yield to such a reply, or would it suggest that there was no presumption that God would reveal to us all truths, from which practical duties would follow supposing he did? "It is highly credible beforehand," is its great general answer, "that revelation should contain many things appearing to us liable to great objection.[1] The analogy of nature shows beforehand not only that we may, but also probably that we will, imagine that we have strong objections against it." "The whole constitution and course of nature shows that God does not dispense his gifts according to our notions of the advantage and consequence they would be to us." "It may be said that a revelation (wanting in certain things) cannot answer its purpose. I ask what purpose? It will not answer all the purposes which it would answer with them, and in the same degree; but it will answer others, or the same in different degrees."

It will be seen that this is an argument from our ignorance. Butler is arguing ultimately, not from analogy, but from something prior to analogy. Prior to all proof from analogy, such an imperfect creature as man must confess the great probability of his ignorance with respect

[1] *Analogy*, Part II. Chap. III.

to the whole designs of God, in His several dispensations, and therefore must confess the valuelessness of his presumptions as to them. Analogy indeed comes in and proves this ignorance demonstrably; because it shows that whereas we had formed various presumptions respecting what a Divine dispensation would be, these presumptions are as a matter of fact falsified by the dispensation of nature before our eyes. We had imagined that God would certainly act in such and such a way, some best imaginable way of our own conception; but we find that as a fact He does not. Well then, argues analogy, here is proof positive of your ignorance. It is indeed absurd that you should want any external proof of it; but here is the proof, as you want one. You have made your guess, and your guess turns out wrong. Now then, at any rate confess your ignorance, and be wise.—This is what is called the negative side of the argument of analogy, that side on which it is conclusive. It is not conclusive on its positive side; far from it: it only gives us probabilities on that side, because on that side it only argues that because such and such a course of things has gone on, it will continue to go on the same. On its positive side it only conjectures future facts; on its negative, it points to present: it is a presumptive argument on its positive side; it argues from actual fact against presumption on its negative. It is arguing on the latter side now. Butler argues from analogy, but from analogy as proving by matter of fact what was sufficiently evident before in itself—human ignorance. "We may see beforehand," he says, "that we have not faculties for this kind of speculation." And analogy comes in as confirmative. "So, prior to experience, they would think they had objections against the ordinary course of nature." "Since, upon experience, the acknowledged constitution and course of nature is found to be greatly different from what, before experience, would have been expected, this renders it beforehand highly credible that they will find the revealed dispensation likewise very different from expectations formed beforehand." And thence the conclusion follows. Men must not "pretend to judge from preconceived expectations." "It is self-evident that the objections of an incompetent judgment must be frivolous." "Since it has been shown that we have no principles of reason upon which to judge beforehand, how it were to be expected revelation should have been left, or what was most suitable to the divine plan of government, it must be quite frivolous to object afterwards to any of them, against its being left in one way rather than another; for this would be to object against things upon account of their being different from expectations which have been shown to be without reason." This negative use of analogy is *the* use to which Butler's work as a whole applies it. " The design of this Treatise is to show that the several parts principally objected against in this moral and Christian dispensation . . . are analogous to what is experienced in the constitution and course of Nature or Providence; and that the chief objections which are alleged against the former are no other than what may be alleged, with like justness, against the latter, where they are found in fact to be inconclusive;" which "argument from analogy is in general unanswerable."[1]

We write the above with reference to what follows.

Mr. Newman, after explaining Butler's reasoning in his own favour, in order to be *utrimque paratus*, proceeds to give reasons for doubting the validity of it; and after proving that the argument from analogy is not against him, opposes the argument from analogy. " Nor can it,

[1] *Analogy*, Introduction.

as I think, be fairly denied that the argument from Analogy in one point of view tells against anticipating a revelation at all; for an innovation upon the physical order of the world is, by the very force of the terms, inconsistent with its ordinary course. We cannot then regulate our antecedent view of the character of a revelation by a test, which, applied simply, overthrows the very notion of a revelation altogether. Anyhow, Analogy is in some sort violated by the fact of a revelation, and the question before us only relates to the extent of that violation."[1] Now here it will be observed that Mr. Newman has glided out of one ground into another. He has got upon the ground of *positive* analogy, and is arguing against *its* conclusiveness; whereas this has not been Butler's argument. He has not been telling us what antecedent views to form of revelation, but dissuading us from giving weight to any; not been arguing that revelation is like to present fact, but proving by present fact that we are ignorant beforehand what revelation should be.

The argument positive indeed of analogy is of undoubted force in its own way, and Butler brings it in. We do unquestionably argue from like to like, "from that part of the Divine government over intelligent creatures which comes under our view, to that government of them which is beyond it; and from what is present collect what is likely, credible or not incredible, will be hereafter." And this argument undoubtedly tells, in a way which we need not describe here, but which is familiar to all readers of Butler, much more against the presumption for a standing revelation than for one. The obvious irregularities, breaks, and limitations in the case of natural knowledge, suggest the same in the case of the revealed. But no one ever supposed that such analogical

[1] Page 122.

presumptions were conclusive. "There is a very strong presumption," says Butler, "against common speculative truths, and against the most common facts before the proof of them, which yet is overcome by almost any proof;" and "presumptions from analogy," he adds, "are overcome by the same proof." The probability of things being like what we see, only holds good of them "in those respects in which we have no reason to believe they will be different"—"real probabilities which rise even to moral certainty are overcome by the most ordinary testimony." Analogy tells us, for example, with all the certainty with which analogy can, that the sun will rise to-morrow; but we know that a day will come when it will tell this falsely,—a day when the heaven and the earth shall be dissolved. Such intrinsic defectiveness, however, in the positive argument from analogy does not prevent Butler from giving the argument weight. In particular, he allows for "a peculiar presumption from analogy" against a revelation in the first instance; and yet continues taking analogy for his guide in his presumptions for that revelation. Mr. Newman appears to see a contradiction here, and says, "We cannot regulate our antecedent view of the character of a revelation by a test which, applied simply, overthrows the very notion of a revelation altogether." But there is no contradiction. Analogy did not "*overthrow* the very notion of a revelation;" it could only *presume* against it. It never pretended to be conclusive, and therefore is not invalidated by being shown not to be. A demonstrative proof is refuted by one contrary case; a ground of probability is not; and exceptions do not undo an argument which, of its own nature, admits of exceptions. After this particular case of violation, just as after any other, the positive argument of analogy goes on and holds good; we continue and cannot help ourselves judging of the unknown from the known; and we apply it to the very revelation against which it has presumed, just as to other things. We regulate, in spite of this or other mistakes which positive analogy may make, our *à priori* views of revelation by positive analogy, though only presumptively, of course not conclusively, and subject to chance of reversal when we come to the fact. Indeed, what Mr. Newman comes to after all, is only that that expectation is weakened in *degree*, and that the violation of it is made *less* of an objection by the consideration he puts forward. He considers still that we *have* that expectation, and that the violation of it *is* an objection.

But he here meets us with a distinction, which seems to him, while he allows the general force of positive analogy, to exempt the particular case of a continual revelation from its jurisdiction. "I will hazard," he says, "a distinction here between the facts of revelation and its principles;—the argument from analogy is more concerned with its principles than its facts. The revealed facts are special and singular from the nature of the case: but it is otherwise with the revealed principles. They are common to all the works of God; and if the Author of Nature be the Author of Grace, it may be expected that, while the systems of fact are distinct and independent, the principles displayed in them will be the same, and form a connecting link between them. In this identity of principle lies the true Analogy of Natural and Revealed Religion in Butler's sense of the word. The doctrine of the Incarnation is a fact, and cannot be paralleled by anything in nature: the doctrine of Mediation is a principle, and is abundantly exemplified in its provisions. Miracles are facts; inspiration is a fact; divine teaching once for all, and a continual teaching, are each a fact; probation by means of intellectual difficulties is a principle."[1] Now with regard to this distinction between "facts" and "principles," considered in itself, we do and can give no opinion, because the value and legitimacy of all such distinctions depend entirely on the way in which they are used. If such distinctions are used, so as faithfully to represent the substantial state of the case, they are convenient; but they must be used with an entire subservience to the substantial state of the case, and not bend the latter to themselves. If a continual revelation is a "fact," it is not a fact like the "Incarnation," in which it is impossible by the nature of the case to look for an analogy. If it is a "fact," it is one in a sense in which probation of the intellect may be called one too: it is a general line of proceeding on God's part toward mankind. The substantial truth in the present case is that we expect an analogy everywhere, except where, by the nature of the case, we are prevented. The nature of the case does prevent us from expecting an analogy or likeness in certain instances, but it does not prevent us from expecting one in the present; and therefore we expect it, and we argue from a certain line of proceeding in nature to a like line in revelation.

Thus much with respect to the positive argument of analogy, and its weight in the present question. But this argument is not—and we have introduced it principally for the sake of showing that it is not—the argument which Butler uses for showing the valuelessness of *à priori* reasonings with respect to revelation. The argument by which he proves that, is an appeal to the simple fact of human ignorance, from which the incapacity for so reasoning necessarily follows. He strengthens this fact, indeed, by a reference to analogy, by showing that the

[1] Page 123.

very things we object to exist in God's natural dispensation, and that therefore the fact proves that we are wrong. But it is analogy as proving ignorance, and not analogy simple and positive, which is the basis of his argument. It follows that to endeavour by various objections and distinctions to weaken the force of the positive argument of analogy is, in the present question, to fight the air, for we do not invalidate one ground by detracting from another. Whatever arguments may be adduced to relax the force of simple verisimilitude, and the inference from the known to the unknown, do not in the remotest way touch the ground on which we have been going in this question. They do not touch that truth of human ignorance which no verisimilitude but actual consciousness witnesses, nor that evidence of human ignorance which no probabilities but actual facts afford us. And on the ground of that ignorance, and that incompetency for *à priori* judgment, we cannot allow any weight to Mr. Newman's presumption that a revelation is to be continued because it has been made.

And now we will make one remark on the whole mode of treating the argument of analogy which has come before us here,—on the general relations which Mr. Newman, as a reasoner, seems to have entered into to that argument. There is an established argument then, to which all this discussion has had reference, called the Argument of Analogy. We have had to view this argument on different sides, but, taken comprehensively, it is an argument which intervenes between the *à priori* reasoner and revelation. It establishes a certain medium through which *à priori* reasoning has to pass, and checks and regulates our presumptions with respect to revelation by an appeal to the course of nature. That there are difficulties connected with the theory of this argument may be true, and Butler invited the attention of philosophers to them when he wrote his treatise; though the invitation, we believe, has never been attended to, and the theory of the argument has remained comparatively uninvestigated to this day. But this is a consideration which does not, of course, affect the practical weight of it, and the Argument of Analogy, involving the medium which we have mentioned, appeals to us like other substantial and practical truth.

Now here, on the other hand, is an argument which makes us reason *à priori* without this medium,—makes us reason from the idea of a revelation to a conclusion with respect to that revelation, straight and directly. It says the existence of a revelation at all is an independent ground of reasoning, from which by itself we draw a sure inference with respect to that revelation, viz., that it will continue and be a standing one. And when the argument from analogy steps in with the veto from nature, *i.e.* the experience which nature gives us of our ignorance, and tells the arguer that he cannot so presume, the arguer replies that a revelation being given is a new ground, which lifts him above this analogy of nature, and is of itself a direct intellectual basis for this conclusion. He tells us that revelation as such supersedes the appeal to nature, and from the fact that it is revelation certifies to a standing revelation. That is to say, here is a view which does not allow the argument of analogy to perform its necessary functions or work at all, for whereas that argument by its own nature intervenes between us and our presumptions with respect to revelation, this view cuts off that intervention.

The argument of analogy, in short, ends where revelation begins, in other words, there is no such thing as the argument from analogy. The very nature of analogy supposes two sides of it, which it argumentatively connects. The whole argument in Butler goes on the principle that although revelation is a new and distinct line of proceeding on God's part from nature—it one thing, nature another—yet that we may and must reason from one to the other, must ever form our presumptions about the former under the veto and through the medium of the latter. But this essential argumentative connection is dissolved if, as soon as revelation comes, analogy goes, and revelation itself supplies the presumptions about revelation. Nor will it alter the case to call revelation a new order of nature, and make its continuation analogous to that new order of nature so called; to say, "The case, then, stands thus: that revelation has introduced a new law of divine governance, over and above those laws which appear in the natural course of the world, and henceforth we argue for a standing authority in matters of faith, *on the analogy of nature and from the fact of Christianity;*"[1] —the analogy of nature meaning here exactly the same thing with the fact of Christianity, *i.e.* revelation here being viewed as nature. For this new order of nature, if revelation be called such, is, in the Argument of Analogy, the very dispensation the view of which an analogy of nature regulates. It is not, therefore, by the argument, that regulating analogy of nature. It is the subject and not the basis of the analogy; and to call it by the name of nature gives it no new function, and makes it no more that course of nature from which the analogy proceeds than it was under the name of revelation. Revelation then, in spite of the verbal change, still presumes about itself: the analogy of revelation to nature is the analogy of revelation to revelation. The argument from analogy, with its parallelism, retreats before one member of it.

[1] Page 124.

One of the lines has become its own parallel; the stream has both banks on one side; revelation is its own analogy. And, therefore, when Mr. Newman speaks of his conclusion of a standing revelation "being forced on him by analogical considerations," he speaks of an analogy which he has explained away, and unsubstantiated altogether. The whole argument has evaporated under his distinctions, and left him an analogy which has no nature to make revelation analogous to, and which he has especially adopted because it has not. He has treated the argument of analogy as the Germans treat inspiration, and under the appearance of explaining it has dissolved it.

It is, however, important before leaving the subject to follow out these two bases of reasoning which we have been contrasting into their respective lines of thought and ultimate positions with respect to religious truth.

We have then, on the one hand, a great presumptive ground asserting that if a revelation is given it must go on; that human nature wants a present infallible guide; that "Christianity must, humanly speaking, have an infallible expounder."[1] Upon this original notion of what is necessary arises immediately the assertion of what is, and with that assertion a whole corresponding view of the existing matter-of-fact Church, and its established body of ideas, however and wherever derived. A whole, to use the word, perfectionist view of the historical progress of thought and growth of truth in the Church earthly, and the Christian world is ultimately imposed by an original basis of presumption like the present. The hypothesis of a standing revelation cannot afford to make any large established ideas in the earthly Church erroneous, it would interfere with such a standing revelation to do so; a pledge for the absolute correctness of all that growth

[1] Page 128.

of opinion which the infallible guide sanctions is contained in the notion of that infallible guide. Thus inevitably arises the great general view that whatever is is right. The fact of certain ideas getting established becomes itself the proof of their truth. We see this view immediately in the tone of the arguer. The arguer reposes in fact; he carries the sensation about with him of largeness, extent, numbers; a doctrine that spreads over a large surface, that is held *de facto* by a large mass, is its own evidence. His tone of reasoning is a perpetual memento of the *de facto* ground. It is almost a condescension for him to argue at all; he has the fact, that is his argument. That his use of the fact is an assumption is lost sight of in the largeness of the fact itself; the authority of fact becomes itself a fact, and is ever seen in the background as the supreme authority, beyond which no appeal lies. The arguer is thus less occupied in proving than in simply unfolding his assumption. He explains how it was that such opinions arose, the need that was felt for them, their convenience in filling up certain chasms in the original revelation. It was thus, he explains, that their truth became known. This desire became, in course of ages, stronger and stronger, till at last it formally expressed itself: the mass of Christendom resolved that these opinions were true, and accordingly they became known truths, and have continued so up to the present day. Such is the account of the rise of this doctrine, of this article of faith: the arguer simply traces the progress of their discovery and adjustment from the very first dawn of the want to the climax of the supply. The completeness and rotundity of the formed system are then urged; the coincidence of the fact that such doctrines exist, with the fact that they were wanted; the coincidence of the various results and ramifications of developed doctrine with each other; the coincidence of the permanency of their reception with the fact of that profession of infallibility which first sanctioned it. "When we are convinced that large developments do exist in matter of fact professing to be true and legitimate, our first impression naturally must be that these developments are what they pretend to be. The very scale on which they have been made, their high antiquity, yet present promise, their gradual formation, yet precision, affect the imagination most forcibly."[1] We need hardly say that Mr. Newman, in accordance with the whole tone of his book, and his appeal to the living and real, as opposed to merely historical and formal, of course understands by these developments of doctrine not the simple statements on paper, but doctrine as generally understood and believed,—the practical and energising opinions of the Christian body. Here, then, is what may be called a perfectionist view of the progress of truth in the Christian world. The ideas which establish themselves time after time in the Church are *ipso facto* true. What exists is right; each successive stage of thought improves on the following one; truth advances with the certainty of a mathematical problem; an infallible centre produces a perfect, ever operating self-correction; and the present state of things, as regards our relations to truth, becomes all that, humanly speaking, we could wish it to be.

The argument of analogy, on the other hand, gives a basis upon which a more qualified system erects itself. Its maxim that we are not judges of what a revelation should be, and consequent confinement of us to the fact of what revelation there has been, tends immediately this way. That there has been a revelation rests upon evidence of fact; its continuance rests upon presumption. That revelation, then, as far as it went, and as much as it said;

[1] Page 135.

the whole of it, in whatever mode communicated; everything for the institution and communication of which, as a fact, there is evidence, the argument of analogy gives us; but for the rest, it tells us that we have no revelation, and that we cannot, by any notion on our part that we ought to have one, make one. It leaves the revelation which God gave, among them to whom he gave it, exposed to the same chances of abuse, perversion, or neglect, in the carrying out, which attend on the truths of nature; in all respects, except those in which it is, as a matter of fact, divinely guaranteed. The Christian revelation *is* divinely guaranteed against total corruption; it has the direct promise that the "gates of hell shall not prevail against it," and stands in a different position from natural religion, in consequence of this promise. With this safeguard, however, the argument of analogy sends it down exposed all the same to common degrees of corruption, and those changes which are consistent with the substance of the revelation continuing. It prepares us, in consequence, for such abuses, if they occur; it makes it most likely beforehand that they will, in a greater or less degree, occur. To the divine truth, thrown into the imperfect human mass, a positive likelihood of distortion and discolourment of some kind attaches. Not to mention lower and rougher causes, the mere tendencies of the human mind to go off upon particular thoughts, refine upon the natural substance of the truth put before it, and idolise its own conceptions and points of view, are against the probability of a revelation which offered the materials and supplied the occasions for abuse, being carried out without it; and running through centuries of intricate and agitating contact with the collective Christian intellect, without any deflection whatever from original soundness. If the rise of such deflections, again, is probable, their permanency is no matter to be surprised at; for the same course of things which originally established them makes them also last: it was their adaptation to some large and prevalent tastes which caused them to spread at first; and the same keeps them going. Again, when they have been going on for a certain time, further accretions to them give them further hold: the appendages of poetry, ornament, association form around them: they colour art and literature, they have aids and alliances in a hundred departments around them, and interweave themselves with the life and sentiment of the mass. If the argument of a standing revelation can explain such facts upon its own hypothesis, the argument of analogy can do the same on its hypothesis; and can do it with exactly the same appeal to coincidence, harmony, and wholeness in its explanation. If truth can systematise and arrange itself, error can do the same; once begun, it is seen going on by a kind of intrinsic force of self-evolving, self-adjusting growth.

To take, for example, the popular and authorised cultus of the Virgin. The argument of analogy can take an unfavourable view of this cultus; offering, in doing so, quite as complete an account, in one way, of the rise, spread, and permanence of it as the argument of infallibility can in another. That the doctrine of the Incarnation, for instance, was likely, humanly speaking, to lead to it, falls in just as well with the former as with the latter argument; for we see, constantly, instances of great truths which slide quite naturally, unless narrowly watched, into error, and seem to produce their own misconstruction. Here, then, analogy tells us we need not be perfectionists, and uphold the whole growth of opinion in the Church as faultless. And it proceeds to give one or two natural answers to some claims and reasons urged on the latter side. It is asked, for example, how we can suppose that God would allow great saints and holy men to have joined in and promoted this cultus if it was wrong? But surely it is not necessary to suppose that, a general tendency to error being granted in the Christian body, good men should not, in particular cases, go along with it, even actively. The general body suffers in its attitude toward truth. If God, with all His vouchsafed grace, has left frailty in the heart of every single member of the earthly Church, from the lowest sinner to the highest saint, you cannot tell what may be the consequences of this fact upon the attitude of the Church, as a body, toward truth. It is natural to suppose that truth and goodness go together; and that if the Church is not pure in one respect, it will not be pure in the other. Subtle evil is an awful mysterious fact, which must be expected to have its results. You cannot tell how it may operate in this respect. And this general tendency in the body may carry away, in particular cases, and even engage the activities of, good members of the body. Moreover, you may ask how God will allow this; but if He allows the element of evil to exist in these good members at all, it is no great additional wonder if He allows that element to do something, and make a real difference in what comes from them, and affect the actual external issues from their minds. Why should not they be subject to their own class of partialities and obliquities, be liable to take up ideas, and then be over fond of them because they have taken them up, and dwell upon them with something like mental luxury, and feel originality with the secret relish of a frail creature, and go on to mould and tune their minds to a favourite line of thought, as men tune an instrument? Let no persons think we are doing injustice here to the minds of really holy men; the degree to which serious evil can co-exist with very high dispositions in the soul is one of the mysteries of our present state. We may add, that apparent symptoms of some ethical unsoundness, and of a degeneracy from the purity and severity of Christian worship, are found in the particular tone which runs through this cultus; which, even in its best form, seems to show an element of what may be called false sweetness in it, and very soon runs out into palpable and unbecoming sentimentalism. Again, if it is such a difficulty that God should permit holy men to think erroneously, how are we to account for the plain fact that He has permitted multitudes, in all ages, of the best and noblest minds to do so, and to worship Him in faulty modes? We are concerned with a principle of Divine government here, and are not, for an instant, comparing Roman Catholicism and paganism. The human souls that have lived and died under pagan systems have had, as far as we can judge, tempers and natures as capable in themselves of the fullest saintly development, and as worthy of the correctest views of truth, as those that have lived and died under Christianity; but they were permitted to think and to worship faultily. Nor is it any answer to this fact to say, that God has distinctly pledged the possession of the truth to good Christians, and did not to good pagans; for it is not denied here that the holy men we are referring to possessed the truth, but only that they possessed it free from all intermixture of error. The general facts of this earthly dispensation show plainly that it is a part of God's providence to permit good men to err. And though it is true that He distinctly teaches that "they who do His will shall know of the doctrine," this cannot be applied as a certain test of truth so long as men do not do His will perfectly. For so long as evil remains in good men, we cannot tell what may be the consequence of that evil, and how far their mental relations to truth may be impaired by it. The rule of doing His will is absolutely true as a practical rule to ourselves; but this rule must be acted up to before it can become an infallible test of the teaching of another, and we know that no human being does act up to it. Nor is this explaining away an obvious meaning, but only excluding a forced one, as regards this scriptural maxim; for its obvious meaning, in the way in which it is brought before us, is that of a practical rule, and the other is a subsequently appended one. The test of personal goodness for deciding truth, though by no means made a useless or unimportant, because it is not an infallible test, nor reduced to nothing because it is not everything, is yet not infallible. If Scripture appeals to it in some places, in others it warns us against it. And the simple fact that on some most important questions which divide the Christian world, equal personal holiness is to be seen on both sides, disqualifies the test of personal holiness in general as an absolute one on the question of truth.

On the whole then, we say—according to the argument from analogy—an original creed or revelation thrown into the world of human intelligence is exposed to all common chances of human discolourment in the carrying out; the substantial original creed remaining throughout notwithstanding, and secured, if there be evidence for this fact, against failure to the end. And however, in reasoning *à priori*, out of our own heads, respecting revelation, we might expect it to do more for us because it did much, and look forward to a progress of truth pure, divinely guaranteed against error: the argument of analogy on the other hand bids us expect no such thing, but take the facts as they stand. It tells us not to expect all must be truth because there is truth; or again, to think all must be error because there is error; but to expect both truth and error. It supplies a dogmatic basis on the one side, and it allows for uncertainty on the other; and bids us neither be unbelievers nor perfectionists. It says—This is a mixed world, and expect mixtures in it. Do not think that the progress of things will be wholly one way, or wholly another; that it will entirely submerge truth, or unfold it unimpeachably. There is much of both good and evil in it. The earthly Church partakes of the mixed character of the world in which it is placed, and which it has more or less received into its own pale. And its best members too are not perfect, but have their own undue biasses of intellect, temper, taste, sometimes more open and palpable, sometimes more refined and internal.

Thus much for Mr. Newman's presumptive argument for a standing revelation, on which he rests the proof of the Papal Infallibility. It only remains now to take a brief view of this line of proof, as distinguished from another line of proof for the same doctrine.

The whole argument, then, of a standing revelation is a very different one from M. De Maistre's argument of simple church government. M. De Maistre argues for the simple necessity of a central government for the Church; the need for a universal empire of a universal head. The simple idea of government, he says, necessarily takes us up, step by step, to one central and supreme seat of government, for there must be some limit to appeal from subordinate authorities, if a question is to be settled at all; and wherever the power of appeal stops, you have *ipso facto* a supreme authority. Now, such an hypothesis as this has certainly the advantage, as an hypothesis, of covering the whole ground. It is, indeed, absurd to expect that the mind should be satisfied with it; because what the mind wants is to believe what is true; and this argument does not touch the question of truth or error in the doctrines themselves decided on by this ultimate authority. It tells us the fact that they are decided on, and no more. It views the Church simply as a polity, and professes to apply the same principles to it which belong to other polities; and wholly omitting its prophetical office of teaching the truth, makes it impose its dogmas on us on the same principle on which the state imposes acts of parliament. However, it has, as an hypothesis, the advantage of covering the whole ground, for every single opinion which is, or can be entertained among Christians is either authoritatively decided, or is not. If it is, it is authoritatively *decided;* and if it is not, it is authoritatively *not* decided: so that, in either case, Christian doctrine has a perfectly complete basis provided for it.

Mr. Newman's argument, on the other hand, though much superior in line to M. De Maistre's, for he does address himself to a real internal craving after truth in the human mind, is not so complete, and does not cover the whole ground. The hypothesis of a standing revelation reaches a point where it ceases to apply, and confesses that it can explain no further. For however largely truth is revealed to us, after all we come to a point where truth is not revealed to us; and it is only a matter of degree whether we stop where an original revelation stops, or stop where a standing revelation stops. As a matter of fact, there are a vast number of questions, and some of them very important ones as regards their intrinsic truth or falsehood, which this standing revelation does not decide. There is the whole question, *e.g.*, of the attributes and position of the Virgin, which this standing revelation has scrupulously avoided deciding; and a person in the Roman Church may either believe, with Mr. Newman, that the Blessed Virgin is all which the Arians supposed our Lord to be, or only believe what the English Church believes about her. It has scrupulously avoided saying whether her conception is immaculate or not.[1] If a standing revelation avoids deciding important questions which come before it, it stops revealing. And though Mr. Newman may say that it may in course of time, though it has not yet done so, turn into dogma or reject a particular view of the Virgin; still here is the fact before us of an important question which this standing revelation has had before it for ages, and has refused to touch: a result (if true) included in the idea of the original revelation, and consequently part of it, and consequently revealed in theory; which, somehow or other, has not been revealed in fact. It is needless pursuing this remark through the whole series of instances in which it would apply. It is evident that in multitudes of cases of theological opinion in the Church public, not to mention the innumerable daily cases in the private life of all Christians in the world, who have been, are, or will be, there is, as a matter of fact, no continuous revelation which decides for us. And wherever it stops, all the objections which apply to the original revelation's continuance, apply in principle to its cessation too.

This defect, indeed, in the hypothesis, is so obvious, that the Roman controversialist attempts to answer it by confessing it; by showing, that is, that it is admitted into the *rationale* of the Papal Infallibility. The idea of a standing revelation which goes to the real extreme of its principle, and reveals everything whatever about religion that people can naturally desire to be told, has its unreasonableness, so far, granted that the Papal authority voluntarily decides a great number of questions

[1] The dogma of the Immaculate Conception was promulgated December 8, 1854.

about religion without revealing; simply commanding as the supreme authority, and claiming obedience on that ground only. All the questions which are decided in this latter way are defined, indeed, to be ones out of "the province of infallibility;" but it is not explained why they should be out of the province; and the case is, simply, that infallibility has come to an arbitrary terminus which it does not choose to exceed, and that a standing revelation stops short. In these cases the Roman *rationale* supplies the defect of one hypothesis by ground from another, and where the profession of a standing revelation conveniently stops, introduces the appeal to mere authority. It constructs a position out of the argument of a standing revelation and the monarchical argument combined; and M. De Maistre and Mr. Newman could only give a unity of hypothesis to its system by each confining himself to one side of it.

Accordingly, the latter, after drawing out his theory for a standing revelation, proceeds to join on to it, as an additional and subordinate one, the simple governmental or monarchical argument; to assert "the impossibility that an infinite wisdom, in decreeing the rise of an universal empire, should not have decreed the development of a ruler;"[1] a certain "absolute need of a monarchical power in the Church; which is our ground for anticipating it;"[2] and of "a necessary centre of unity for preserving the sacrament of unity." We have not space for a regular discussion of this further subject; and contenting ourselves with the general answer that all the arguments quoted above against the validity of *à priori* reasoning on the point of a standing revelation apply to the same line of reasoning on the point of an absolute monarchical authority and necessary centre of unity in the Church, shall make but one or two reflections here.

[1] Page 171. [2] Page 170.

With respect, then, to the direct proof of the existence of an absolute monarchical authority somewhere in the Church, drawn from the fact of the Church being intended to be one external society;—of the proof of the existence of a local centre of unity, drawn from the idea itself of unity;—we do not see the force of it. The idea of unity does not imply a particular local centre of unity. Take a drop of water, or any fluid substance; it is one drop, but there is no centre of unity in it. The particles of any substance can adhere together by some equal pervading adhesion; and do not involve the existence of a central force in it attracting them to itself, and preventing them from flying off. The Church might certainly continue, as far as the nature of the case is concerned, one external society, without a monarchical head over it, or centre in it. What if all Christians had from the first obeyed the spirit of unity, and kept together upon their own individual will? The idea, of course, implies much more perfection in Christians than there has been; but it shows that the Christian society does not, metaphysically, and in the nature of the case, as one society, imply a local centre and head. Indeed Christians *did* keep together for many centuries in fact, without any local head. So much for the nature of the case, and the metaphysical reason. Nor does the practical argument, again, of the expediency of such a local head for preserving unity, prove such a necessary centre of unity as is wanted: for an expedient for preserving unity is not the substance itself of unity. Water cannot rise above its level: an argument cannot prove more than its basis supports. The argument here proceeds on simple expediency as its basis, and therefore cannot confer any sacramental character as its result. The Papal power is, on this argument, a means to an end; a practical instrument for making men keep a Christian ordinance—that of external unity. If it fails to do this, and does not secure the preservation of that ordinance, either from its own excesses or the fault of the material it has to do with, it fails just as any other instrument may fail in doing its work : the ordinance is broken, and there is all the evil, whatever that may be, of external schism in the Christian body. But it is the division in the unity of the body at large, and not the separation from the Papacy, which is that evil; and no sacramental virtue is conferred by this argument on special union with Rome.

Again, the necessity of the Church being one external communion is urged as a practical argument in this direction; and for that necessity the most common argument urged is a *reductio ad absurdum* one.

A *reductio ad absurdum* argument then, to prove that the Church can be but one intercommunicating body in the world, proceeds thus :—If there can be two branches of the true Church not intercommunicating, why may there not be a thousand? and why may not every single Christian diocese in the world split off from every other, and yet all continue real Churches ? If two Churches can be Churches without intercommunicating, there can be no such thing as a schismatical Church. We must be allowed to say here that the *reductio ad absurdum*, as a whole form of argument, is in an unsatisfactory, we may say neglected state,—there are no recognised rules for the use and management of it; and each side on every question, worldly or religious, wields it in a loose irregular way, as it serves a turn, and inflicts a temporary stroke. In the present instance we shall only ask, would it be a *reductio ad absurdum* of the extreme doctrine of the Papal Infallibility, to suggest that there is nothing whatever in the nature of things to prevent a Pope turning Gallican, and proclaiming the truth of Gallicanism by a formal bull ?

Such an argument would be considered puerile; and yet we see no difference in principle between it and the argument here advanced respecting schism. Neither of these contemplated absurdities have occurred, and nobody expects that they will occur. It may be said that there is a tendency, an apparent beginning of the fact in one case, which there is not in the other; but what difference does this make, so long as in neither case the fact will actually take place, *i.e.* so long as the right to say that the fact will not take place is the same on either side? And this right is the same. For that evil exists to a certain degree, is no kind of evidence in itself that it will proceed to the greatest possible degree. There are multitudes of beginnings and tendencies in the world which are no sort of evidence, even to the remotest probability, that the extremes of which they are the abstract beginnings, and to which they do abstractedly tend, will follow. Every human being tends to diabolical and insane wickedness, if by saying so be meant that he has the beginning of that which, if followed out, would become such; but no one would say that an excellent religious man actually tends to such a character, for there is not the remotest prospect, from the fact of his having evil in him, that he will become evil to that amount. In the same way there may be a beginning of unlimited schism in the Church; but it does not at all follow from that, even in the way of the remotest probability, that such unlimited schism will ensue. There is a difference of degree, which is, for all argumentative purposes, a difference of kind: a difference of degree in which there is no actual sequence from the one extreme end of the series to the other extreme end. The Church ought by rights to be one external society; if she is split up into two or three large branches, she is so far divided, and there is so far schism;

the principle of unity is violated. But this is one state of things. A state of things in which Christians, instead of loving one another, had grown to hate one another to such an extent, that no one single particle of the Church would cleave to any other, and which would seem to show that Christian principle, and with it the Church upon earth, had evanesced, is another state of things. And there is no actual sequence from the one to the other. And therefore in the two cases of *reductio ad absurdum* before us, one side has as much right to disown the hostile supposition which its opponent presses as the other has. What we assert is that all division does not take away churchship, and that more than one external communion may be the Church. The proper mode of answering this is to prove that all division *does* unchurch, and that the Church *can* only be one external communion. If the necessity of this external oneness is not established by direct proof, it cannot be established by this *reductio ad absurdum;* for because the fact of existing division has to be accounted for, we have not therefore to account for the fact of a vast amount of division which does not exist.

But we must go from these reflections on certain lines of reasoning on the subject before us, to the examination of a statement. Mr. Newman asserts that, as a matter of fact, all Christianity outside of the Roman obedience has been a failure, and that therefore there is the evidence of fact to the divine institution of the Papal Monarchy. "Wherever the Pope has been renounced, decay and division have been the consequence."[1] "The Church is a kingdom; and heresy is a family rather than a kingdom: and a family continually divides and sends out branches, founding new houses and propagating itself in colonies,

[1] Page 170.

Theory of Development. 133

each of them as independent as its original head; so was it with heresy."[1] And this observation is meant to be applicable to all that is outside of the Roman obedience. Now to bring this statement to the test of fact. There is a large and important branch of the Church, which, never having been under the Roman obedience from the first, refused about a thousand years ago to conform to it, and has consequently been separate from the Roman see ever since. This portion of the Church has not exhibited, since that separation, division or decay. With respect to division: The Eastern Church—the portion to which we allude— was very fertile in division and heresy *before* the separation of East and West; and when, therefore, not the East by itself, but the whole Church, East and West together, as one body, were responsible, so far as responsibility was incurred, for such events. It was very fertile in schism in early times, as the Western Church has been in later. But the Eastern Church has had, since the separation of East and West, comparatively no division or heresy rising out of it; the Nestorian heresy and the Monophysite, which subsequently split into the Armenian, Jacobite, and others, date prior to that era. The Eastern Church again has not exhibited decay. It was overwhelmed by Barbarians in its more Eastern domains, just as the African Church was overwhelmed by the Vandals; but it found other ground, and soon after its Asiatic reverses shot up with marvellous vigour and success in the North of Europe. Its conversion of the North, the largest and most striking of all the conversions of the middle ages, took place, it is to be remembered, after the separation from Rome; and the result is now before us in the shape of the Russian Church, with its history, saintly names, and associations, and all the

[1] Page 146.

ecclesiastical accumulations of a thousand years. The Eastern Church presents at this day the phenomenon of a Church, comprehending about eighty millions of Christians, in perfect doctrinal unity with itself, chanting the same creed and the same liturgies now which it has chanted every day of every year since the time of St. Basil, the Gregories, and St. Chrysostom, up to this present hour at which we write,—a Church in full possession of the popular affection throughout its domains, and fertile in examples of the most holy, self-denying, and severe Christian life. Such is the Church which is asserted to have exhibited nothing but decay and division since the separation from Rome.

Mr. Newman's line with respect to the Greek Church is indeed a feature in the Essay to be observed. His ordinary view supposes it not to exist; and the argument, proceeding as if there were no such body, is of course not encumbered by the fact at all. But he is necessarily brought into contact with it occasionally, and then he supposes it as a totally different fact from what it is. He supposes Eastern Christianity to be an effete and stagnant superstition, showing no life and producing no fruits. Its permanence confronts him as an obstacle to his theory of a corruption, which makes corruption "the end of a course, a transition state leading to a crisis, and as such a brief and rapid process;"[1] and the same theory, which proved that corruption could not attach to Roman doctrines, because they were permanent, has to be explained when it comes across the doctrinal permanence in the East. And the explanation is the one mentioned. "Decay," he says, "which is one form of corruption, is slow. . . . We see opinions, usages, and systems, which are of venerable and imposing aspect, but which have no soundness within them,

[1] Page 90.

and keep together from a habit of consistence and from dependence on political institutions; or they become almost peculiarities of a country, or the habits of a race, or the fashions of society. . . . Such are the superstitions which pervade a population, like some ingrained dye or inveterate odour, and which at length come to an end because nothing lasts for ever."[1] "Whether," he continues, "Mahometanism, external to Christendom, and the Greek Church within it, fall under this description, is yet to be seen." And so the case of the Eastern Church is dismissed. But surely upon this very statement, highly unfavourable as it is to Eastern Christianity, the case of Eastern Christianity cannot be so dismissed. For the only conclusive proof of the theory of decay, viz., dissolution, it confesses to be wanting here, and it allows that whether the Eastern Church "comes to an end" or not "is yet to be seen." It has not then, at any rate, come to an end yet; and so long as it has not, it is the phenomenon of a permanent Christian doctrine and society outside of the Roman obedience, and is therefore a real difficulty which his theory has to surmount,—a difficulty, we must add, which is but imperfectly covered by coupling its permanence and that of Mahometanism (which is no difficulty to Rome whatever) together. The "barrenness, if not lifelessness,"[2] of the Greek Church, however, is the one idea taken for granted throughout the Essay, and is aided by side remarks here and there, such as the casual suggestion that it is mere accident that it did not fall with the rest of early heresy contained in the quotation from Gibbon, that perhaps the "Greeks would be still involved in the heresy of the Monophysites if the Emperor's horse had not fortunately stumbled. Theodosius expired, and his orthodox sister succeeded to the throne."[3]

[1] Page 91. [2] Page 72. [3] Page 46.

With respect then to this assertion of lifelessness in Eastern doctrines, we do not know what particular standard of life in a Church may be implied here, but we will propose one to which there can be small objection. Doctrine is not barren and lifeless which produces good works. Other things may be wanting; but if they are there, after all they are the surest sign of life, of a Church having something in her, being a reality, being solid. They show that her doctrine is not mere sound,—that it has a spirit in it; they show that she is animated,—that she is not a corpse, a husk. Learning, science, intellectual refinement, and many of the human media by which a Church expresses and adorns its spiritual life, there may not be; but if the Christian type has worked, and an awful unspeakable moulding power has resided within her, seizing human souls as if it were some physical principle, mastering and overwhelming weak and carnal nature in them, and making them new creatures, with thoughts and hopes estranged from earth, and passing through this world as through a wilderness,—if some powerful mould within her has formed wonderful spiritual beings on whom the inhabitants of the earth have gazed in reverence and awe, this shows something more than the dead dry husk and shell of a Church. This presence of the Spirit, and these deep movements of grace, the Eastern Church can show. She has formed saints and holy men in all their various gradations; has produced great spiritual deeds of self-denial, love, and fear; and, from the highest and severest ascetic down to the humblest of the Church's flock, has trained in every age, and does train now, souls for heaven. If she has done this, she has been a living Church. We may be answered, perhaps, that a congregation of Baptists produces good men amongst them, and yet is not the Church.

But this is no answer to meet the case. Here is a body that has the whole external form and system of a Church which the early Church exhibited; and which is the representative, by uninterrupted descent, of the ancient Eastern Church. It believes and teaches the self-same dogmatic Christianity which the ancient Church did. There is not the smallest question that the dogmatic creed of the Eastern Christian at this day is the creed of St. Basil and St. Chrysostom. Now this whole corporate and doctrinal identity with the ancient Church the Baptist congregation wants; and those appearances of life are a mere isolated note in the case of the Baptist congregation, which come in to complete a whole body of other notes of a Church in the Eastern case. Moreover, it may do very well as an off-hand answer, to say that all sects can produce their good men; but the note of sanctity which belongs to the Eastern Church is a totally different one from what sectarian piety affords us. We are concerned with a question as to a phenomenon here—the apparent life of the Greek Church; and we say that Eastern sanctity is one phenomenon, and what we call sectarian piety is another; and one phenomenon cannot be put aside by identifying it with another, which is totally different from it.

Indeed, the controversial line taken upon this subject is one which we must notice. It is objected, on the part of the Roman controversialist, to the English Church that she does not exhibit notes of sanctity. Her defenders reply that she has them, though in her own form, and though she cannot show the same extraordinary manifestations in individuals which some other Churches can. And they are told that this is not enough; that the truth is, we have no saints, and that, therefore, we are not a Church. With this decision the controversy steps over to the East. Now the Eastern Church on this subject produces what is something like evidence. The Greek points to twelve thick volumes, one for each month, containing the Hagiology of his Church. We open the volumes, and there, at any rate, are portrayed real saints. There is no distinction there between sanctity and its form, to be offered and to be overruled; there are real saints, spirit, form, and all; men who lived literally in caves and dens of the earth, who passed life in spiritual contemplation, or in converting rude tribes to Christ; men who laid the foundation of the monastery in the wild forest, and whose cells, hollowed with their own hands out of the solid rock, or mountain, or lake side, far from human habitations, still collected disciples, attracted by the fame of their sanctity, to hear their voice, and crowds of simple folk to touch their garments. Here are the lives of holy monks, hermits, bishops, from a thousand years ago to recent times, the canonised saints of the Eastern Church, and as true and unquestionable saints as any Church can show. And what does it gain to the Eastern Church in the controversy to show them? Nothing. The advocate of Rome as completely excludes the Greek Church from the universal Church of Christ as if it had not one single saint to show. The line is the same with respect to miracles. The English Church is told she has not the note of miracles. But the Eastern Church has the note of them, upon quite as good evidence as the Roman; and it does her no good whatever to prove it. No wonder if some people think all controversy hollow and unreal when they see arguers simply dealing out their arguments for the occasion, and allowing no weight to, and claiming the greatest weight for, the same evidence at the same time, according as others or themselves are to be benefited by it.

But to return to what we were saying about the character of the phenomenon here before us : for our own part, we look in vain to discern any essential distinction as to the note of sanctity (including miracles in that note) between the Eastern and the Western Church. We see on each side a vast collection of wonderful saintliness, accompanied by a considerable amount of miraculous agency, asserted and recorded, and professing to be so upon evidence. It would disturb a devotional mind, and make the latitudinarian smile, to attempt to establish any solid distinction, either as to evidence or internal character, between the miracles of the Eastern and the Western Church. Moreover, at the Council of Florence, as the terms of the meditated reconciliation implied, the Church of Rome herself was quite willing to recognise this sanctity. She was willing to allow the whole Eastern Church to retain its calendar, and go on in future exactly as it had gone on in this respect; to continue regarding as undoubted Christian saints the self-same persons whom it had all along regarded as such, and paying them, to all time, the same honours,—observing their festivals, chanting their praises, recording their miracles, invoking their intercession. In fact, the Roman Church was willing to receive the whole body of Eastern canonised saints. We must add, that to be willing to do so was to be willing to allow the real churchship of the Church of which they were members. How could they be made Christian saints, unless they were made members of the Christian Church ; and how could they be made members of the Christian Church after their death, if they were not so during their life ? How can a fact be created *ex post facto*, and a thing which was not, be afterwards made to have been ?—an act of power which, Aristotle says, the gods themselves are not equal to. It may be said that it is possible to suppose them members of the Christian Church in heaven, without supposing them to have been members of the Christian Church upon earth. But it is the latter of these two which the Church of Rome was willing to allow the Easterns to believe, and not the former only. It is the latter of these two beliefs which is involved in the act of a whole Church keeping up the memory of departed saints. You allow a whole Church to go on taking the same view of a certain body of saints which it had done; but it *had* always regarded them as members of the earthly Church, therefore it is allowed to continue to do so. And really, without anything more being wanted, if you allow millions of Christians to go on reciting the holy deeds and miracles of their departed saints, observing their festivals, and dwelling in thought upon the examples of their earthly lives; to say that you need not allow them, in doing so, to regard them as members of the same earthly Church as themselves, would be at once inane and trivial. On the principle here mentioned, the Church of Rome could canonise the Hindoo saints on converting a Hindoo population. You may suppose the Hindoo saints, as saints in heaven; "for in every nation, he that feareth God and worketh righteousness is accepted of Him." But you could not make them Christian saints; and why not, but because they were not members of the Christian Church upon earth? If then you *do* recognise a body of Christian saints, you *do* imply that they were members of such a Church.

The substantial subject, however, with which we are concerned throughout these reflections, is simply the sanctity of the Eastern Church, as an ordinary and common sense fact discernible in it, without bringing in other aspects or considerations. All we want to say is, that there are discernible in the Eastern Church real, and high, and solid effects of some spiritual life, as we must needs suppose it to be; that its sanctity is upon the primitive and ecclesiastical type; that it holds up the standard of Christian mortification to its people; and that that standard is not a practically unproductive one, but has had all along, and has now, its genuine fruits. If that Church exhibits the same spiritual marks which the Roman Church can, the latter cannot call her decayed, or her doctrine a dead and lifeless one; and such Christianity cannot be put aside under the designation of "an inveterate odour." Certainly, Eastern sanctity shows marks of the soil on which it grows; and the world is much mistaken if Roman sanctity does not do the same. Eastern sanctity, too, presents features of uncouthness, rudeness, strange simplicity—in a word, some barbarian features to the European eye; but we have yet to learn that the Gospel distinguishes, so long as men love God and hate their own flesh, whether they are barbarians or not. Many a saint of the early Church must be rejected on such a rule. The Eastern Church has gone on comparatively outside of the great movement of intellect, science, and civilisation in the world; and, therefore, its Christianity is open to remarks on this head. But it is a small thing to be judged of by man's judgment. Mr. Newman must permit us to say that his judgment on this head has signs of being something very like "man's judgment." He refuses, in a certain case, to see and recognise the Christian type, because it does not come before him in the Latin shape, and with the accompaniments of intellectual grace and refinement which it has incorporated on its European area. It comes before him in the shape which antiquity, and not "movement," has attached to it; and he puts it aside under the name of "an inveterate odour," the "venerable peculiarity" of a particular population; analogous, it might seem, to any case of old custom, law, or costume. This is "man's judgment," we must say. The early Church gloried in a religion which made all men equal—the refined Greek or Roman, and the barbarian, whose name had but just reached the threshold of the civilised world—absolutely equal. The genius of Christianity broke down the barriers of artificial types and standards in character, and with a holy violence levelled the formations of human genius, philosophy, and will, to make way for one substantial, fundamental character for man. That was love. Pervading all Christian natures, and, running the same invariable substance through all outer character, and all modifications of human sentiment and feeling, the principle of love was his moral being and life; and one universal type converted all other distinctions into childishness and nullity. Rudeness, civilisation, ignorance, science, uncouthness, grace, were all one—for love was deeper than all, and men were new-formed, "after the image of Him who had created them; where there was neither Greek nor Jew, circumcision nor uncircumcision, Barbarian, Scythian, bond nor free, but Christ was all, and in all."

To return to our main subject.

We have examined the presumptive part of Mr. Newman's argument for the Papal Infallibility. It is not our intention to follow him into the historical, or examine how far his original presumption is sustained by the evidence of fact. That has been already ably, acutely, and in the most fair, candid, and tempered tone of controversy, done by a writer whose work was noticed in the last number of this Review. Mr. Newman himself admits that his presumption is the strongest part of his argument, and alludes to the historical evidence for the Papacy as a subordinate and secondary part of it. "All," he says, "depends on the strength of that presumption."[1] "The

[1] Page 170.

absolute need of a spiritual supremacy is at present the strongest of arguments in favour of its supply."[1] With respect to the historical evidence—the evidence, that is, of early Church history to its divine institution, as a matter of fact—he is content if it only gives a negative support: "Supposing there is *otherwise* good reason for saying that the Papal supremacy is part of Christianity, there is nothing in early Church history to contradict it."[2]

Having gone through these two stages of argument on the main question which Mr. Newman's Essay brings before us, we approach a third. It has appeared that the principle of development in itself, however enlarged upon, cannot be any pledge for absolute correctness in development, or secure the truth of a certain mass of developments which has grown up. It has appeared that for the existence of what alone can secure this absolute correctness in developing, and alone can prove the absolute truth of certain developments, as well as the right to impose them as articles of faith;—for the existence of a constant, infallible, developing authority, or standing revelation in the Church—the argument advanced is an insufficient one; inasmuch as this argument is based on a presumption for which we have no warrant. The argument of the Essay now takes another line, and one of a very different character from what it has hitherto. It adopts the line of a *reductio ad absurdum*. It asserts that the fundamental doctrines of Christianity are developments; and that therefore we must either give them up, or admit that continuing developing authority in the Church which established them. It instances the Nicene Creed. That, it proceeds, is regarded by both sides as essential, and that is a development; we are therefore committed already to the principle of development, and must either receive

[1] Page 127. [2] Page 170.

the whole cycle of Roman doctrine, or be prepared to give up Nicene. It says, in short, that we have no standing ground between Rome and Infidelity. Let us admit then, though not logically required to do, the conditional truth of this argument; we then say, truth is the end of controversy, and this is a fair argument if its fundamental fact is a true one. At the same time it is not too much to say that considerable responsibility attaches to the use of such an argument as this.

Now here the first question to be settled is obviously that of the sense in which the word development is used. The creed which contains our fundamental articles of faith is called a development; in what sense is it meant that it was one?

One sense of development makes it a simply explanatory process. Development is explanation; explanation is development. A man in conversation makes an assertion, which another misapprehends; in reply, he explains the meaning, or develops the meaning of his assertion. His meaning is exactly the same with what it was before; it is in order to show what it was before that the explanation is given; the meaning before the explanation or development of it, and the meaning after, are by the very nature and aim of the process the same. It so happens that language, or the medium by which we convey our ideas to one another, is capable of misinterpretation; we have therefore often to alter or add to the language in which we expressed an idea, and express it anew,—not because our idea itself was imperfect, or was different at all from what it is, but because some person has construed our language in a way in which we did not intend it to be construed. This explanation again, inasmuch as language still continues our medium, may be misinterpreted, and a second explanation become necessary for the benefit of some second objector. A third, a fourth, a fifth, an indefinite number of explanations may succeed on the same principle which produced the first. An idea may thus, in course of discussion, be said to be developed; *i.e.* may go through fresh successional stages of language, according as preceding stages are found not adequate to prevent it from being mistaken and confused with some other idea, different from, or short of it. Each misconstruction, as it shows itself, makes a fresh defence necessary: when three or four defensive explanations have been made, these again have to be reconciled to each other; and the creation of language becomes larger and larger. The case is not unfrequent of a single arguer having to maintain in conversation a particular point against a whole circle of opponents. He adheres firmly, consistently, and with all unity and simplicity, to the one point which he defends, and is only bent on defending it. But, with that one object in view, what a vast formation of language does he raise as he goes on! what distinctions accumulate, and what protests and safeguards grow up out of, and surround the original statement! He would be surprised at the end of the argument to see the edifice he had built. And yet nobody would say that his idea had altered, and was not just the same as it was when he began. It was for the very purpose of so maintaining it, that he explained it again and again anew, as misconstruction threatened it, and so formed all that body of expression around it; and a bystander will make the special remark on such an occasion, that the arguer has kept to his own point, amidst a varied and complex opposition. Cases of legal amplification illustrate the same principle. What a testator or seller of an estate wants to do, is able to be expressed in two words for any fair man's understanding; but the law has the responsi-

K

bility of guarding against all the possible constructions which may be put upon a statement, and not only that of satisfying an ordinary and simple construction. The case, in short, is a common everyday one, in which the idea in a person's mind is exactly the same, whether more shortly and simply, or more fully and guardedly expressed. It is not meant that it may not become clearer by such a process ; but the additional clearness is an external argumentative one ; not affecting its substance, or making it, as regards natural straightforward thinking, any other than the identical idea which it was before. Such is simply explanatory development.

On the other hand, there is a kind of development which is a positive increase of the substance of the thing developed,—a fresh formation not contained in, though growing out of, some original matter. The developed substance here is not the same actual one with the original, but a very different one. Growth-out-of is a wholly different thing from identity-with. The development of a seed into a plant is one of growth, for example ; and it does not carry with it identity. It is a pure metaphor by which we say the acorn is the oak ; it is so, if by saying so be meant that the acorn is the thing in consequence of which (coupled with other causes) an oak will exist, but it is not identical with it actually. As things actual, things cognisable, an acorn is one thing, an oak is another : the one is a smooth oval piece of vegetable matter, about an inch long, and of that consistency and appearance of which it is ; and the other is a large, wide-spreading tree, with rough bark, and thick branches bearing leaves. When one of these phenomena exists, indeed, the other does not, and this succession in two things is able to be called the existence of one and the same thing in different stages ; but it is self-evident that they are not actually one and the same thing, and that, however intimate may be the relation of growth in the two, they have not the relation of identity. This is, perhaps, the most common and natural sense of development; the word, either from etymological or from conventional reasons, is suggestive of an actual enlargement of substance in the thing developed. Power develops, *i.e.* becomes actually larger; there is more of it. Rome was a small power at first; it developed into a larger one. The "march of mind" development is of this kind; it consists of new ideas and forms of thoughts, new discoveries in science, new social comforts and conveniences arising. Philosophical development may be partly explanatory only, partly an actually enlarging one. Such are two sorts of development; that of explanation simply, and that of substantial growth. The one begins with what the other ends in; explanation starts with its substance, growth arrives at its substance gradually. In growth it is the ultimate formation of all which is the substance of the thing growing; the substance before that point only existing on a kind of antedating view. The oak is the grown oak, not the acorn; the Roman empire is Augustan and not Romulean Rome. The original thing is not the real, the substantial thing, in this kind of development; it is only the imperfect, half-existing, ambiguous, and struggling element of future reality and proper being.

Now, of these two kinds of development, the former is of course conceded in the case before us. All allow that Christian fundamental truth has been explained. The whole of scientific theology is an explanatory development of it. To take the doctrine of the Incarnation, the truth that God became man. A whole body of Christian theology, from the short decrees of the earliest councils to the full volumes of the Schoolmen, explain this truth.

The former guarded it from misconstruction; the latter, besides this, brought out, in detail, the logical contents of the truth. There are inexhaustible logical contents in it. God comprehends all that God is; man comprehends all that man is. All that was logically comprehended under these two terms was brought out; and all that was logically comprehended in the idea of the union of the two was brought out. There is question upon question in Aquinas, *De Modo Unionis Verbi Incarnati*, extending from the most fundamental to the most distant parts of the truth:— "*Utrum Unio Verbi Incarnati sit facta in natura vel personâ; Utrum Unio Verbi Incarnati sit facta in Supposito vel Hypostasi; Utrum Hypostasis Christi post Incarnationem sit composita; Utrum natura humana fuerit unita Verbo Accidentaliter; Utrum Unio sit aliquid creatum; Utrum idem quod assumptio; Utrum facta per gratiam; Utrum merita præcesserunt; Utrum gratia Unionis fuerit homini Christo naturalis.*" There follow questions, "*De Modo Unionis ex parte Personæ assumentis;* and then questions, "*De Modo Unionis ex parte Naturæ assumptæ;*" the former runs out into the questions, "*Utrum Personæ Divinæ conveniat assumere naturam creatam; Utrum Naturæ Divinæ conveniat; Utrum una Persona sine alia possit assumere; Utrum plures Personæ Divinæ possint; Utrum una Persona Divina possit assumere duas naturas humanas;*" and many others. The latter runs out into the questions, "*Utrum Filius Dei assumpserit personam; Utrum assumpserit hominem; Utrum assumpserit humanam naturam abstractam ab omnibus individuis, vel in omnibus individuis.*" Then succeed questions, "*De modo Unionis quantum ad ordinem; Utrum anima à Filio Dei prius fuerit assumpta quam caro; Utrum tota natura fuerit assumpta mediantibus partibus, vel partes mediante toto:*" Questions, "*De Gratia Christi; Utrum in*

Christo gratia habitualis; Utrum virtutes; Utrum fides; spes, timor:" Questions, " *De Scientia Christi; De Scientia Christi in Communi; De Scientia Beata Animæ Christi; De Scientia Indita; De Scientia Acquisita:* " Questions, " *De Potentia Animæ Christi,*"—all running out into their respective subdivisions. Here, in short, is a field of explanatory theology, which takes the idea of the Incarnation, and brings out all the possible inferences and aspects which can be elicited from it, some nearer and more obvious, others remoter and minuter, till the subject multiplies into a whole world of subtle, and, so to call it, microscopic theological science. But such manifold evolutions do not profess to add anything to the substantial idea of the Incarnation,—the truth that God became man. There is a great difference between the clearness, accuracy, and circumstantiality in the intellectual image of the doctrine, which such an explanatory development as this produces, and the intellectual image in an ordinary Christian mind unversed in scholastic divinity; but the doctrine entertained is the same identical one.

But it is the latter kind of development, that of growth and not that of explanation only, which Mr. Newman's argument desiderates in the present case. His argument parallels the Roman doctrinal developments with the doctrinal development at Nice. The latter, therefore, to make the argument hold, must be a development in the same sense as the Roman ones. That is to say, that as the doctrines of purgatory and the Papal Infallibility are obviously positive substantial advances upon the doctrines of the early Church on the subjects of the intermediate state and the Roman see, so the doctrine of the divinity of our Lord, as declared at the Nicene Council, was a positive substantial advance upon the earlier teaching of the Church with respect to our Lord's nature. It is not enough for the consistency of this argument, to say that the doctrine as to our Lord's nature was explained, defended, and secured by additional language from misconstruction at that Council: it is necessary to say that the doctrine positively itself grew, was itself more than it had been, more at the Nicene epoch than it had been formerly. No instance of simple explanation, however extensive and copious, can afford a parallel case to that positive growth to which Mr. Newman has to find a parallel. According to Mr. Newman, those Roman developments to which he parallels the Nicene, though called developments, still are distinct doctrines[1] from the elementary ones on the same subject; that is to say, other truths than what were known before, different pieces of knowledge from former ones; a person might know the former and not know the latter: when he comes to know them, he knows something which he did not know; he has positive fresh truth, a substantial idea in his head, which he had not before. Consequently to the Nicene doctrine of our Lord's divinity, for the parallel to hold, the same must apply. There is, first of all, a development which is identical with simply understanding a statement. "When it is declared," says Mr. Newman, "that the 'Word became flesh,' three wide questions open upon us at the very announcement. What is meant by 'the Word?' what by 'flesh?' what by 'became?' The answers to these involve a process of investigation, and are developments;"[2] but this kind of development will not do here. There is then a further development which explains a statement, and carries it into additional and more formal statements—"a multitude of propositions, which gather round the inspired sentence of which they come, giving it externally the form of a doctrine."[3] And

[1] Page 55.   [2] Page 97.   [3] Page 98.

this development will not do here either. There must be more here. There must, in the case of the Nicene doctrine of our Lord's nature, be positive growth of, and such substantial addition as growth implies to, a former elementary doctrine of the Church on that subject.

This kind of development and this basis of essential doctrine being necessary for Mr. Newman's argument in the present instance, it is to be observed that the line of thought which runs through his Essay as a whole does not keep back such a theological position, and that his language extends the hypothesis of growth to the fundamental articles of Christian faith, making them to be developments from some former elementary and seminal doctrines on the subjects to which they refer; just as the Papal Infallibility is made the development of the early respect to the see of St. Peter, and just as the doctrine of purgatory, of the deification of St. Mary, and others, are made the developments of former shadowy, primordial, and scattered anticipations of those doctrines. He puts both these classes of doctrines on the same ground with respect to development. "That the hypothesis he adopts," he says, "accounts not only for the Athanasian Creed, but for the creed of Pope Pius, is no fault of those who adopt it. No one has power over the issues of his principles; we cannot manage our argument, and have as much of it as we please and no more."[1] Reverse the order of the two *credenda*, and the hypothesis he adopts accounts not only for the creed of Pope Pius, but also for the Athanasian creed. The same appeal to Church testimony, he proceeds, "cannot at once condemn St. Bernard and defend St. Athanasius;"[2] that is to say, that if the former taught what was new about the Blessed Virgin, the latter taught what was no less new about our Lord's divinity. With

[1] Page 29. [2] Page 9.

this alternative, he boldly meets the use of the Vincentian rule, "*Quod semper, quod ubique, quod ab omnibus.*" The Vincentian rule, as applied by English divines, claims for certain doctrines the evidence of early and general testimony; testimony to the fact that they were originally taught by the Apostles, and received through successive generations of Christians ultimately from their hands. It asserts this of the doctrine of our Lord's divinity taught by the Nicene and Athanasian Creeds, and of other doctrines. Mr. Newman does not meet this application of the rule with a direct, but a conditional answer. He says, *if* the rule proves the one set of doctrines,—the English,—it proves the other too, the Roman; *if* it does not prove the latter, it does not prove the former either. He meets the rule itself with a demand for fairness and impartiality in its application, whether in the negative or affirmative, and protests against the "Lesbian" use of it, upon which English divines have proceeded. This conditional answer, reduced into a direct one, is simply that the rule *does* not prove the later doctrines, and therefore *does* not prove the earlier either. His application of the rule is negative in the former case; and is therefore negative in the latter also. Indeed what he professes to supply in this Essay—it is his very object in writing it—is a basis for later Roman doctrines, which is not Vincentian; that is, which does not appeal to an original reception, but to a law of growth as their proof; and which does not assert the fact of an early belief, but gives a rationale for a later one. He applies, therefore, this law and this rationale to the case of earlier doctrines as well. He claims anticipations in the case of the Roman doctrines; and he will claim anticipations in the case of the Nicene; but his argument does not claim more for Nicene than for Roman, and asserts in either case the existence of a seminal elemental doctrine, anterior to that of the subsequently, and now, established one. How far indeed that early received doctrine respecting the nature of our Lord, for example, went, or what it was, his argument does not inform us; but its parallel does not require more than a very seminal elemental one. The seminal doctrine in the case, for instance, of the Papal Infallibility is confessedly very small and shadowy. In the case, then, of the Nicene doctrine of our Lord's divinity, it need be no more. But, without entering into the details of the parallel, the argument asserts with sufficient force the general point, that the Vincentian appeal to early reception cannot be supported in the case of the Nicene, any more than it can in the case of later Roman doctrine; and that the anterior and primordial idea with respect to our Lord's nature, is not, going by such evidence, the same with, but the seed of, the Athanasian doctrine on that subject.

Thus commences and proceeds, then, the great course of doctrinal development which this Essay maintains. Starting from the small and seminal beginning of primitive doctrine, it gradually grows and enlarges, and goes through a career analogous to the progress of science and the march of civilisation. Truth gains fresh augmentations at Nice, at Ephesus, at Chalcedon, at the Lateran Councils, at Florence, at Trent: its first one is at Nice, where our Lord's divinity is declared; that step gained, in course of some centuries it proceeds, under the infallible sanction, to establish the cultus of St. Mary. "Christianity came into the world as an idea,"[1] and an imperfect idea. In the case of such an idea arising, "Its beginnings are no measure of its capabilities nor its scope. At first no one knows what it is or what it is worth. It remains perhaps for a time quiescent; it tries, as it were, its limbs, and

[1] Page 116.

proves the ground under it and feels its way. . . . It seems in suspense which way to go : it wavers.[1] There will be a time of confusion, when conceptions and misconceptions are in conflict; and it is uncertain whether anything is to come of the idea at all."[2] "The dogmatic principle was in the history of Christianity what conscience is in the history of an individual mind. . . . Conscience mistakes error for truth; and yet we believe, that on the whole, and even in those cases where it is ill-instructed, if its voice be diligently obeyed, it will gradually be cleared, simplified, and perfected. I would not (but he gives no reason why he should not) imply that there is indistinctness so great as this in the knowledge of the first centuries."[3] "The statements of the early fathers," we are told, "are but tokens of the multiplicity of openings which the mind of the Church was making into the great treasure-house of Truth; real openings, but incomplete and irregular."[4] "The Church went forth from the world in haste, as the Israelites from Egypt 'with their dough before it was leavened, their kneading-troughs being bound up in the clothes upon their shoulders.'"[5] But out of this indistinct, vague, and chaotic state of the original Christian idea, at last "some definite form of doctrine arose." When one "generation of teachers was left in ignorance, the next generation of teachers completed their work, for the same unwearied anxious process of thought went on."[6] "The doctrine of the Holy Trinity," found at most only in its "rudiments"[7] in earlier writers, grew up. When they had "duly secured in the affections of the faithful the supreme glory and worship of God incarnate, . . . they determined the place of St. Mary in our reverence."[8] "The conduct of Popes, Councils, Fathers, betokens the slow, painful,

[1] Page 38. [3] Page 348. [5] Page 107. [7] Page 396.
[2] Page 36. [4] Page 349. [6] Page 354. [8] Page 145.

anxious taking up of new elements into an existing body of belief."[1] This course of doctrine moved on; and time, which "is necessary for the full comprehension and perfection of great ideas,"[2] gradually brought out and substantiated the original idea of Christianity.

We are not at present engaged in disproving, but only in representing Mr. Newman's doctrine of development, and showing in what sense he uses the word. We will, however, just allude to one or two arguments used about it. The analogy of the development of the Mosaic dispensation appears to us, then, an obviously untrue one. The Mosaic dispensation was not a final but a preparative one; it suggests its own want of finality; it ever prophesies its own issue in a higher revelation, and confesses throughout its own incompleteness and shortcomings. The Christian dispensation, on the other hand, is a final one. As a dispensation which is not final proceeds, by the very force of the hypothesis, towards something which is, tends to an issue, and aspires to a development different from, and higher than, itself, so a dispensation which is final, by the very force of the hypothesis, does not. The Law was a shadow of good things to come. When those good things came, therefore, they, and not things still further on and beyond them, were the substance. Otherwise one side of a relation is met by what is not its correlative one; and type is responded to by type, and not by antitype. Substance is the correspondent to shadow, as son is the correspondent to father, giver to receiver, ruler to subject: father does not generate father, nor shadow introduce shadow. The Law's foreshadowings, the gradual evolutions of prophecy, anticipation strengthening, type becoming clearer, a preparation growing age after age more critical, and step by step approximating to that to which it led,—

[1] Page 353. [2] Page 27.

this ascent to a climax, this slowness and solemnity in ushering in an end,—the whole course of development, in a word, in the Jewish Dispensation, so far from affording a parallel for the same in the Christian, makes us expect the very contrary, for it points to that Revelation as itself the development which that course of Judaism had developed into, and therefore opposes it, instead of paralleling it to that course, on the development point. We do not argue from the length of the journey the length of the end of the journey; or from the time it takes learning the time it must take knowing; or from the gradual nature of acquisition the gradual nature of possession. We cannot argue from the development of the seed to the development of the fruit; nor from the growth of Judaism to the growth of Judaism's consummation—Christianity. It will be said that a Revelation may be the development of an anterior one, and may yet be developed itself into a further and larger one, but, if so, it is not *the* development of that anterior revelation. It may be said that the Christian Revelation is only as a whole, and including all subsequent growth, the development of the Jewish; but this is an ambiguous explanation here. The question is, Was that particular revelation which immediately succeeded to Judaism itself the development of Judaism, or only the seed of a prospective grown revelation which was to be? If the latter, all we can say is, that it falsifies the whole process by which it was introduced. That whole course of preparation in which Judaism consisted, designed and adapted as it professedly was for ushering in something ultimate and perfect, certainly fell short of its obvious purpose, and balked expectation, if it ushered in with so much pomp of gradual evolution, not a climax and end, but a small beginning, a seed and element of a future grown revelation. The same kind of answer may be given to another argument urged in behalf of this sort of development in Christianity, the argument, viz., that the Apostles brought out the truth by degrees in their preaching; for this kind of reserve is, of its own nature, only temporary, and has reference to the individual addressed only, and not to the condition of the truth itself, —the very fullest and most perfect knowledge of the truth being able to be coincident with the most gradual method of communicating it.

Again, there is a general argument which has considerable weight with some minds in favour of such a development of Christianity as we are speaking of,—an argument which appeals to their intellectual prepossessions and aspirations. There is something imposing in the idea of a revelation growing and enlarging; stationariness appears to them like stagnation; and to be tied to an original Revelation looks like adhering to "beggarly elements." They see an apparent poverty and meagreness, an antiquarian dryness and narrowness in the latter view; that of growth and development seems a larger one. Largeness, freedom, and depth of mind seem thus concerned in its reception, and mental qualities are appealed to which we value and encourage in ourselves. We like the sensation of growth and progress in our own minds; we sympathise with such a progress in the system of truth to which we belong; we identify ourselves with the system, and like progress in both together. Of this feeling, then, there is a right side and a wrong. The love of progress, considered as the love of truth, is right. We ought to be glad of truth growing, provided it does grow; and if it was less yesterday, there is a disinterested pleasure and triumph in its being more to-day. But there is another feeling which mixes very subtly with this disinterested triumph, and that is the feeling arising from the consideration of that knowledge, as possessed by ourselves, in favourable contradistinction to others. The tone of speakers who talk of the "march of mind," and the discoveries of the nineteenth century, for example, has obviously a considerable mixture of the flattery of comparison in it. An age likes to imagine itself on some highest ground; sharpens the vertex for itself to stand on, and dwells with complacency on the slowly unfolding knowledge of its predecessors. This is applicable to religion. The idea of a fixed settled Revelation, simply continuing, impressing the self-same truth from century to century upon the human heart, and only guarding itself from time to time against misconstruction; applied to a thousand different cases, and meeting a thousand different positions as ages roll on, but itself standing still, and being neither more nor less than what it was eighteen centuries ago, does not satisfy the feeling we speak of so well as the idea of its substantially growing up to the present day. And under this feeling the principle of progress may proceed to claim more ground than it has a right to, may begin to usurp, and make out a case of elementary commencement, in order that it may enjoy the sensation of subsequent growth. It may raise prejudices to the disadvantage of earlier times, in order that it may gain by the contrast; elevate unnaturally and untruly present thought and system; give sensations of largeness and height at the expense of humility; use truth as a material for mental exercise and prowess; and idolise movement and advance, because it feels itself the mover.

On the other hand, the mind has another and counteracting line of thought to this; if it has a love for progress, it can also see through progress; it can see through the accumulation of the verbal reflections of truth into the substance which they reflect, and see that they after all only reflect it. It can say to itself, in surveying some highly, —in appearance,—developed department of Christian doctrine, Certainly here is a vast machinery of language and apparatus of divisions and defences; here is much detail of thought and minuteness of evolution: I see that one idea has a quantity of questions and inferences contained in it, which issue out of it, just as all the mathematical aspects of a triangle issue out of the triangle; nevertheless, I have only more expressions than the early Christian had, and he had quite as full and rich a substance, because the self-same one. The doctrine of the Incarnation, for example, the truth that God was man, and man God, furnished to his devout imagination all that the greatest multiplication of mathematical issues from it can give me. He had all those issues in the idea before him. He did not consciously apprehend them indeed; and no more do Christians now apprehend them. If an early Christian lived before the times of scholastic and controversial divinity,—with the great body, not of ordinary only, but of the most spiritual and deep Christians now, it is the same as if they did. Nay, the very theologian whose subtlety elicited them, could only, by a painful effort of his intellect, momentarily arrest his own eductions: his mind, like that of the primitive Christian, reposed in its natural devotional state, upon the one fundamental idea. His meditation carried that idea indeed into all those directions where meditation could naturally follow it; could dwell on all the graces of our Lord's human, and the mystery of His divine, nature; and so could the meditation of the early Christian too. The same deep, rich, mental development of this truth was admissible to his devotion, which was to the schoolman's. He had the same devotional imagery, because he had the same doctrinal substance. Mr. Newman's argument of development indeed gives these inferential issues a sort of separate substantiality, and converts them into actual growth of the body of the doctrine: "the treasure-house of truth" is opening to the Church's theological search, and she is beginning to enjoy, in these issues, the real substance of the doctrine, of which she has hitherto only had the element. Her "unwearied process of thought" has at last brought her to the solid reality of that faith of which she has only had as yet the foretaste. But another view exhibits them as only the manifold reflections and aspects of that substance which existed one and the same all along: tells us that the devotional thoughts of St. Ignatius and St. Polycarp dwelt on the same identical perfect truth of an Incarnate God on which St. Thomas Aquinas or St. Bernard dwelt; presents them following the mystery into all that region of awe and love into which it leads the highest Christian of to-day; soaring in contemplation as far as any Christian souls did after them; and enlightened by the self-same mentally enlarging, expanding, enriching dogma, which has enlightened, and will enlighten, all saints, past and present and to come.

Such a line of thought as this, we say, will not compel us to give an artificial elevation to mere additions of definition, to convert mere shadows of language into actual new knowledge, and so attach an unreal and mechanical character to truth. We will give a case in point. In the year 1215, an opinion of a certain Abbot Joachim on the subject of the unity of God was condemned by the Council of Lateran. Joachim maintained, as the Council tells us, a "Unity of the Divine Nature which was not a true and proper unity, but a collective and metaphorical one: a unity in the sense in which many men are called one people, and many faithful one Church." Joachim adduced the texts—"The multitude of them that believed were of one heart;" "He that planteth and he that watereth are one;" and others of the same kind: and especially the text, "That they may be one, even *as we are one.*" He said "they," the faithful, are not one thing (*"una res quæ communis sit omnibus"*), but only one in the sense of being one Church and one kingdom; and thence argued that the Divine Nature was not one thing either, but only one in the way in which one Christian society is one. For this the Council condemned him, and asserted that the Divine Nature was one thing—"*una res.*" Upon this Mr. Newman's comment is, that the numerical unity of the Divine Nature had, till the year A.D. 1215, only existed as "an impression or *implicit* judgment in the mind of the Church,"[1] and was now for the first time declared. Ideas, he says, go on in the mind of an individual often in a vacant, half-conscious way: "The impression made upon the mind need not even be recognised by the parties possessing it. . . . Nothing is of more frequent occurrence, whether in things sensible or intellectual, than the existence of such unperceived impressions. What do we mean when we say that certain persons do not know themselves, but that they are ruled by views which they do not themselves recognise?"[2] Such an "unperceived impression," such an "unrecognised view" on the subject of the unity of God does he consider there to have been in the Church up to the year 1215, when, for the first time, there was a direct and distinct ecclesiastical decision upon the numerical unity of the Divine Nature. Now, we ask, what does the "*numerical*" unity or "*una res,*" declared by the Lateran Council, mean or convey to us more than simple unity, as the Church had all along used the word? Here is a certain Abbot Joachim who gives a plainly evasive and polytheistic meaning to the word Unity, and

[1] University Sermons, ed. 1872, p. 323.   [2] *Ibid.* p. 321.

the Council asserts that it has not that polytheistic meaning. Any other Abbot Joachim who chose to contradict the plain meaning of a word, might explain "numerical" unity exactly in the same way in which his predecessor explained unity; nor in either case, the two being condemned, is anything more done by the Church than simply repelling an absurd meaning from the word. To speak of such a declaration as the coming to light of an "implicit judgment of the Church" which had been indeed the "*secret* life of millions of souls"[1] hitherto, but only as secret unconscious truth,—to speak of it as an instance of the "birth of an idea, the development in explicit form of what was already latent," the realisation by the Church of "an unperceived impression," "an unrecognised view," which had lain hidden in her from the first, waiting for this moment of emission,—does appear to us, we must say, a very obvious case of making a great deal out of nothing. The truth which Abbot Joachim contradicted was not declared for the first time at the Council of Lateran; it was declared long enough before on Mount Sinai. No orthodox Jew or Christian ever dreamed of a unity of God which was any other than numerical unity; and the Lateran condemnation of the notion that the Divine Nature was only one Divine Nature in an inclusive sense, as human nature, which contains all the individuals in it, is one human nature, was a simple assertion of God's unity, and no more. What we mean by God being one, is that he is one as truly as one thing (*res*), one man, for example, is one. "Una *res*" is not mentioned indeed in the Nicene Creed, but has any Council yet defined that God is good? Yet supposing that formally declared, would it not be, or would it be, self-evidently absurd to say that an implicit unconscious judgment in the Church

[1] University Sermons, ed. 1872, p. 323.

as to the Divine goodness, now became explicit and positive knowledge?[1]

But to return: we have seen the kind of development which Mr. Newman means, and of which he maintains the Nicene Creed to be an instance, viz., a development of positive growth, parallel to the later Roman ones of Purgatory, the Papal Infallibility, and others.

Now a development of this kind the Nicene Creed was not. The Nicene Creed only asserted and guarded a doctrine which had been held from the first, viz., that of Christ's true and proper Divinity. The original Christian Revelation declared that Christ was God. If Christ was God, He was true God; He had true and proper Godhead. The Nicene Creed asserted this of Him, and no more; it expressed this truth, and no more, by the word *Homoousion*. The word *Homoousion* declared that Christ was very God with God the Father. His oneness of substance with the Father was the term by which the Nicene Fathers declared His true Godhead with the Father. And this true Godhead was attributed to Christ by the original Christian Revelation, which declared Him to be God, and commanded Him to be worshipped as God. Should it be said that the word God is doubtful, and might mean secondary as well as true Godhead, let it be well observed to whom the Christian Revelation was given. The Christian Revelation was not engrafted on Paganism, which had not the belief, but on Judaism which had the belief in the unity of the Divine nature. "Hear, O Israel," was the Law's voice, "the Lord thy God is one Lord." The unity of God was the great dogma of the Jewish dispensation; the Jews were separated from the rest of mankind, and made a peculiar people in order to preserve that doctrine amid the polytheism of the whole world around

[1] *Ibid.*

them, and be a standing protest against it. Christ, therefore, being revealed as God to the Jews, was revealed as the one God, for they had none other God but one. Had the Christian Revelation been made to Pagans in the first instance, and the Godhead of Christ been communicated to people whose notions of Godhead were altogether corrupted and polytheistic, we cannot say what additional safeguards would have been necessary in order to distinguish the revealed true Godhead from the false godheads of numerous other divinities. But to a Jew it was sufficient to say that Christ was God, to express the meaning that he was true God. The Revelation came to a people whose ideas of Godhead had been purified and preserved in strictness. Their education under the Law presented them guarded from the risk of misapprehending Christ's Divinity when it should be revealed; and the faith of the old dispensation was a security for the faith of the new. We can hardly, indeed, understand what Mr. Newman means by saying that there was little importance attached to religious opinion under the old dispensation. He says "that opinions in religion are not matters of indifference, but have a definite bearing on the position of their holders in the Divine Sight, is a principle which, . . . I suppose, had hardly any exercise under the Law; the zeal and obedience of the ancient people being employed in the maintenance of Divine worship and the overthrow of idolatry, not in the assertion of opinion."[1] Surely in overthrowing idolatry, in maintaining a certain worship, they asserted an opinion, and a belief, and that a strong one. Nor was Jewish thought in that neutral and indistinct state as to the nature of God which would fit it for being the receptacle of an indistinct shadowy doctrine of Christ's Godhead. The Apostles and first Christian preachers were

[1] Development of Christian Doctrine, p. 339.

Jews then, and came to the new truth of Christ's Godhead with the Jewish doctrine of the unity of God in their minds. And Christianity gave its own strict sense to the word God by the fact of its speaking to minds who understood it in such a sense. In this true sense, then, the Divinity of Christ, along with the Divinity of God the Father, and consistently with the unity of the Divine Nature (Christianity retaining all the truth of Judaism while it added to it), was handed down to the succeeding Church. But in course of time a heresy arose, denying that Christ was God, and asserting Him to be a creature. The Nicene Fathers met this heresy at the Council of Nice, and framed a test to exclude it. That test was the "Homoousion." The Arians used the word God in their own sense, and therefore the word God did not exclude in their case the wrong sense, and was not a test. But the "Homoousion" was a test, and did as a fact answer in excluding their sense, and therefore the orthodox adopted it. And the Nicene Creed was an explanation, and not a growth, of the doctrine of our Lord's Divinity.

Moreover, this ground of development is a totally different and directly opposite ground from that which the Nicene Fathers themselves professed in their enunciation of doctrine. A modern theorist may plead development for them, but would they have pleaded it for themselves? Would they have been thankful for the explanation, or would they have anathematised *uno ore* the broacher of it? A person must know very little of ecclesiastical history who does not see what they would have done. Imagine any one of that age, with a benevolent wish to extricate the Fathers from what he considered a difficulty, informing them that they were developers, and that their ground was perfectly good on that view. It appears to us tolerably certain that if such a person had maintained his theory after his publication of it, he would have maintained it outside the Church, and not inside. The Fathers would have been utterly astonished at his audacity; and they would have told him to communicate his assistance to heretics, for that they wanted none of it. To have called them developers would have been to take away, in their opinion, the very ground from under them, and to falsify their whole position. The hypothesis would have come into direct collision with the special declared ground on which the whole of their doctrinal teaching went, and would have just interfered with the very essence of their argument. Their argument, on every occasion of heresy arising, was one and the same thing, viz., that they had received a certain doctrine from the first, and that this heresy was contrary to it. They said, This is the old doctrine that we have, the old doctrine which the Apostles delivered, which has been the doctrine of the Church ever since, which we received from our predecessors as they received it from theirs, and which we now here maintain as we received it. The same, the very same, they repeated; they professed to hold it because it was the same, and for that reason only. They would not receive or listen to any other, for the simple reason that that other was not the same. They shut their ears in horror, the very sound of novelty shocked them, and they seemed polluted by the mere contact of their ears with it. "Who ever heard of such things?" was the universal cry of the orthodox on Arianism appearing; "Who is not astounded at them?" The Arians positively ridiculed the extreme and obstinate simplicity of their arguments; they taunted the Nicene Fathers with being ἀφελεῖς καὶ ἰδιώτας, poor unintellectual men, who neither had nor put forward any reasoning whatever as the basis of their doctrine, but kept on one unceasing, unvarying, untiring appeal to simple fact. They would have drawn them by taunts from this ground, but the Nicene Fathers were not to be taunted off a ground of which they were sure. And they went on, and the whole Church with them, appealing *uno ore* to a simple fact; asserting *uno ore* that the doctrine they had, and which they now at the Nicene Council enunciated, was the same, very same, self-same, original doctrine which the Apostles had delivered and handed down. Compare, *e.g.*, the whole mode in which the doctrine of the "Homoousion" was maintained against Arius, and the mode in which the doctrine of Transubstantiation was maintained against Berengarius; there is just the difference which the fact of the one being an old fundamental received truth, and the other being a view of gradual, later growth in the Church, would naturally make.

Here, however, Mr. Newman introduces a counter argument, and, to the actual inference which would be drawn from this universal testimony, opposes certain asserted deficiencies and ambiguities, in the expression of the doctrine of our Lord's proper divinity in the documents of the ante-Nicene age, now extant. He asserts that the ante-Nicene documents do not of themselves prove the reception of this doctrine in those times, and takes us upon the ground which Bishop Bull went over with Petavius. On this point we have a word to say to begin with.

It does not, we conceive, devolve upon us then, in this state of the case, to refute a doubt which is a contradiction to the plain traditional testimony of the Church Universal. The Church Universal has had those documents before them since the time they were written, and it has, from the time they were written down to the present day, asserted the fact that the doctrine of our Lord's true and proper divinity was the received doctrine of the Primitive Church, and communicated to it straight by the Apostles. As far as the unanimous testimony of age after age from the first, receiving and handing down in turn the report of a fact, can settle the truth of that fact, the truth of this fact is settled. The Church Catholic now at this moment in all her branches, Eastern and Western, from every authorised book of instruction, declares this fact. It does not devolve upon us to argue for the truth of a fact under such circumstances against an all but unsupported contradiction to it. Still less, when a view approximating to Mr. Newman's on this subject was put forward about a century and a half ago in the Church by a particular writer, and was formally, and with great weight of solid intellect and learning, answered by another,—of which answer no notice worth the name has been taken by Mr. Newman,—does it devolve upon us to repeat that defence of early belief which the latter writer made. When Mr. Newman puts forward an answer to Bishop Bull's arguments on this subject, it will then be proper time for somebody to reconsider Bishop Bull's arguments in connection with Mr. Newman's reply. But as yet Bishop Bull has received no reply, and therefore as yet his arguments stand good. A note on the πρὶν γεννηθῆναι, showing that Bull has made a mistake (as what theologian, however accurate and solid, has not in some matter of detail?) in his interpretation of that clause; and a hint thrown here and there, intended to create a disparaging impression of Bull's argument, but hardly tangible enough, or indeed sufficiently declaratory even of the objector's own meaning or purpose, to be able to be replied to, are not an answer to Bishop Bull. An objection must be made in a certain way to be properly fit for argumentative notice at all; and if indefiniteness makes it unanswerable, it makes it also nothing to be answered. When Petavius threw doubts upon the orthodoxy of the ante-Nicene period, Bull met him with a regular answer, in which he went in detail through the whole extant body of theology of that period, and first brought forward copious positive evidence from that theology of those writers having held the Nicene doctrine; and then, as another part of his treatise, brought forward arguments explanatory of certain passages in it, which appeared out of harmony with that doctrine. Now such a work cannot be thrown aside with such a notice as the following:—

"In the question raised by various learned men in the seventeenth and following century, concerning the views of the early Fathers on the subject of our Lord's Divinity, the one party estimate their theology by the literal force of their separate expressions or phrases, or by the philosophical opinions of the day; the other, by the doctrine of the Catholic Church, as afterwards authoritatively declared. The one party argues that those Fathers *need not* have meant more than what was afterwards considered heresy; the other answers that there is *nothing to prevent* their meaning more. Thus the position which Bull maintains seems to be nothing beyond this, that the Nicene Creed is a *natural key* for interpreting the body of ante-Nicene theology. His very aim is to explain difficulties; now the notion of difficulties and their explanation implies a rule to which they are apparent exceptions, and in accordance with which they are to be explained. Nay, the title of his work, which is a "Defence of the Creed of Nicæa," shows that he is not seeking a conclusion, but imposing a view. And he proceeds both to defend the Creed by means of the Fathers against Sandius, and to defend the Fathers by means of the Creed against Petavius. He defends Creed and Fathers by reconciling one with the other. He allows that their language is not such as they would have used, after the Creed had been imposed; but he says in effect that, if we will but take it in our hands and apply it to their writings, we shall bring out and harmonise their teaching, clear their ambiguities, and discover their anomalous statements to be few and insignificant. In other words, he begins with a presumption, and shows how naturally facts close round it and fall in with it, if we will but let them. He does this triumphantly."—Page 158.

That is to say, Mr. Newman puts aside the whole work of Bull's *ab initio;* and in order to justify that attitude to it, fixes a particular aspect upon the work. The writer of it, he says, "imposes a view," and shows "how facts fall in with a presumption, *if we will but let them;*" in other words, colours facts according to an hypothesis; assumes without evidence a Nicene belief in these writers in the first instance, and then interprets their language to signify this belief. This view of Bull's work relieves an opponent of all necessity of going into the contents of it, and meeting his facts; he has only to deny Bull's hypothesis, and the erection upon it falls to the ground at once. He can even afford to allow that Bull proves what he wants *upon* his hypothesis *triumphantly:* a thing, by the way, impossible for him in the nature of things to avoid doing on this view, seeing Bull's hypothesis, as thus made for him, *is* itself the exact thing which Bull wants to prove. But surely to answer Bull's work thus is simply to avoid it. It is to answer an opponent's evidence by not hearing what he has to say; by assuming at starting that his evidence is valueless, and that he gets his conclusion out of his own head. Instead of meeting what a writer's argument brings forward, his argument itself is assumed to be a totally different one from what he declares it to be, and metamorphosed into one which an opponent can afford to call "triumphant," because he has made it nugatory. The whole aspect here fixed on Bull's work requires wrong statements to support it,—statements which are made here: "The one party argues that these fathers *need not* have meant more than what was afterwards considered heresy: the other (Bull) answers that there is *nothing to prevent* their meaning more." This is not Bull's answer. Bull's answer is that they *must* mean more,—that there is satisfactory positive evidence from their own statements that they *did* mean more. Again, "The position which Bull maintains seems to be nothing beyond this, that the Nicene Creed is a *natural key* for interpreting the body of ante-Nicene theology." The position which Bull maintains is a great deal beyond this. He expressly tells us what it is in his preface to his work.—"*Duriora veterum dicta catholicum sensum non modo admittere sed et postulare, observato cujusque auctoris scopo et proposito, adductisque etiam ex singulis sententiis aliis, luculentioribus, solide probare conatus sum.*" And if it be objected that a writer gives a partial view of the nature of his own argument, it is sufficient in answer to refer to the work itself, which unquestionably does what the writer says it does. Bull, that is to say, does not explain the *duriora dicta* of these writers by an appeal to subsequent doctrine, but by an appeal to much fuller and clearer statements from, and to the whole pervading fundamental teaching of, those very writers themselves. The plain state of the case is, that Bull asserts a fact and brings forward evidence for it. If books teach something, it is surely possible for them to show from their own language what they do teach: he asserts that the language of the books in question shows that they teach the Nicene truth of our Lord's absolute Divinity. It is open to any one to call proving a fact "imposing a view," and a person who brings forward evidence for a particular fact in a court of justice, may be looked on as "imposing a view" upon the evidential matter which he brings forward; but a judge would hardly interfere with an arguer on such a ground, and stop him *in limine* with the distinction that he must not "impose a view, but seek a conclusion."

There is no call then upon us, we repeat, to reply to an argument to which a reply has been already given and not answered. But as our readers may require some specimens of Mr. Newman's mode of arguing, we will subjoin one or two.

In the first place, then, he maintains that there is not evidence enough in quantity, in these extant ante-Nicene documents, to show that certain, now considered, fundamental truths were held by the early Church. "One divine is not equal to a Catena. We must have a whole doctrine stated by a whole Church. The Catholic truth in question is made up of a number of separate propositions, each of which, if maintained without the rest, is a heresy. In order then to prove that all the ante-Nicene writers taught it, it is not enough to prove that each has gone far enough to be a heretic,—not enough to prove that one has held that the Son is God (for so did the Sabellian, so did the Macedonian), and another that the Father is not the Son (for so did the Arian), and another that the Son is equal to the Father (for so did the Tritheist), and another that there is but one God (for so did the Unitarian),—not enough that many attached in some sense a threefold power to the idea of the Almighty (for so did almost all the heresies that ever existed, and could not but do so, if they accepted the New Testament at all); but we must show that all these statements at once, and others too, are laid down by as many separate testimonies as may fairly be taken to constitute a 'Consensus of doctors.'"[1] Again, "The creeds of that early day make no mention in their letter of the Catholic doctrine at all. They make mention indeed of a Three; but that there is any mystery in the doctrine that the Three are One, that They are co-equal, co-eternal, all increate, all incompre-

[1] Page 11.

hensible, is not stated, and never could be gathered from them."¹ Again, "If we limit our views of the teaching of the Fathers by what they expressly state, St. Ignatius may be considered a Patripassian, St. Justin arianises, and St. Hippolytus is a Photinian."² Again, "It may be questioned whether any ante-Nicene Father distinctly affirms either the numerical unity, or the co-equality of the three persons."³ One large class of statements, he decides, in early writings, is thus not sufficiently clear and explanatory. He adds that that class of statements which is sufficiently clear and explanatory, is not sufficiently large. "We find the word Trinity used by St. Theophilus, St. Clement, St. Hippolytus, Tertullian, St. Cyprian, Origen, St. Methodius; and the Divine *Circumincessio*, the most distinctive portion of the Catholic doctrine, and the unity of power, or again of substance, are declared, with more or less distinctness by Athenagoras, St. Irenæus, St. Clement, Tertullian, St. Hippolytus, Origen, and the two SS. Dionysii." "This," he concludes with saying, "is pretty much the whole of the evidence,"⁴ and this is not enough.

We will forestall our answer here, so far as to say that unless the want of evidence from other quarters as well is shown, the mere insufficiency of evidence in ante-Nicene documents, were it even conceded, has nothing decisive in it;—especially such a kind of insufficiency as is instanced here, which simply proceeds from the inability of writers to express all the aspects of the truth they are speaking of at once; and that perhaps when they are purposely giving prominence to some one or other aspect. To say that no one of the statements in these writers, taken singly, would logically contain the whole, *i.e.* all aspects of the doctrine in question; that a Sabellian interpretation may be put upon one, a Macedonian upon another, an Arian

[1] Page 12.   [2] Page 14.   [3] *Ibid.*   [4] Page 115.

upon another, a Tritheist upon another, an Unitarian upon another, according as each statement in succession does not of itself supply all the enunciations of truth which would be the contradictions to those errors, is not saying much. Who could possibly expect such completeness of them? Is it to be found in writers of the latest age even? Take up the last volume of sermons of ever so orthodox a divine, and could not just the same remark be made, that different statements in it were in themselves incomplete, and that the void might be filled up with Sabellian, Macedonian, Arian complements, as might be? What human being ever could possibly write a single page, on the condition that he was to express the whole of the truth which he believed in each sentence? To make such a demand as this of the ante-Nicene Fathers, would be as much as to say, do what you cannot do, accomplish some feat of language which the constitution of human thought makes impossible, and then you may command my attention.

But besides this negative ground of insufficiency, Mr. Newman has a positive one in the actual discrepancies of language in ante-Nicene and post-Nicene writers, which appear so great to him, that he infers an actual difference in their respective doctrines themselves on the fundamental points in question,—such a difference as is parallel to the primitive and later state of the doctrine of Purgatory, the Papal Infallibility, and the like. Early Fathers reject expressions which later ones use, and use expressions which later ones reject, on the subject of our Lord's nature.

Now the question of certain discrepancies of language, and the inferences to be drawn from them, is evidently one that comes under the general head and department of language; and is to be settled in accordance with the rules and principles by which we decide on questions of language in general. And, speaking generally, it is not, we hope, explaining away language, but simply and literally explaining it, to say that language, in the case of the persons using it, only means what they mean by it. Language, as language only, has no meaning whatever. A certain collection of sounds or marks, as such, no more means one thing than another. The question is, what people using them understand by such sounds and marks? We are speaking here of the matter practically, the only way in which we are here concerned with it, and do not enter at all into the great and important metaphysical controversies on the subject of language. Mr. Newman himself says, "Ideas may remain (remain the same ideas we presume he means, not different ones) when the expression of them is infinitely varied."[1] This common sense truth about language leads necessarily to a certain line of judging with respect to discrepancies of language. It is evident that it is not enough in such cases, for proving the discrepancy of the ideas, to point to the discrepancy of the language. In ordinary literature words alter their meaning often in the course of ages; and we do not infer, because one word is used in one age, and another in another, that therefore the ages had different ideas; but only that the words themselves have different senses. And this rule applies to the department of theological language as well as that of others. It is not enough to say that the early Fathers, in particular instances, used language which later ones avoided, to prove a difference of doctrine in the two; it must appear that they used it in the same sense in which the others avoided it. It may turn out, on a reference to history, as the plainest matter of fact in the world, that they did not. A great deal may

[1] Page 60.

actually appear in history with respect to this matter, of the meaning in which words were regarded, whether to use or not use them. Writers may tell us *totidem verbis* in some cases, in others by the context and whole drift of their writing, that they do not use or reject such a word or phrase in the obnoxious meaning in which it was regarded afterwards. Indeed, such language in them may often not only show no incorrectness of idea, but in the writers no incorrectness to the very smallest extent even of language. For the bad meaning we see constantly in the history of theological language arose after the use of the phrase. The early Fathers expressed themselves in language such as suggested itself in the act of writing on certain sacred subjects: heretics afterward used this language in an obnoxious sense, and so the language itself became obnoxious; but the heretics and not the early Fathers made it so. Language is able to bear different senses; and you cannot, by using it in one sense, prevent others after you from using it in another. From such a law, as from a mathematical principle, proceeded inevitably some changes in theological language in the early Church; such changes proving simply, not that bad language was used, but that language was. Language was used; and having been used, was perverted. What was to prevent this course of things? Nothing, except that no language should have been used to begin with at all. Some persons must live before others; write before others: in language antecedency is enough to create perversion. Had the early Fathers never spoken, their words would never have been used in an unfavourable sense; if they afterwards were, it only proves that they spoke. Some limitation, in particular instances, theological language thus underwent as the necessary condition of its existence. It was more free at first, because it was then anterior to its misuse; and the early Fathers wrote more naturally and pliably, and were less afraid of venturing on some of the tender parts of doctrine; and shrunk less from some mysteries which later theology, though holding their truth, avoids; were less stiff, and trusted themselves nearer the verge. And who can say that diminution of that freedom of language is in itself a privilege; or, while he respects the orthodoxy which subsequently avoided what was misinterpreted, elevate avoidance so caused, from a remedy for an evil, into an advantage in itself? Such facts are interesting ones in the history of theological language; but the history of language is one thing, and the history of doctrine is another. And to go up straight from modern language to ancient, and accuse the ancient of unsoundness because we ourselves bring with us associations of unsoundness to it, is not philosophical or just.

We have said thus much on the point of language, to show that words may be rejected at an earlier time and used at a later, or used at an earlier time and rejected at a later, without any difference of idea and doctrine being proved.

An instance of the former we have in the history of the word "Homoousion." Mr. Newman makes a point of the word "Homoousion" having been rejected at the Council of Antioch sixty years before it was received at the Ecumenical Council of Nice. "There is one and only one great doctrinal council in ante-Nicene times. It was held at Antioch, in the middle of the third century, on occasion of the incipient innovations of the Syrian heretical school. Now the Fathers then assembled, for whatever reason, condemned, or at least withdrew, when it came into the dispute, the word "Homoousion," which was received at Nicæa as the special symbol of Catholicism against Arius."[1] Now we have already, in what we have said, answered this statement; for Mr. Newman says, "for whatever reason," as if it made no matter, so long as the word was rejected, what reason it was rejected for; whereas we have maintained that that makes all the difference.

It so happens, however, that we have an explanation of this fact from St. Athanasius himself, who expressly vindicates the Antiochene Fathers from having meant, in rejecting the word, any other than the same precise doctrine which the Nicene Fathers meant in adopting it; and attributes the difference of their respective lines about it entirely to an accidental difference of view about the word itself. He says, "If we examine their real meaning, we shall find that both Councils agree. The former was condemning the heresy of Samosata, the latter the Arian heresy. They who condemned the Samosatene heresy took the word 'Homoousion' in a corporeal sense. For Paul sophisticated, and said, if Christ was consubstantial with the Father, it necessarily followed that there must be three different substances, one which is prior, and two other sprung from that. To avoid that sophism of Paul, the Fathers said that Christ was not consubstantial, *i.e.* that He was not in that relation to the Father which Paul said the word meant. On the other hand, those who condemned the Arian heresy saw through the cunning of Paul, and considered that in things incorporeal, especially in God, consubstantial did not mean this, and asserted the Son to be begotten of the substance of the Father, and yet not to be separate from the Father. . . . The more simple Antiochene bishops did not apply that nicety and discrimination in their treatment of the word consubstantial, but gave it the meaning which they were told it had. They wished to condemn Paul, and they

[1] Page 13.

were wholly intent on that."[1] Here is an explanation of the fact, then, from an authority which nobody can dispute. It appears that there was a heretic, Paul of Samosata, at that time, who held the modern Socinian view, or something near it, that Christ was only a man naturally, and was *made* God from being a man. They wished to test Paul by the word "consubstantial," and make him say or deny that Christ was of one substance with the Father. He had a subtler head than his judges, and perplexed them with an inference which he drew from the word, that if the Son and the Holy Ghost were of the same substance with the Father, the original substance of the Father was divided into three substances. The Fathers not seeing their way at the time as to whether the word implied this or not, simply withdrew the word, and condemned Paul without it. Here, then, is no difference whatever from strict Nicene doctrine, though an abstinence from a Nicene word; and so far from abstaining from the word, because it went too far for them, the Antiochene Fathers actually wish to use the word for the very purpose for which it was used at Nice, viz., for expressing the proper divinity of the Son; and are only turned from doing so by the sudden suggestion of an unfavourable meaning which the word might bear in another direction from that in which they were then specially employing it.

We will add that, in other ways besides the one just exemplified, the word "Homoousion" has a history of its own, as many words have; and that, when it is objected that it was sometimes bestowed in early times where it was afterwards withheld, just as we have seen it withheld where it was afterwards bestowed, it is saying no more than that the word "Homoousion" is, as a word, recipient of different meanings, which it undoubtedly is. As far

[1] S. Athanas. de conciliis Arimin. et Seleuc., ch. iii., § 45.

as the word itself is concerned, it does not tell us whether it means that oneness of substance with God which the *Deus ex Deo* has, or such oneness of substance with Him as might mean simply coming from Him, and which creatures might have; for we express creation sometimes as a kind of derivation, meaning nothing in so calling it more than creation. If instances then can be found in which, as says a modern reviewer of the Petavian school, angels and souls were called by early writers " Homoousioi" with God, what does the fact prove? Simply that the word was sometimes used then in a vaguer meaning than that to which it was afterwards confined. To argue from such a fact, that a certain doctrine, afterwards tested by that word, was then only partially held, would be to imply that the word itself made the doctrine which it tested. The Church had a doctrine which she wanted to preserve and guard: she had to choose from the words which language gave her for this purpose, and she took the word " Homoousion." It did not in itself necessarily convey that one exclusive meaning which she wanted it to convey, but her own use of the word in that exclusive meaning, in time gave it that exclusive meaning. But for this imposition of a meaning on the word "Homoousion," a modern Socinian might use it; there is nothing in the word itself to prevent him from putting his own sense upon it, and in that sense acknowledging our Lord to be " Homoousion" with the Father. It is a great, providential mercy, indeed, that the Church is thus enabled to conquer the essential uncertainties of language. Had the whole Arian party taken the test of the " Homoousion," her difficulties would have been greater than what they were. But this mercy is shown to her. By a course of steps which we cannot analyse or follow, a word gets to have a particular meaning so stamped upon, and connaturalised with it, that it becomes an obvious hypocrisy and deceit for any one to take that word in a different sense of his own. The history of language, indeed, would, we doubt not, if accurately and deeply examined, exhibit in this very point of view as signal proofs of the overruling providence of God as any other department of history. The Church, by her use of the word "Homoousion," had fastened her exclusive sense upon it so strongly before the Nicene Council, that the Arians encountered it defined and pre-occupied, and were shut out by it. But all this belongs to the history of language and not of doctrine. The Church gave her own definite meaning to the word "Homoousion;" that definite meaning, therefore, preceded her use of the word, and her doctrine must have been antecedently the same with that which the "Homoousion" subsequently expressed, in order to have made the "Homoousion" express it.

We have anticipated, in these remarks, the other point we are coming to. We have, then, in the second place, particular phrases and expressions rejected in after times used in earlier. The expressions brought forward by a writer of the modern Petavian school are such as St. Ignatius's, the Son of God, "according to the will and power of God;" St. Justin's, "Him who, by the will of the Father, is with God, as being His Son, etc.;" St. Justin's again, "Derived from the Father before all creatures by His power and will;" Tatian's, "The word springing forth from the Divine simplicity at His will;" St. Hippolytus's, "Whom God the Father having willed, begat as He willed;" Novatian's, "From whom, when He willed, His Son the Word was born:" that in the Recognitions attributed to St. Clement, that "God begat Him, *voluntate præcedenti:*" Tertullian's, "As soon as God willed:" that in the Apostolical Constitutions, "At the pleasure of the Father:" the ὑπουργία (ministration) of the Son of God, found in St. Theophilus and St. Irenæus: St. Hippolytus's again, "God over all, because God the Father has put all things under his feet;" St. Justin's again, "called God from His being the first-born Son of all creatures." Now, without entering into the question of the genuineness of all the passages in which these expressions are found, or the genuineness of all works in which the passages are, or the comparative authority of the different writers (for some names here are heretical ones, and others of unsound estimation from the first), it is evident that we have here a set of expressions on a particular subject, one of a most mysterious, incomprehensible, and awful character, the subject, viz., of God the Son's derivation from, and subordinateness to, *qua* derivation from, God the Father. It is obvious that this is a subject on which it is most difficult to speak with perfect accuracy, so as to avoid, in expressing the idea of derivation and subordinateness, the ideas of posteriority in time, and inferiority of nature. Our natural and ordinary idea of derivation connects posteriority with it, and proceeds to connect a certain inferiority of nature with that posteriority. Here is a subject, then, on which it would be most unfair to judge particular expressions on a standard of literal accuracy, and throw upon them the whole meaning which can be extracted from them by themselves without alleviation or set-off. Persons in expressing one side of truth will sometimes express it too boldly, while, after all, they only profess it to be an expression of one side of truth, and not to contradict another. We have, accordingly, a set of expressions put before us, which, taken as a whole (though of some of them we doubt whether even this can be said), are not what later writers would use; and they are extracted from the books of all their respective writers, and put before us in that collective insulation which tells upon the imagination. But what, after all, can any fair mind draw from this, which can seriously shake our confidence in the faith of the writers, if their works, as a whole, and any other valid evidence about them, exhibit them as sound? What if St. Ignatius says, "The Son of God, according to the will and power of God;" we really cannot see the harm of the words, though such expressions may doubtless be perverted. If it is true that the Son is derived from the Father, it cannot be in itself wrong to say that He is derived from the Father in accordance with the Father's attributes; and will and power are attributes of the Father. He is not derived against the Father's will and power, and therefore He is derived in accordance with them. The idea of "will," indeed, carries one or two of the expressions before us into the idea of precedence in that will, because we naturally look upon will as precedent to what it wills; and so in the order of nature it is, though in order of time the eternal will and eternal act are coeval,—a truth with which these expressions are compatible. However, the writers are here wishing to express a sacred truth most difficult to express; and if, before the experience of the perversion of such modes of speaking by subsequent heretics, they do occasionally, and quite as an exception, carry such modes of speaking too far, it proves very little. Indeed, in some instances which are urged, it is quite obvious on the surface that the writer is really wishing to express the idea of the Son's generation being absolutely coeval with the eternal Being of the Father; and is using the examples from the natural world, where the derivation is most immediately consequent upon the existence of the thing derived from, in order vividly to impress that idea of coeval upon the reader's mind. "The Son," says St. Clement of Alexandria, "issues from the Father *quicker* than the light from the sun." Here, however, the very aim of the illustration to express simultaneousness is turned against it, and special attention is called to the word "*quicker*," as if we were to infer that the writer had only degrees of quickness in his mind, and only made the Son's generation from His source "quicker" than that of light from its, not absolutely coeval with it. We have no time, however, for dwelling on the frivolity of such criticism. We only want to have it understood what the task of these early writers was, and what the subject they had to deal with, in the instance of these casual expressions quoted from them.

In connection, again, with these modes of speaking, and with the general doctrine of our Lord's derivation and subordinateness as the Son, is the view held by some of the early Fathers of the λόγος ἐνδιάθετος and λόγος προφορικὸς, which we will just notice, as an interpretation is suggested by Mr. Newman for it. Some early Fathers, besides the eternal generation of the Son, attributed a second and external generation to Him on His going forth to create the universe. He had, from all eternity, resided as the Λόγος, the second Person in the Godhead, in the bosom of the Father. But He left the bosom of His Father, in a sense, when He went forth to create; and therefore the act of creation was described as a kind of second generation on the Son's part. He was thus spoken of, occasionally, as generated in time, just before the creation of the world—the Λόγος προφορικὸς; such generation, in reality, not at all interfering with His eternal generation and Personal existence from all eternity, as the Λόγος ἐνδιάθετυς, to which the same writers perpetually testify. The doctrine is thus first stated, and then has an explanation suggested for it.

"Five early writers, Athenagoras, Tatian, Theophilus, Hippolytus, and Novatian, of whom the authority of Hippolytus is very great, not to speak of Theophilus and Athenagoras, whatever be thought of Tatian and Novatian, seem to speak of Divine generation as taking place immediately before the creation of the world, that is, as if not eternal; though at the same time they teach that our Lord existed before that generation. In other words, they seem to teach that He was the Word from eternity, and became the Son at the beginning of all things, some of them expressly considering Him, first, as the λόγος ἐνδιάθετος, or Reason, in the Father, or (as may be speciously represented) a mere attribute; next, as the λόγος προφορικὸς, or Word. This doctrine, when divested of figure, and put into literal statement, might appear nothing more or less than this,—that at the beginning of the world the Son was created after the likeness of the Divine attribute of Reason, as its image or expression, and thereby became the Divine Word; was made the instrument of creation, called the Son from that ineffable favour and adoption which God had bestowed on Him, and in due time sent into the world to manifest God's perfections to mankind,—which, it is scarcely necessary to say, is the doctrine of Arianism."—*Note upon Athanasius against the Arians*, p. 272.

With respect to such an explanation as this, whether Mr. Newman means to suggest it as a true or false one, from whatever quarter it comes, we might make some obvious remarks, and say that, on such principles of criticism, it will be utterly impossible for any author to protect his meaning. If writers directly attribute personality from all eternity to the Λόγος before His going forth to create the world, and a critic interprets that personality into a metaphor, and leaves the λόγος a mere Divine attribute, he has taken the law simply into his hands. But we are calling attention now to the Patristic view itself, and the particular subject upon which it and the ambiguities of expression likely to be connected with it turn.

Here, then, is a whole line of expression before us, which is, be it observed, *the* line of expression which is urged against the early Fathers, and which has, as we see, reference to and gathers round a particular doctrine. It is to be remarked next that that doctrine is one which has been allowed by the Church, since their time, to fall into the shade; and so been made, with all the language connected with it, comparatively strange to modern ears. The doctrine of the subordination, *qua* origination, of the Second Person of the Trinity, with all that mode of viewing and speaking of it which went along with it, has been thrown into the background in later ages; and the Church has, since that day, avoided all verbal dangers on this subject, by avoiding the subject itself altogether. "As the Arian controversy proceeded," says Mr. Newman, "a tendency was elicited to contemplate our Lord more distinctly in His absolute perfections than in His relation to the First Person of the Blessed Trinity. Thus whereas the Nicene Creed speaks of the 'Father Almighty,' and 'His only-begotten Son our Lord, God from God, Light from Light, Very God from Very God,' and of the Holy Ghost, 'the Lord and Giver of Life,' we are told in the Athanasian of 'the Father eternal, the Son eternal, and the Holy Ghost eternal;' and that none is afore or after other, none is greater or less than another." "The doctrine of the Son's subordination to the Eternal Father, which formed so prominent a feature in ante-Nicene theology, comparatively fell into the shade."[1] By "having fallen into the shade," we suppose he does not mean ceased to be true: for once true, it must be so always; and we recite it in the Nicene Creed at this day. And therefore what such a statement of the case on the whole amounts to, is

[1] Page 400.

little more than this : That a very mysterious and awful doctrine, connected with our Lord's nature, was contemplated and treated of by theologians of the early Church; but that though a perfectly true and sacred doctrine in itself, its tenderness as a matter of theological handling led to expressions, occasionally, among theologians, which Arians and other heretics took advantage of, and that therefore the Church thought it wisest to discourage further dwelling upon it. Such a statement of the case as this, we say, does not make the real doctrinal meaning at the bottom of all these expressions an erroneous and unsound one, but only one which has been thrown into the background and not attended to in later times; and therefore, at the worst, make such expressions overstatements of real truth, and not statements of error.

Upon objections, then, in general to the orthodoxy of the ante-Nicene Fathers, on the ground of this whole line of expression which is found in them, there is one very obvious remark, suggested by what we have been saying, to be made, and that is, that the modern objector forgets, in making such a charge, that those Fathers held a deep view on this subject, which is not put forward in the Church now, and with which the objector himself is not familiar. He comes to a particular part of their language, without carrying their idea to it, and says, what strange language! But carry their idea to it, and the language is not strange. It is just like any other case of theological difference of view on a subject. One theologian charges another with unsound language: the latter says, You accuse my language because you do not understand my idea : let me acquaint you with my idea, and if you think that wrong, then you have a good and solid ground against me; but do not go on assailing fragments and outsides, this word, and that phrase, blindly and without having the key to them. The ante-Nicene Fathers may make the same answer to their modern interpreters. They may say, You are judging our language, and yet, in the same breath, you confess that you have allowed the idea which animated and explains it "to fall into the shade." You come to us, you confess, without the key to us, and then judge us as if you had it. You attack our language, here and there, in this and that word, half word, half sentence; is not this poor work? What if you can pick a hole in our mere language here and there? you prove nothing more in our case than what, in the full light of all post-Nicene doctrine, happens in your own every day. Condemn our idea, our doctrine; and that is a fair, solid argumentative line to take. But if you cannot do this,—if that idea and doctrine confronts you in the Nicene Creed, and you can only say that, though perfectly true, "it has fallen into the shade,"—it is trivial and frivolous work carping at particular expressions of it. Such appears, we say, to be the state of the case with respect to ante-Nicene writers. The modern interpreter comes and sees occasional language there which he is not accustomed to. He instantly assumes that such language expresses a rude, incipient, and elementary state of Christian truth, and forgets that it may only express, after all, a particular truth which he is not familiar with: he assumes that it expresses the absence of a doctrine which has been now arrived at, and forgets that it may express the presence of a doctrine which has been laid aside. Mr. Newman is constantly referring to the "Catholic doctrine of the Trinity," as not having been held by the early Fathers, *i.e.* being then only in process of formation, in an incipient and elementary state. But would it not be much truer to say that they held it just as much as he himself does, but held a particular doctrine in connection with it, which, with him, has "fallen into the shade." He has one mode of holding the doctrine of the Trinity which puts aside the doctrine of the subordination of the Second Person; the Fathers had another mode of holding it which put forward that doctrine. Their theology on the subject was different from his. But it is a further question, if this doctrine is true, as it undoubtedly is, and the Fathers held the doctrine of the Trinity with, and the modern interpreter without, the appeal to it, whether their theology is, therefore, less sound and less perfect than his.

Thus much for the alleged insufficiency, arising either from defects or difficulties of ante-Nicene documentary evidence: and now for a concluding remark upon this argument as a whole. The argument then is, that coming to the ante-Nicene documents with no other evidence to depend on for the fact in question but those documents themselves,—coming to them with nothing to prepossess or guide our judgment from any other quarter, coming to them as simply so much extant covered parchment, with our minds blank,—we could not gather the fact from them that the writers held the true orthodox belief which the Church held afterwards. Now to this we might answer that we did not admit such insufficiency in those documents even upon this isolated basis; that if the New Testament would as a whole, without other aid than its own letter, prove to a really candid and religious mind the proper Divinity of the Son of God, the ante-Nicene documents would do the same. And we might appeal to statement upon statement of the doctrine of the *Deus ex Deo* as accurate, subtle, and unquestionable as could be found in any post-Nicene writer. But it is not necessary to recur to such a ground as this.

For, be it observed, the whole line of argument which

we have been dealing with here, simply omits the strong positive historical testimony there is, before we come to examine the documents of the ante-Nicene Church, to the fact of what the doctrine of that Church was. We have the unanimous testimony of the whole body of Nicene Fathers to the fact that they had received the doctrine they asserted from their predecessors in the Church; which predecessors had asserted that they had received it from their predecessors, and so on up to the age of the Apostles. It was the full historical belief of the Nicene Church that its doctrine had been the doctrine of the ante-Nicene up to the commencement of Christianity. Mr. Newman appears, indeed, to acknowledge this evidence, but does not; for though he maintains the "subsequent *profession* of this doctrine as a presumption that it was held before," he only means the presumption from the subsequent profession of a truth that there were previous elementary anticipations of it; and makes no mention of a declaration ever *accompanying* that subsequent profession, which spoke to that truth's antiquity and existence as the same identical truth as then professed from the first. So here is a body of plain, historical evidence, before coming to ante-Nicene documents, which the argument before us simply omits. And whereas Mr. Newman invalidates all explanation of difficulties in the ante-Nicene Fathers, on the ground that to enter upon it "is to assume that they are all of one school, which is the point to be proved:" here is this very point proved upon unanimous historical testimony; that is, if, as orthodox members of the Church of their day, to have all one creed is to be "of one school." We have, we say, this positive evidence as to what the creed of the ante-Nicene Church was, prior to coming at all to the examination of the documents of the ante-Nicene Church. We come to the examination of them, as we do to that of the Scriptures, with the rule of historical tradition to guide us,—a tradition speaking directly to the fact of what the belief from which those documents issued was. Every rule of proof requires that the insufficiency of evidence in one quarter should be no obstacle whatever to the weight of evidence in another; and not only permits, but compels the weaker and obscurer part of evidence to receive light from the stronger. Granting, then, ever so much insufficiency in the ante-Nicene documents, taken by themselves, to prove the point of ante-Nicene belief, here is positive evidence from another quarter, on that point, which only requires the absence of positive counter-evidence to be of force and hold its ground. Let but the ante-Nicene documents not positively contradict the historical testimony which accompanies us to them; let them but simply fall in with, and negatively coincide with it, and that negative coincidence becomes at once a confirmation of the positive truth, instead of that positive proof being weakened by the negative one. It is a case which we meet with every day in questions of evidence. How much more than this negative proof there is in the ante-Nicene writings we are not, as we say, concerned with proving here; it is sufficient that they only bear out this universal and undoubting testimony with respect to the faith which produced them, and that the tradition of the Nicene age on that point is clear, unanimous and uncontradicted.

It will be said, perhaps, that this argument is, after all, only an appeal to the later doctrine as a key to the earlier one, and that is just what the doctrine of development does. It appears to be thought by some impossible to refer to subsequent evidence with respect to early belief, without referring to it as a proof of the elementary state of that belief prior to the age of this subsequent evidence;

and, accordingly, they meet all appeal, of whatever kind, to evidence of a later age, with the general assertion that we are implying an after-growth by appealing to it. But this is to confound two totally distinct things; later evidence may prove what was early doctrine, without later growth having formed it. An historian does not create by relating; evidence does not make by proving. Nicene testimony can appeal to ante-Nicene fact as its subject simply, and not as its work. If it *is* testimony it must do so. For testimony must act as testimony, and cannot possibly act in any other capacity.

Such is the fact, then, which the argument before us omits. We will add that Mr. Newman does notice it in another place, and out of this argumentative connection; and we will give first his notice, and then his explanation of it.

"Christians were bound to defend and to transmit the faith which they had received, and they received it from the rulers of the Church; and, on the other hand, it was the duty of those rulers to watch over and define this traditionary faith. It is unnecessary to go over ground which has been traversed so often of late years. St. Irenæus brings the subject before us in his description of St. Polycarp, part of which has already been quoted, and to it we may limit ourselves. 'Polycarp,' he says, when writing against the Gnostics, 'whom we have seen in our first youth, ever taught those lessons which he learned from the Apostles, which the Church also transmits, which alone are true. . . .' Nor was this the doctrine and practice of one school only, which might be ignorant of philosophy; the cultivated minds of the Alexandrian Fathers, who are said to owe so much to Pagan science, certainly showed no gratitude or reverence towards their alleged instructress, but maintained the supremacy of Catholic Tradition. Clement speaks of heretical teachers as perverting Scripture, and essaying the gate of heaven with a false key; not raising the veil, as he and his, by means of tradition from Christ, but digging through the Church's wall. . . . 'When the Marcionites, Valentinians, and the like,' says Origen, 'appeal to apocryphal works, they are saying, "Christ is in the desert;" when to canonical Scripture, "Lo, He is in the chambers;" but we must not depart from that first and ecclesiastical tradition, nor believe otherwise than as the Churches of God by succession have transmitted to us.' And it is recorded of him in his youth that he never could be brought to attend the prayers of a heretic who was in the house of his patroness, from abomination of his doctrine—'observing,' adds Eusebius, 'the rule of the church.' Eusebius too himself, unsatisfactory as is his own theology, cannot break from this fundamental rule; he ever speaks of the Gnostic teachers, the chief heretics of his period (at least, before the rise of Arianism), in terms most expressive of abhorrence and disgust. The African, Syrian, and Arian schools are additional witnesses; Tertullian, at Carthage, was strenuous for the dogmatic principle, even after he had given up the traditional. The Fathers of Asia Minor, who excommunicated Noetus, rehearse the creed, and add, 'We declare as we have learned;' the Fathers of Antioch, who depose Paul of Samosata, set down in writing the creed from Scripture, 'which,' they say, 'we received from the beginning, and have, by tradition and in custody, in the Catholic and Holy Church until this day by succession, as preached by the blessed Apostles, who were eye-witnesses and ministers of the word. . . . Who ever heard the like hitherto?' says St. Athanasius, of Apollinarianism: 'who was the teacher of it? who the hearer? "From Sion shall go forth the Law of God, and the Word of the Lord from Jerusalem;" but from whence hath this gone forth? What hell hath burst out with it?' The Fathers at Nicæa stopped their ears; St. Irenæus, as above quoted, says that St. Polycarp, had he heard the Gnostic blasphemies, would have stopped his ears, and deplored the times for which he was reserved. They anathematised the doctrine, not because it was old, but because it was new."[1]

Now, such a passage as this appears to, and to an ordinary reader would, convey the notion that Mr. New-

[1] Page 343.

man thoroughly estimated the testimony we have been alluding to for the perfect identity of Christian doctrine in subsequent and in earliest times; for the antiquity, in the obvious sense of the word, as opposed to the after-formation of Christian fundamental knowledge. But on coming to what immediately follows it, we find that all this acknowledgment of early testimony has been introduced for the very purpose of stopping this natural inference from it. The writer proceeds immediately to turn this very testimony against itself, and to draw, by an ingenious turn of reasoning, from that express witness to the fact that such doctrine was old, the immediate inference that it was new. Let us see: Christians were very much startled at the contrary doctrine, as soon as ever taught by heretics, and shut their ears in horror. The obvious inference from such a fact would be, that this doctrine contradicted some old known familiar truth. But no, says Mr. Newman, it shows just the contrary: "The doctrine in question being strange and startling, it follows that the truth, which was its contradictory, had also been unknown to them hitherto."[1] We must really say that we hardly know how to reply to such reasoning as this. There is something so strange in inferring from the intensity with which men felt a contradiction,—the fact that they had never known that which it was a contradiction to. Ordinary people would ask with some surprise, how the contradiction could be seen before the truth was; but Mr. Newman asks, with equal and quite as sincere surprise, how the truth could be seen before the contradiction was. Is no truth, however, seen till it is contradicted? And is it in the power of shameless and unlimited

---

[1] Page 344. In the recent edition (page 351) the passage stands, "It follows that the truth, which was its contradictory, was also in some respects unknown to them hitherto."

paradox to create at any moment the new truths, that fire burns and water flows, that the eye sees and the ear hears, and that we have bodies and souls? Contradiction certainly cannot do this. And if it cannot, we do not see how it could create and make known the great Christian dogmas. The dogma, as plain, simple, and matter-of-fact to the belief as it is incomprehensible to the intellect and unfathomable to meditation, the early Christian knew as he knew a fact, because he was told it; —just as persons know other things, because they are told them. You tell a person a thing; he apprehends what you tell him; then he knows that thing. It is not necessary that somebody else should come and contradict it in order that he may know it. There is something indeed which contradiction does do, but will what it does do be much to Mr. Newman's purpose in this argument?

Contradiction, undoubtedly, has the effect of sharpening our logical view of a truth, and we gain in the process of answering a contradiction a more definite and fuller logical image of the truth we defend. Contradiction to what we know elicits new expressions of that knowledge, and new aspects and inferences of that class which is identical with it. But to do this is not to give us that knowledge in the first instance. All that it gives us, which we had not before, is that series of aspects and inferences, that argumentative and mathematical issue from the substance, which is identical with the substance. As we find ourselves only taken back, however, here to an old subject, and have in this view of the powers of contradiction only another name for the view of development itself, we need not repeat arguments which we have already given; and need only say that the new expressions of truth which contradiction elicits, just as the expressions which explanatory development, *i.e.* explanation, makes, being one and the same thing, are neither of them additions of substantial truth; that there is an inference from truth which the precise answer to contradiction expresses for the first time, and that there is a truth itself which it does not; and that to perceive one of these inferences from the truth for the first time, is not to perceive the truth for the first time; and that it must be shown that it is the truth itself which is so seen, in order to answer the purpose of the arguer in the present case.

One remark, however, before leaving this subject. It appears that the unanimous testimony of the early Church, age after age, asserts that the doctrine it taught was the same identical doctrine with the doctrine which was delivered by the Apostles, and was received in the most primitive days. It appears there was a doctrine so strong, so decided, so familiar, that it was able on the very first rise of any contradiction instantly to see and reject it. The process of actual rejection was long, because heretics argued and explained, and it took time to expose their sophistries. But the feeling of rejection was full and immediate. Orthodox Christians closed their ears in horror at the plain contradiction to plain known sacred truth. Here then is strong, plain, unanimous testimony to what was early doctrine. An ordinary thinker would certainly say, Here, in the first place, is so much deliberate testimony to that point; and here, moreover, is the *ipso facto* unconscious testimony which the doctrine itself gives to its own antiquity, by being able from the very first to reject immediately anything contradictory to it. We argue the existence of substance from what comes against it being immediately cast off: we argue the existence of the truth, from its immediately casting off the error opposed to it. How could anything but the idea that the

Son was Very God, ever exclude the idea that He was not Very God: and this latter was immediately excluded as soon as it arose, and nobody can doubt that it would have been immediately excluded from the first. Nicene doctrine's antiquity and simple identity with the truth of original revelation is thus what these facts naturally take us to. But here comes an argument which does not bring counter evidence—a different step altogether, and quite a legitimate one,—but which explains away this very evidence itself into meaning something quite contrary to what, upon a plain common sense view, it does mean. For here is an argument which proves that this very testimony of the Church to the fact of its doctrine being old, is a testimony to the fact of its being new; and infers from early Christians being astonished at error, that they did not know the truth. Here is an argument which explains away, and turns against itself, the very fact of that universal testimony to its own antiquity, by which the Church's teaching, to a natural view, establishes that antiquity. An esoteric interpretation explains the loud assertions of the Nicene Fathers and all the after Church as to this fact, to mean something different from what one would naturally understand from them; or says that the assertors themselves did not really mean what they thought they meant; and that thinking they meant that they had exactly the same doctrine with the early one, they only *really* meant that that early doctrine was the seed and rudiment of their own, it having grown so imperceptibly that they did not perceive the change. A philosophic criticism, that is to say, refines upon the facts of history, analogously to the way in which one school of speculation refines upon the idea of Inspiration, and another upon the idea of Conscience. And the plain witness to the absolute identity of later doctrine with early melts away.

What we maintain then is, that the Nicene truth is not a development in the sense in which Mr. Newman uses the word, that the whole testimony of antiquity declares the contrary, and that Mr. Newman's arguments to prove that it was not held, but only some rudiments of it, in ante-Nicene times, are forced and unsatisfactory.

Our argument has now to take another direction, and to call Mr. Newman's attention to a certain result of his theory, if true, which we cannot see how it can avoid. If it be really true, as his theory implies, that the doctrine of the Divinity of our Lord maintained at Nicæa was not the received doctrine of the earlier Church, we cannot, for our own part, understand how he can believe that that doctrine was an original doctrine of the Christian revelation, and one which the Apostles and first promulgators of Christianity taught. We are, of course, dealing with Mr. Newman's argument here, and not for an instant with his personal belief. His argument appears to us to run, distinctly and quite inevitably, into the denial of the doctrine of our Lord's Divinity as an original doctrine of revelation. For if that doctrine was not the received one of the early Church, and of the age of the ante-Nicene Fathers, it could not possibly have been communicated at the Apostolic era. If it had been, it would have been preserved, and been the received doctrine; not being preserved, the necessary inference is that it had never been delivered. The argument throws us back upon an early Christianity, of which the doctrine of our Lord's Divinity was no part, and denies that doctrine to be a revelation from the mouths of the first teachers of Christianity; in other words, to be an immediate truth of inspiration at all.

Indeed, Mr. Newman is himself not insensible to this tendency of his theory, and he endeavours to ward it off. He does this by occasional disclaimers, by the balance of clauses, by protests in a succeeding sentence against the obvious meaning and necessary force of the immediately preceding one; and he endeavours to counteract the substantial tendency of the argument by arbitrarily putting aside its result when he comes across it. His whole mode of arguing here shows the uneasy and conflicting position. He glides out of one statement into another, and glides back again, as the argument itself, or as its check, requires; he leaves the reader in doubt what he really means to say: he asserts, he denies: though how the denial is reconcilable with the assertion does not appear, and which of the two he means to stand does not appear. Under the general haze and ambiguity which conflicting sentences create, he admits what he wants to admit into his development theory, and excludes what he wants to exclude; and while he makes Nicene truth the development of something before it, does not fairly face the result that what was before it was not Nicene truth. For example, the ambiguity between denial of the fact, and denial of the evidence for it. He leaves us in doubt whether he means to say that the Nicene doctrine was really not received in early times, or that it was received, and that there is only not *evidence* for its reception. For, after a refutation of the evidence for that doctrine, of which the apparent effect is to prove that there really was not that doctrine, he adds, "It is true that the subsequent profession of the doctrine creates a presumption that it was held even before it was professed;"[1] and of certain early Church documents he says, "The Creeds of that early day make no mention in their letter of the Catholic doctrine (of the Trinity) at all. They make mention indeed of a Three; but that there is any mystery in the doctrine that the Three are One . . . is not stated, and never could be gathered from them. Of course

[1] Page 12.

we believe that they imply it, or rather intend it. God forbid we should do otherwise;"[1] as if he meant to say that the doctrine was held, but only that certain evidence was wanting. And after arguing against the ante-Nicene Fathers, he adds in the same way: "I must not be supposed to be ascribing any heresy to the holy men, whose words have not always been sufficiently full or exact to preclude the imputation."[2] "Let it not be for a moment supposed that I impugn the orthodoxy of the early divines."[3] Again we have the old ambiguity in the meaning of the word "development" itself, as to whether development affects the substance, or only the expression and mode of representing a doctrine. In the latter sense it does not, of course, prove that the doctrine did not exist before; and he leaves it doubtful on particular occasions whether he does not use it in the latter sense only, calling the "developments in the doctrines of the Holy Trinity and the Incarnation mere portions of the original impression and modes of representing it."[4] Again, a general distinction between explicit and implicit doctrine suggests that doctrine may be held implicitly before it is held explicitly, held latently and unconsciously before it is held distinctly and positively. Mr. Newman's Roman Catholic opponent in America describes his theory here powerfully and accurately. Mr. Newman, he says, maintains

"a slow, painful, and laborious working out, by the Church herself, of dogmatic truth from implicit feelings,—though what kind of feeling an *implicit* feeling is, we are unable to say. 'Thus St. Justin or St. Irenæus might be without any digested ideas of Purgatory, or original Sin, yet have an *intense feeling*, which they had not defined or located, both of the fault of our first nature and of the liabilities of our nature regenerate.' It is obvious from the whole course of

[1] Page 12. [2] *Ibid.* [3] Page 15. [4] Page 55.

Mr. Newman's reasoning, that he would predicate of the Church, in their time, what he here predicates of St. Justin and St. Irenæus. The Church had a vague yet intense feeling of the truth, but had not digested it into formal propositions or definite articles. She had a blind instinct, which, under secret, supernatural guidance, enabled her to avoid error and to pursue the regular course of development. She had a secret feeling of the truth, as one may say, a natural taste for it, and a distaste for error; yet not that clear and distinct understanding which would have enabled her at any moment, on any given point, to define her faith. She only knew enough of truth to preserve the original idea, and to elaborate from her intense feelings, slowly and painfully, as time went on, now one dogma and now another. What in one age is feeling, in a succeeding age becomes opinion, and an article of faith in a still later age. This new article gives rise to a new intense feeling, which, in its turn, in a subsequent age becomes opinion, to be finally, in a later age yet, imposed as dogmatic truth. This is, so far as we can understand it, Mr. Newman's doctrine of development, and what he means by 'working out dogmatic truth from implicit feelings.'"—Brownson's *Quarterly Review*, No. XI., for July 1846, Boston, U.S. (a Roman Catholic periodical.)

Such is the mode of explanation which would reconcile the fact that the Nicene doctrine of our Lord's Divinity was the development of anterior doctrine, with the fact that it had been the doctrine of the Church from the first; and denies its primitiveness at one argumentative call, and allows it at another.

Now, with respect to these ambiguities and modes of warding off the plain consequences of an argument, we have one answer, and that is the argument itself. Here is an argument before us, and the question is, what does that argument go to prove? For example, with respect to the ambiguity first mentioned: Does that argument allow Mr. Newman really to oscillate between denying the reception itself of a certain doctrine in those early times, and only denying the evidence of it? Certainly not. However he may alternate himself between both grounds, his argument stands upon one. His argument requires that, really and as a fact, the belief entertained by the Nicene Fathers should not have been held by the ante-Nicene. For his argument wants a parallel case to the growth of later doctrines, such as Purgatory and the Papal Infallibility. It must, therefore, maintain that there *is* that parallel case, and not only that there is no evidence that there is not. It urges a case in point, viz., that of Nicene growth as sanctioning Roman growth: it must, therefore, maintain that there *is* Nicene growth, and *is* ante-Nicene shortcoming. Moreover, where is the difference between saying that there is no evidence at all for, and that there was not, the belief of Nicene doctrine in those times? An arguer, indeed, who maintains the existence of any positive evidence in *one* channel for a fact, can, in proportion to the strength of that evidence, afford the silence or neutrality of another channel, for that silence or neutrality does not negative that evidence; but an arguer who comes with no evidence from any one channel, to no evidence in any other too, has no evidence at all for a fact, and therefore that fact does not exist in his opinion. A person who takes the unanimous witness of the Nicene Fathers to the early belief in Nicene doctrine as decided evidence for that early belief, can afford silence or neutrality in ante-Nicene quarters without displacing that fact; but Mr. Newman, who does not do this, and comes with his mind blank to the ante-Nicene region of evidence, if he disallows the evidence there for the early belief in question, disallows all evidence for it at all, and therefore must hold that there was not such early belief. However, we need not go into such considerations as these. Mr. Newman's parallel requires Nicene doctrine to be a real substantial development of an earlier doctrine as to our Lord's nature. Requiring the fact of an earlier doctrine, he cannot possibly have the right to take the tone of allowing the then reception of the later one, in spite of want of evidence for it. His argument does not regret the veil over a complete truth, but demands the existence of a seminal one.

So, again, with respect to the ambiguity of the meaning of development, which makes Nicene development mean substantial growth when it has to bear out Roman, and only explanation when it has to guard itself: the answer is the same. Here is an argument before us. That argument proceeds upon a parallelism,—that parallelism is the parallelism of Nicene growth to Roman growth. Let the arguer then choose whichever he likes of these two meanings of the word development, as far as himself is concerned; but if his parallel commits him to one, that one he must take, and he must keep to it. He says that the doctrines of Purgatory, of the Papal Infallibility, of the cultus of the Virgin, are the developments of the primitive ideas on those subjects. Does he mean to say that they are simple explanations of those ideas, and that if an intellectual primitive Christian had explained to a simple one the Church's then idea of the authority of the Bishop of Rome, and had said, 'The Bishop of Rome is the absolute Monarch of Christendom, and has the power himself of imposing articles of faith,' that the simple one would have replied that that was what he believed, and that the explainer only expressed his belief accurately and scientifically? If Mr. Newman does not say this, and by the argument of his book he does not; if the Roman development is a vast, solid, substantial change upon the primitive rudiment, then those Roman doctrines are more than explanations of the primitive ideas on these subjects, and therefore Nicene doctrine, to support the parallel, must be more than an explanation of the primitive idea on its subject.

So, again, with respect to the distinction between explicit and implicit knowledge: the answer is the same. Here is an argument. Here is a parallelism. We must go where they lead us, and take what they give us. Mr. Newman may allow an implicit knowledge of the truth of our Lord's proper Divinity in the Primitive Church; but it makes no difference calling it by a particular name, if whatever he allows can only be what his argument allows, and just as much and no more. Indeed, to allow an implicit knowledge is not to allow much; because implicit knowledge in multitudes of cases is no knowledge at all, and there is no saying what a man does know and what he does not, in the sense of this implicit knowledge. A man may be in time present, and as far as any actual perception and all that we mean by knowledge goes, totally ignorant of a truth; and yet when the truth afterwards is brought to him, he may discover, on looking back into the state of his own mind, some implicit unconscious idea of it before,—some knowledge which did not know; and some perception which did not perceive. In this sense the world has from its commencement known the theory of gravitation, the theory of the arch, the principle that water finds its own level, and numberless other scientific laws. But such implicit knowledge as this is not what we mean by knowledge. Knowledge is a definite perception of something: we go on for a long time not knowing; then there is a positive change from this not knowing to knowing: we know a thing then, and before we did not. No mental analysis can penetrate to the point of transition, but practically a point of transition there is, where the mind passes from ignorance to knowledge. The world went on for ages with the phenomena of water and its movements before it; and men knew that water moved, and that it moved in the way in which it did; and their mental eye gazed sleepily and vacantly on it, and there were some inert tendencies, which they could not help having, from the fact of seeing such phenomena, to the knowledge of a law about them. At last the law struck some one in whom the tendencies were rather less inert than in the rest, and a spring in his mind was touched; something was lit up, and knowledge took place: he caught the point; he knew the principle that water finds its own level. Then as soon as he had made the discovery, the rest of the world might say that they had had implicit knowledge of it all along. But it is evident that the knowledge which they had was not what we mean by knowledge: it was ignorance with the capacity of knowledge. A mere implicit knowledge then, attributed to the Primitive Church, of subsequent truth need not amount to much. However, if we were left to words to guide us in the present case, we could not extract any plain result from them, however their obvious meaning might seem to contain it, for the arguer frequently says under such circumstances that he means more than you mean by the words. The mere words, we say,—seed and growth, elementary doctrines and developed, implicit and explicit knowledge, and other modes of expressing a certain relation of primitive truth to Nicene,—ought not simply as such, however naturally they may convey a particular meaning to our minds, to have that meaning imposed upon them, if the writer gives us to understand, by his argument, that he does not use them in that meaning. Nay, and if a writer's argument is not attended to in interpreting his words, it will very frequently happen that much injustice will be done him in giving meanings to his words which they do not according to the argument bear. And one writer will under such circumstances sometimes go on for a whole controversy, totally misunderstanding another, and arguing upon a supposed meaning in his adversary's words, which his real line of thought does not give them. But, as we say, we are not left to words here. We have a parallel to guide us to the meaning of them: we have an illustration from fact of the kind of knowledge which implicit knowledge in the present case is; of the kind of relation which doctrine implicit has to doctrine explicit. Nicene development is made to sanction Roman; Roman development appeals to Nicene as its parallel. Whatever relation therefore the explicit doctrine has to the implicit in the Roman development, that same relation must it have in the Nicene. Now in the case of the Roman development it cannot possibly be asserted that the ultimate doctrines on the subject it is concerned with, are what could upon any common sense and natural standard, be called the same doctrines with the primitive ones. It could not possibly be asserted that the Roman doctrine on the intermediate state is the same with the primitive one; that the Roman view of the *sedes Petri* is the same with the primitive one; that the Roman regard to St. Mary is the same with the primitive one. To speak of the primitive Christian holding the Roman Purgatory, Papacy, and Cultus of the Virgin, would be a solecism, which would have immediately to be explained into meaning quite another thing than the words naturally suggest. It is obvious that in these instances the development has been of a kind which leaves the primitive doctrine a mere element and seed, compared with the real substantial later one. Who would deny that in the instance of the Papal Infallibility,—to fix our eye upon one,—the growth had not been so enormous that the ultimate grown doctrine was, as far as anything cognisable goes, literally one thing, and the asserted primitive element of it another thing? Indeed, as we have said, Mr. Newman does not call these the same doctrines, for the very object of his Essay is to dispense with the necessity of this identity, and give a rationale for change. Thus on the Roman side of the parallel, the implicit doctrine has the relation to the developed of no more than a seed or element. Then on the Nicene side it must be the same. The Nicene doctrine of the proper Divinity of our Lord must be the development of an early doctrine as to our Lord's nature, as truly seminal and elementary as the early asserted anticipation of Roman doctrine is. And if it be argued that the Nicene growth was only the first sample and beginning of a course, and need not be equal in amount to, in order to sanction, later growth, the same thing has still to be repeated; if it sanction the later, it must be real growth: now the Nicene doctrine as to our Lord is no more than that He was very God; the primitive doctrine then must have been less. The conclusion still is that as an anterior doctrine preceded the Roman one of the Papal Infallibility, which was substantially a different one from that of the Papal Infallibility, so an anterior doctrine preceded the Nicene one of the proper Divinity of our Lord, which was not the doctrine of His proper Divinity.

Such is the result of an argumentative parallel, though far be it from us to press it in any other than this connection, or to impose the result if the parallel is not imposed. But if Mr. Newman has the advantage of the parallel, he must take the disadvantage of it. He has, on the one hand, the option of allowing the Nicene development to be of a different sort from the Roman;

and if he takes that, he escapes this result with respect to Nicene doctrine, but has no benefit of parallel with respect to Roman. He has, on the other, the option of saying that they are the same sort of development and of asserting the parallel; and if he takes that, he has the benefit of it with respect to Roman doctrine, and the disadvantage of it with respect to Nicene. We are unable to see any middle ground between these two.

It does, then, as we have said, appear to us to be a necessary result from this line of argument, that the doctrine of the proper Divinity of our Lord was not a doctrine of inspiration. If it was not the received doctrine of the Primitive Church, the first inspired teachers of that Church could not have communicated it to her. For to say that it was communicated and not at first understood by the Church, or anything of that nature, would be so much mere hypothesis. We can only know of its original communication by the fact of its early reception. Moreover, if it was not communicated, we have no ground for saying that the Apostles themselves knew it, and were inspired as to that truth. For vain would be the distinction, if attempted to be urged, between what inspired men might know from God and what they communicated to men. We have no presumption for saying that they knew from God any other doctrines than what they were commissioned to communicate, or that inspiration had esoteric dogmas for the individuals inspired to keep to themselves. It follows that, on this theory, we have no reason for saying that the Apostles themselves were believers in, *i.e.* knew this doctrine, or therefore that, as far as any conscious meaning in the minds of the writers is concerned, the New Testament, from beginning to end, contains it. A great number of texts, which Arians and Socinians have taken advantage of, receive as a consequence a very different interpretation from that which we have been accustomed to give them. The New Testament becomes an ante-Nicene document, containing those errors and shortcomings which are charged upon the ante-Nicene Fathers, and containing them in the same sense; not simply in the sense, that is, that the words of the writers are to be explained to mean what universal tradition witnesses that they did, as a fact, mean, but in the sense that the actual doctrinal *meaning* of the writers was a rudimental and defective one,—that what St. Paul, St. John, St. Peter actually meant in what they wrote was not the Nicene truth of the proper Divinity of our Lord, but an earlier truth, the truth of that day as to our Lord's nature, whatever that was; an elementary truth indeed, which was capable of being expanded in the course of centuries by the "unwearied thought" of the Church and her theologians into that truth, but which was not that truth itself, any more than the acorn is the oak. In short, if a doctrine of inspiration means, as everybody supposes it to mean, a doctrine of which the Apostles were informed by inspiration, and being informed of, taught, the doctrine of our Lord's Divinity is, upon the theory we are dealing with, not a doctrine of inspiration; and a whole view of early Christianity and apostolic teaching, different from what we have been ever taught, goes along with that fact.

And now it is time that this article should draw to an end; a prospect which affords as much satisfaction to ourselves as it will to our readers. We have trespassed almost unprecedentedly upon established limits; and the task of the arguer, hard, cold, and hostile, and though lengthy enough to be tedious, short enough to oppress him with the continual memento of points wholly omitted, and thought just begun and left off, has not been relieved by the consideration of that name which the Essay he has been examining bears, and which he has had so often to repeat, in a very different tone and connection from that in which the pages of this Review have mentioned it in former times.

What we have to say now is little more than what the reader will gather for himself, if he has gone along with us. We have to say, that having followed Mr. Newman's argument through the three stages through which it has taken us, we do not feel ourselves convinced by it. His tests of a true and false development did not convince us in the first place; his argument for the Papal Infallibility, the only logical hypothesis which could then settle that question of development in his favour, did not convince us in the second place; his argument of *reductio ad absurdum*, which imposes that development upon us as a thing to which we have already committed ourselves in the acceptance of the fundamental doctrines of Christianity, and thrusts upon us the alternative between Rome and infidelity, does not convince us in the third place.

Some obvious reflections, first upon the way in which this theory of development affects the Roman controversy in general, and then upon this theory of development itself in particular, shall follow in conclusion.

With respect, then, to this whole theory of development, we have to observe that its propounder introduces it into the theological arena with this assertion: "This is an hypothesis to account for a difficulty."[1] There is, then, a difficulty, acknowledged in the Roman development of Christianity; and an hypothesis is said to be wanted to account for it. The phenomenon does not explain itself; it has to be explained upon an hypothesis. We recommend this observation, in the first instance, to the

[1] Page 27.

attention of some who appear to think that they decide the question against the English Church, if they can appeal to obvious difficulties on her side. It seems that there are difficulties on both sides; and that if one side has to explain, the other has to explain too. Christianity has now run through eighteen centuries, says Mr. Newman, and has a history. "Christianity," therefore, "may now *legitimately* be made the subject-matter of theories." "It has been long enough in the world to justify us in dealing with it"[1] in this way. Moreover, that history has brought along with it difficulties; for them an hypothesis is absolutely *demanded*. The writer of this Essay, then, does not give much encouragement to what may be called the simple method of deciding the question between the Roman and English Churches. He gives the Roman Church a "theory," "an hypothesis," which accounts for "her difficulties;" but he does not profess to say that she has a position free from them. We might suggest a comparison between the Roman Church with this ground, and St. Augustine's Church with its: the latter had a good deal more simple a position, if we are to judge by the greater simplicity of the argument; which was, if we mistake not, a simple appeal to people's eyes. The phenomenon of St. Augustine's Catholic Church explained itself; but the phenomenon of the Roman Catholic Church, it seems, does not explain itself, but requires an hypothesis. But we must proceed.

Having observed, then, that the thing before us is an hypothesis, our next observation is that it is an additional and a directly counter hypothesis to another, which has always had, and has now, the general, public, and authoritative acknowledgment of the Roman Church. The

[1] Page 1.

public and authoritative hypothesis of the Roman Church is that the whole of the Christian faith was revealed entire from the first : Mr. Newman's hypothesis is that the whole of the Christian faith has been a development from the first. It is wholly needless for us to cite the names of all the Roman divines who have, without hesitation or qualification, maintained this as the regular hypothesis of their Church : it would be, with hardly an exception, simply transcribing the whole index from beginning to end. It is enough to say that it is the ground of Bellarmine. The list exhibits at the end some distinguished names of the present day; and the present representatives of Roman theology at Rome, and in England, appear as the undoubting and dutiful supporters of it. " We believe," says Dr. Wiseman, " that no new doctrine can be introduced into the Church, but that every doctrine which we hold has existed and been *taught* in it, ever since the time of the Apostles." " The Apostles," says the Jesuit Perrone, the present Professor of theology at Rome, " having been instructed by Christ in the truths of the faith, delivered these same truths to successors chosen by them, that they in like manner might transmit them entire, even to the latest posterity, *such as they had received them.*" I admit [progress], he says, *i.e.* greater elucidation *of the doctrine already received;* I deny [progress] by the introduction of new dogmas." " The doctrines of the faith are so many truths divinely revealed, which the Church received from Christ to be transmitted to posterity, and inviolably preserved from the gnawing tooth of innovation." " The Pontiffs and Councils never obtrude anything of their own, but are witnesses of the doctrine which Christ taught and the Apostles delivered." " It is the constant rule of Catholics," says another living theologian of the Roman Church, that "no change can take place in what concerns the doctrines of revealed religion." With respect to Purgatory, says Dr. Wiseman, "Nothing can be more simple than to establish the belief of the universal Church on this point. The only difficulty is to select such passages as may appear the clearest. These passages contain *precisely* the same doctrine as the Catholic Church teaches." With reference to Indulgences, the same writer says, "The Church in the earliest time" claimed and exercised this power. With reference to the Invocation of Saints, he says, "I can have only one fear in laying before you passages on this subject. It is that in the authorities from the Fathers, their expressions are so much stronger than those used by Catholics at the present day, that there is a danger (if I may so speak) of proving too much; they go beyond us." In a word, the ground of the Roman Church hitherto has been, that all the Roman doctrines were actually revealed to the Apostles, and really in the Church from the first, though some were not taught publicly. This hypothesis Mr. Newman denies. He says of the "hypothesis put forward by divines of the Church of Rome, called the *Disciplina Arcani*, It is maintained that doctrines which are associated with the later ages of the Church were *really in the Church from the first*, but not publicly taught,"[1] "This is no key to the whole difficulty,"[2] that is to say, it is not a true hypothesis; and he puts forward the hypothesis of development expressly to supply its place. So then here are two directly conflicting hypotheses put forward in the Roman Church as the account of her faith.

Now, upon this state of the case, one reflection, which necessarily arises, is that with regard to general antecedent claim upon attention and respect, both hypotheses

[1] Page 25. [2] Page 26.

are considerably weakened by this opposition. So long as one account of her creed is put forward by a whole Church, that account comes with a certain imposing introduction to us; but if another account is put forward which directly conflicts with the old one, it is natural for a person to say, 'You come to persuade me, and yet you are fighting among yourselves as to the very foundation upon which your own whole belief rests. The early Church had one account, but you have two contrary ones. You must really make up your own mind before you come to persuade me. Choose which of the two you please, but if they oppose each other, do let me have one of them, and not both together. Otherwise you simply puzzle me.' The Roman Church, we say, if she admits two contrary hypotheses, ceases *ipso facto* to argue at all. Schools and individuals in her argue, but the Church does not. As a Church, she abandons the field of controversy because she contradicts herself. For, be it remembered, this is not an affair of simple phenomena, the truth of which is visible to the eye, and does not depend at all on the hypothesis which explains them, such as the fact that matter falls to the ground, the truth of which does not at all depend on the hypothesis of gravitation; but it is a case where the hypothesis is appealed to for the truth of the fact itself. We want to know why we are to believe a doctrine, say Purgatory or any other. Bellarmine gives one reason, and Mr. Newman a totally contrary one. Nor would the remark that it was the Church's teaching all the same in either case be to the purpose, for the reason of the Church's teaching is the argumentative ground on which we believe the Church's teaching; and this reason is a contrary one as Bellarmine and as Mr. Newman give it.

We must add, that Mr. Newman's hypothesis is

especially affected by this state of the case. We have naturally and reasonably so little confidence in our own private judgment, that when an individual writer comes before us with the information that he has an hypothesis for, a rationale to give of, the whole of Christian doctrine, we first ask him whom he represents, and what testimonials he can give *primâ facie* recommendatory of it. And when he says that it is a new one, that it is only his own, or that of a particular circle of thinkers, and that it is not only not borne out by, but opposed to, and intended to supplant the whole account of the Christian faith maintained by the Universal Church from the first, it is then natural to say that we should not trust our own reason enough to accept such an hypothesis, even supposing it to exhibit, upon examination, great argumentative force. Nor are we surprised at Mr. Newman's Roman Catholic opponent putting the question to him rather sharply.

" In regard to all this, we simply ask, Does the Church herself take this view ? Does she teach that she at first received no formal revelation,—that the revelation was given as ' unleavened dough,' to be leavened, kneaded, made up into loaves of convenient size, baked, and prepared for use by her, after her mission began, and she had commenced the work of evangelising the nations? Does she admit her original creed was incomplete, that it has increased and expanded, that there have been variation and progress in her understanding of the revelation she originally received, and that she now understands it better, and can more readily define what it is, than she could at first? Most assuredly not. She asserts that there has been no progress, no increase, no variation of faith ; that what she believes and teaches now is precisely what she has always and everywhere believed and taught from the first. She denies that she has ever added a new article to the primitive creed ; and affirms, as Mr. Newman himself proves in his account of the Council of Chalcedon

(p. 145), that the new definition is not a new development, a better understanding of the faith, but simply a new definition, against the 'novel expressions' invented by the enemies of religion of what, on the point defined, had always and everywhere been her precise faith. In this she is right, or she is wrong. If right, you must abandon your theory of developments; if wrong, she is a false witness for God, and your theory of developments cannot make her worthy of confidence. If you believe her, you cannot assert developments in your sense of the term; if you do not believe her, you are no Catholic."—Brownson's *Quarterly Review*, p. 352.

We say if any person maintained that he did not feel a logical call even to give a consideration, in the first instance, to an hypothesis coming before him as this does, we should not be prepared, for our part, to contradict such a view. If the bare possibility of turning out true gave an hypothesis a claim upon our consideration, we should be living every hour of our lives in the greatest possible neglect of our duties as rational beings; inasmuch as many a theory comes before us daily, of which we cannot say that it is self-evidently false, and which we yet do not feel called upon to consider; and these theories too upon important subjects. To draw the line between hypotheses which have a claim upon our consideration and those which have not, appears to be an important part of practical logic, and one perhaps which, however intimately depending upon each man's common sense, might be brought, to a certain extent, under rule, as ordinary logic is.

To proceed. There being then now two contradictory hypotheses put forward by the Roman Church, or schools in her, each of which is weakened,—and especially the latter, as far as the *a priori* claim upon our attention goes, —by this contradiction; what we thirdly observe is, that on an actual examination and comparison of the two hypotheses, we do not see that the new one is more free from difficulties than the old one. Its difficulties indeed have another character, and lie in another quarter; but they are as real. The old one lies under a great disadvantage with respect to the department of later doctrine, for it has to assert of such doctrine that it was actually revealed to the Apostles, and communicated by them to the Church,—an assertion which is contradicted by all history. The new one, on the other hand, is able to take a natural view, as far as history is concerned, of the origin of later doctrine, and fairly to face and acknowledge the fact of its lateness; but it compensates for this advantage when it comes to the department of earlier; and the necessity of proving growth becomes as onerous to it as the necessity of proving antiquity was to the old one. It is now its turn to falsify history, to be unreal and artificial, to make much out of nothing. It has to convert explanation into growth, new expression into new substance; to raise the definition of a truth,—because it moulds it into more verbal accuracy,—into truth's rising manhood compared with former infancy, into the plant compared with the seed; it is to be obviously hollow and bombastic. Nor is this all which the new hypothesis has to do, for it has to explain away the loud, clear, unanimous assertion of the whole Nicene Church that its doctrine was not a development. It has *not* to see a whole body of evidence on this subject, which stares it in the face; or to put ingenious aspects upon such evidence when it does come across it; and make out that it is evidence for the very contrary of what it professes to be evidence for. Nor is this all, for arriving at last at the era of Revelation it has to face the awkward result of its own argument, that the fundamental doctrines of Christianity were not in existence then; and a whole Socinian view of early

Christian theology meets it. Such are the two hypotheses; and if the old has difficulties on the later ground, the new one has no less on the earlier.

To this new hypothesis, then, a member of the English Church has the same answer to make that he had to the old one. He has only to take his stand on the old ground. As a matter of evidence, he maintains that there is a distinction between these two classes of doctrines, between Nicene doctrines and Roman, between primitive and later; and whereas here are two hypotheses, which, in different ways,—one by making the whole an original revelation, another by making the whole a development, —attempt absolutely to identify the two, he says that, looking to facts and history, he cannot do so. He observes that each of these hypotheses falsifies fact according as they maintain their respective modes of identifying these two classes of doctrines; according as one makes Roman doctrine originally revealed, and the other Nicene doctrine subsequently developed. And he accordingly adheres to his ground which distinguishes between them, and, avoiding the unnatural, takes the natural part of both hypotheses. Upon this distinction of evidence, again, it necessarily follows that he makes a distinction in his belief as to the two respectively, and accepts the one class of doctrines as articles of faith, and not the other. And whereas each of these hypotheses presses the charge of illogicalness upon him for making this distinction in his belief, calling upon him to accept all or none, and denying a standing ground between Rome and infidelity, he naturally replies that, supposing he took that view of evidence which they take, it would be very illogical for him not to accept all; but that making a distinction in evidence, it would be very illogical for him not to make a distinction in belief. Again, if he is taken off the ground of evidence into the only other one, the *a priori* ground, he takes his stand upon the argument of analogy; and whereas his opponents argue *a priori* that there must be an Infallible Authority always at hand in the Church, and therefore that there is one, he does not allow the presumption, and therefore does not allow the fact built upon it. And here again he considers he is logical, for though if he allowed the necessity of a Standing Infallible Authority, it would be illogical for him to deny the fact; not allowing that necessity, it is not illogical for him to deny it. But the denial of the *a priori* ground leaves him perfectly at liberty with respect to other grounds. And, therefore, if an Authority presents itself to him claiming on other grounds to be an Infallible Authority, he may on consideration of such grounds accept it as such, and for the purpose for which there are grounds for thinking it infallible. And such an authority he admits in the Universal Church, accepting all those definitions of the faith which it has given, or may hereafter give. But this does not commit him to the decrees of the Roman Church, because he believes, upon evidence, the Roman Church not to be the Universal Church.

But after making the comparison between Mr. Newman's hypothesis and the old one, and deciding that the former has equal difficulties with the latter; the fourth and last observation we shall make is one which we should not like to omit on taking leave of the present subject.

For we must confess that, after the most attentive consideration which we have been able to devote to this Essay, viewing it as a whole, we are unable to discover that Mr. Newman has any regular hypothesis at all. We have supposed him indeed to have one, because he tells us he has one, and has given it a name and called it a Theory of Development. If a person comes forward with a theory, it is right to presume that he will fairly go upon it, and fairly make it his theory, by argumentative consistency, till we find the contrary. And therefore we suppose beforehand Mr. Newman will do so. But on coming to inspect his own argumentative relations to his own theory, we discover a looseness and inconsistency which seems to break up his theory as a theory altogether.

Mr. Newman's professed theory is indeed a simple one. All grows out of one seed. Christianity came into the world an elementary idea; and from that idea all that it subsequently gained of belief and organisation grew. So —first on the point of belief—here is a theory which commits the holder of it to a certain elementary exordium of Christian belief. Now, ask a Socinian what was the exordium out of which Nicene belief grew, and he will give you an exordium and a very simple one; he will say that Christians began with thinking our Lord a mere man, and that the idea of His nature then grew, till at the Nicene era it arrived at the idea of Godhead. This is an intelligible exordium of Christian doctrine, supposing Christian doctrine is really a growth. But going into the substance actual of Mr. Newman's theory, we cannot discover what exordium it makes, or if it makes any exordium at all, which can be said legitimately to answer to the assertion of growth. If the theory of development enlarges forward, it must diminish backward; if you say that such a doctrine is a growth, then you imply that it was a seed,—you must make it less as you trace it to its beginning, till you come to some ultimate atom which it originally was. Such should, according to the theory, be Mr. Newman's original "Christian idea," when he says "Christianity came into the world an idea," and develops all doctrine and institution whatever out of that idea. We naturally say, Here must be the original atom of

Christianity; and what is it? Your theory demands a real *bona fide* exordium: show it. But we make the demand in vain; we try in vain to find out what this original idea is; it nowhere appears; we can make out nothing of it. As soon as ever Mr. Newman's theory approaches its elementary region, it disappears, and we are left without any theory at all to make out the original idea of Christianity, to be as much or as little as we like. We may make it out to be full Nicene doctrine if we like; he does not prevent us: he scrupulously abstains from preventing us, and says he has only meant to say that there is not *evidence* for that doctrine having existed then, but that we may believe it did if we like. In fact, this exordium, on the elementary nature of which we have, in accordance with the theory, counted all along, turns out to be a regular dogmatic creation when we approach it. After all the assertion of the Nicene " Homoousion " being a growth, he actually allows us to assume "that there is a consensus in the ante-Nicene Church for the doctrines of our Lord's Consubstantiality and Co-eternity with the Almighty Father." He says, "There is not an article in the Athanasian Creed concerning the Incarnation which is not anticipated in the controversy with the Gnostics; there is no question which the Apollinarian or the Nestorian heresy raised which may not be decided in the words of Irenæus and Tertullian."[1] Why, then, he has taken us as far back as he can in the Christian history, and instead of an elementary idea we have a full dogmatic Nicene belief. Nor is the expedient by which he tries to make this dogmatic belief a seminal one again, and restore consistency to his theory after he has destroyed it, a very fortunate one. What does he say?—" Let us allow that the whole circle of doctrines of which our Lord is the

[1] Page 10.

subject was consistently and uniformly confessed by the Primitive Church, though not formally ratified by council. *But it surely is otherwise with the Catholic doctrine of the Trinity."* But what is the Catholic doctrine of the Trinity, but that the Father, Son, and Holy Ghost are each God, and all Three but one God? So, on Mr. Newman's view, the Godhead of the Father and the Godhead of the Son being acknowledged as the doctrine of the early Church, and the doctrine of the Trinity not acknowledged, we have for the belief of the early Church, Dualism. But surely Mr. Newman will not assert the absurdity that the creed of the Church was ever a Dualistic one. If the doctrine of the Trinity is defective in such circumstances, it can only be by the non-acknowledgment of the Divinity of the Holy Ghost, or by His oneness with the Consubstantial Father and Son not being acknowledged: in either case there is Dualism. Or if we have not Dualism, what is it that we have? And this is the elementary idea of Christianity which the theory comes to after all; —a full dogmatic belief as regards one doctrine, arbitrarily made to stop short of another, which it is quite absurd to suppose it should stop short of, if it existed at all. We naturally say, Let us have one thing or another: a seminal origin fairly agrees with your theory; a full dogmatic origin fairly disagrees with it. But here is neither a genuine dogmatic nor genuine seminal origin for Christianity, but an artificial, arbitrary, grotesque, unmeaning medium between the two. Such is the course which the theory takes when it has to make itself actual, and embody itself in fact.

So then we ask Mr. Newman what is his theory? For we confess we are unable to make it out. He calls upon the member of the English Church for his theory: What is his own? As far as he has explained it hitherto, it is a theory of growth without a seed,—development without an exordium. We come to what is his original idea of Christianity, and expect to find a philosophical elementarity in it; but we find nothing of the kind. The truth is, the author is afraid of his own theory as soon as ever it comes to its trying part; he finds it—it is not a grave word, but we use it gravely—beginning to pinch him, and he drops it. He then begins, as we said before, arbitrarily to balance, and qualify, and do what he has allowed none of his opponents to do in his whole Essay —explain. His theory goes on with an easy swing enough over its easy ground; but it comes to its difficult ground, and it begins to halt. Now is its turn to be lame, feeble, confused, and unnatural; to be as impotent as it is arbitrary, and expect to be believed for no kind of reason. The Theory of Development gets over the ground of later doctrines with a bold assurance; but when it comes to fundamental ones, it stops and wavers. It dares not face its own result. But surely it does not deserve the name of a theory if it does this. Any theory can get over its easy ground well: it is the difficult ground which tries it. Theories geological, chemical, astronomical, all go on successfully enough over their easy ground, and nobody thinks anything of them for doing it.

Again, with respect to the ecclesiastical question. We must confess ourselves unable to see how Mr. Newman can get a Church at all, much less a Papal Church, with its local centre and monarchy, out of an "idea." To quote his American opponent:—

"Mr. Newman evidently proceeds on the assumption that Christianity can be abstracted from the Church, and considered apart from the institution which concretes it, as if the Church were accidental and not essential in our holy religion. 'Christianity,' he says, 'though spoken of in prophecy as a kingdom, came into the world as an *idea* rather than an institution, and has had to wrap itself in clothing, and fit itself with armour of its own providing, and form the instruments and methods of its own prosperity and warfare.' . . . Its Divine Author, then, sent Christianity into the world a naked and unarmed idea. By its action on us, and ours on it, it gradually develops itself into an institution, which, feeble at first, as time and events roll on, strengthens and fortifies itself, now on this side and now on that; pushes deep its roots into the heart of humanity, sends out its branches, now in one direction and now in another, till at length it grows up and expands into that all-embracing authority, those profound and comprehensive dogmas, those pure and sublime precepts, and that rich and touching ritual, which together make up what we to-day call the Roman Catholic and Apostolical Church."—Brownson's *Quarterly*, pp. 354, 355.

All this is to come out of the "idea," but the writer adds—

"Ideas, not concreted, not instituted, are not potencies, are not active, but are really to us as if they were not. The ideal must become actual before it can be operative. If Christianity had come into the world as an idea, it would have left the world as it found it. Moreover, if you assume it to have come as an idea, and to have been developed only by the action of the human mind on it, the institutions with which it is subsequently clothed, the authorities established in its name, the dogmas imposed, the precepts enjoined, and the rites prescribed, are all really the products of the human mind; and instead of governing the mind, may be governed, modified, enlarged, or contracted by it at its pleasure. The Church would be divine only in the sense philosophy or civil government is divine."—*Ibid.* p. 356.

We do not see how Mr. Newman can escape this reasoning, so far as the point for which we have quoted it is concerned. He educes all Christianity whatever out of an "idea." Then how can that idea become ever more than an idea? It may expand indefinitely, but it must expand as an idea. It was that to begin with, and that it must continue. Whenever it becomes an "institution," something arises quite additional to the idea and the philosophical simplicity of the theory gives way. It may be said that an idea can clothe itself with such an institutional body in course of time; but an idea can do no such a thing. What is wanted is an external institution or society, membership of which is necessary on its own account; and not merely as expressing agreement in certain ideas. It is not enough for a man to think with the Church : he must be in it. An idea cannot develop into an institution such as this;—into a body of which membership is, as membership, sacramental. It may form an association certainly, such as the Platonic philosophy did; the virtue of belonging to which was no more than that of agreement in the philosophy. But this would be a school and not a Church. As soon as ever the principle of a Church comes in, and there is a body which it is necessary to belong to, as such, there is something which the "idea" does not give us. The ideal exordium which Mr. Newman assigns to Christianity must, unless added to from without, make Christianity continue to all time a philosophy and not a Church. This is what the German Rationalist educes from it; and it is the fair legitimate issue of it. But Mr. Newman brings it to another issue, and contrives to incorporate with it, as he works it up, the adventitious principle of a Church.

What we say then is, that Mr. Newman has no consistent theory whatever. He professes a theory, but admits, as circumstances require, into it, things which contradict it, and things which it does not account for. He has a theory on paper, and none in fact : he begins with philosophical simplicity, and ends in arbitrary mixture. His theory is an inclusive one simply, and not an explanatory one; embracing a great number of heterogeneous facts within one pale, but leaving them as far as ever from making one whole. We expected on opening this Essay to find Mr. Newman's theory for Roman facts, but we find nothing of the kind. What he does is to assert the old ultra-liberal theory of Christianity, and to join the Church of Rome; but he does not show—what it was the object of his Essay to show—the connection of the two,—the accordance of his theory with his act. And after professing to give us an hypothesis which accounts for and fits on to the facts of Ecclesiastical History, he ends with having an hypothesis indeed, and having facts, but having his hypothesis and his facts in separation.

May, 1878.

A CLASSIFIED CATALOGUE OF BOOKS

Selected from the Publications of

MESSRS. RIVINGTON

WATERLOO PLACE, LONDON

MAGDALEN STREET, OXFORD; TRINITY STREET, CAMBRIDGE

Contents.

	PAGE		PAGE
1. THE PRAYER BOOK AND THE CHURCH SERVICE	1	6. SERMONS	47
		7. RELIGIOUS EDUCATION	65
2. THE HOLY SCRIPTURES	7	8. ALLEGORIES AND TALES	70
3. DEVOTIONAL WORKS	17, 88	9. HISTORY AND BIOGRAPHY	73
4. PARISH WORK	32	10. POETRY AND MISCELLANEOUS	84
5. THE CHURCH AND DOCTRINE	37	11. INDEX	89

EDUCATIONAL WORKS—*see* RIVINGTON'S SCHOOL CATALOGUE.

---

1. The Prayer Book and the Church Service.

The Compendious Edition of the Annotated Book of Common Prayer, forming a concise Commentary on the Devotional System of the Church of England. Edited by the Rev. JOHN HENRY BLUNT, M.A., F.S.A., Editor of the "Dictionary of Sects and Heresies," &c., &c. Crown 8vo. 10s. 6d.; in half-morocco, 16s.; or in morocco limp, 17s. 6d.

[B—250]   Waterloo Place, London

The Annotated Book of Common

Prayer; being an Historical, Ritual, and Theological Commentary on the Devotional System of the Church of England. Edited by the Rev. JOHN HENRY BLUNT, M.A., F.S.A., Editor of the "Dictionary of Sects and Heresies," &c., &c. Seventh Edition. Imperial 8vo. 36s.; or in half-morocco, 48s.

[This large edition contains the Latin and Greek originals, together with technical Ritual Annotations, Marginal References, &c., which are necessarily omitted for want of room in the "Compendious Edition."]

"*Whether as, historically, shewing how the Prayer Book came to be what it is, or, ritually, how it designs itself to be rendered from word into act, or, theologically, as exhibiting the relation between doctrine and worship on which it is framed, the book amasses a world of information carefully digested, and errs commonly, if at all, on the side of excess.*"—GUARDIAN.

"*The most complete and compendious Commentary on the English Prayer Book ever yet published. Almost everything that has been written by all the best liturgical and historical authorities ancient and modern (of which a formidable list is prefixed to the work) is quoted, or referred to, or compressed into the notes illustrative of the several subjects.*"—JOHN BULL.

"*The book is a mine of information and research—able to give an answer almost on anything we wish to know about our present Prayer Book, its antecedents and originals—and ought to be in the library of every intelligent Churchman. Nothing like it has as yet been seen.*"—CHURCH REVIEW.

Liber Precum Publicarum Ecclesiæ

Anglicanæ. A GULIELMO BRIGHT, S.T.P., Ædis Christi apud Oxon. Canonico, et PETRO GOLDSMITH MEDD, A.M., Collegii Universitatis apud Oxon. Socio Seniore, Latine redditus. Editio tertia, cum Appendice. [In hac editione continentur Versiones Latinæ—1. Libri Precum Publicarum Ecclesiæ Anglicanæ; 2. Liturgiæ Primæ Reformatæ; 3. Liturgiæ Scoticanæ; 4. Liturgiæ Americanæ.] With Rubrics in Red. Small 8vo. 7s. 6d.

The First Book of Common Prayer of

Edward VI. and the Ordinal of 1549. Together with the Order of the Communion, 1548. Reprinted entire. Edited by the Rev. HENRY BASKERVILLE WALTON, M.A., late Fellow and Tutor of Merton College; with Introduction by the Rev. PETER GOLDSMITH MEDD, M.A., Rector of North Cerney; Canon of St. Albans; late Senior Fellow of University College, Oxford; and Rector of Barnes. Small 8vo. 6s.

The Prayer Book Interleaved; with

Historical Illustrations and Explanatory Notes arranged parallel to the Text. By W. M. CAMPION, D.D., and W. J. BEAMONT, M.A. With a Preface by the LORD BISHOP OF WINCHESTER. Ninth Edition. Small 8vo. 7s. 6d.

An excellent publication, combining a portable Prayer Book with the history of the text and explanatory notes."—SPECTATOR.
"This book is of the greatest use for spreading an intelligent knowledge of the English Prayer Book, and we heartily wish it a large and continuous circulation."—CHURCH REVIEW.

"The work may be commended as a very convenient manual for all who are interested to some extent in liturgical studies, but who have not time or the means for original research. It would also be most useful to examining chaplains, as a text-book for Holy Orders."—CHURCH TIMES.

The Book of Common Prayer, and

Administration of the Sacraments and other Rites and Ceremonies of the Church, according to the use of THE PROTESTANT EPISCOPAL CHURCH in the UNITED STATES of AMERICA, together with the Psalter, or Psalms of David. Royal 32mo. French roan limp, 2s. 6d.

An Illuminated Edition of the Book

of Common Prayer, printed in Red and Black, on fine toned paper; with Borders and Titles designed after the manner of the 14th Century. By R. R. HOLMES, F.S.A., and engraved by O. JEWITT. Crown 8vo. 16s.

A Book of Litanies, Metrical and Prose.

With an Evening Service. Edited by the Compiler of "The Treasury of Devotion." And accompanying Music arranged under the Musical Editorship of W. S. HOYTE, Organist and Director of the Choir at All Saints', Margaret Street, London. Crown 4to. 7s. 6d.

Also may be had, an Edition of the Words, 32mo., 6d.; or in paper cover, 4d. The Metrical Litanies separately, 32mo., 5d.; or in paper cover, 3d. The Prose Litanies, with an Evening Service, separately, in paper cover, 3d. An Evening Service separately, 1d.

---

and at Oxford and Cambridge

A Key to the Knowledge and Use of

the Book of Common Prayer. By the Rev. JOHN HENRY BLUNT, M.A., F.S.A., Editor of the "Annotated Book of Common Prayer," &c. New Edition. Small 8vo. 2s. 6d. Also a Cheap Edition, 1s. 6d.

Forming a Volume of "Keys to Christian Knowledge."

"*Impossible to praise too highly. It is the best short explanation of our offices that we know of, and would be invaluable for the use of candidates for confirmation in the higher classes.*"—JOHN BULL.

"*To us it appears that Mr. Blunt has succeeded very well. All necessary information seems to be included, and the arrangement is excellent.*"—LITERARY CHURCHMAN.

"*A very valuable and practical manual, full of information. It deserves high commendation.*"—CHURCHMAN.

Sacraments and Sacramental Ordi-

nances of the Church; being a Plain Exposition of their History, Meaning, and Effects. By the Rev. JOHN HENRY BLUNT, M.A., F.S.A., Editor of the "Annotated Book of Common Prayer," &c. Small 8vo. 4s. 6d.

A Commentary, Expository and De-

votional, on the Order of the Administration of the Lord's Supper, according to the Use of the Church of England; to which is added, an Appendix on Fasting Communion, Non-communicating Attendance, Auricular Confession, the Doctrine of Sacrifice, and the Eucharistic Sacrifice. By EDWARD MEYRICK GOULBURN, D.D., Dean of Norwich. Sixth Edition. Small 8vo. 6s.

Also a Cheap Edition, uniform with "Thoughts on Personal Religion," and "The Pursuit of Holiness." 3s. 6d.

The Athanasian Creed: an Examina-

tion of Recent Theories respecting its Date and Origin. With a Postscript referring to Professor Swainson's Account of its Growth and Reception, which is contained in his Work entitled "The Nicene and Apostles' Creeds, their Literary History." By G. D. W. OMMANNEY, M.A., Vicar of Draycot, Somerset. Crown 8vo. 8s. 6d.

Waterloo Place, London

Notitia Eucharistica; a Commentary, Explanatory, Doctrinal, and Historical, on the Order for the Administration of the Lord's Supper, or Holy Communion, according to the use of the Church of England. With an Appendix on the Office for the Communion of the Sick. By the Rev. W. E. SCUDAMORE, M.A., Rector of Ditchingham, and formerly Fellow of St. John's College, Cambridge. Second Edition, revised and enlarged. 8vo. 32s.

The Athanasian Origin of the Athanasian Creed. By J. S. BREWER, M.A., Preacher at the Rolls, and Honorary Fellow of Queen's College, Oxford. Crown 8vo. 3s. 6d.

The "Damnatory Clauses" of the Athanasian Creed rationally explained in a Letter to the Right Hon. W. E. GLADSTONE, M.P. By the Rev. MALCOLM MACCOLL, M.A., Rector of St. George, Botolph Lane. Crown 8vo. 6s.

Comment upon the Collects appointed to be used in the Church of England on Sundays and Holy Days throughout the Year. By JOHN JAMES, D.D., sometime Canon of Peterborough. New Edition. Small 8vo. 3s. 6d. Also a Fine Edition, on Toned Paper. Crown 8vo. 5s.

A Commentary, Practical and Exegetical, on the Lord's Prayer. By the Rev. W. DENTON, M.A. Small 8vo. 5s.

The Psalter, or Psalms of David. (The Prayer Book Version.) Printed in red and black. Small 8vo. 2s. 6d.

---

and at Oxford and Cambridge

The New Mitre Hymnal, containing New

Music by Sir JOHN GOSS, Sir GEORGE ELVEY, Dr. STAINER, HENRY GADSBY, Esq., J. BAPTISTE CALKIN, Esq., BERTHOLD TOURS, Esq., JAMES LANGRAN, Esq., and other eminent Composers; together with Scandinavian Tunes now first introduced into this Country. Royal 8vo. 5s.

An Edition of the Words without the Music may also be had. 18mo., cloth limp, 1s.; or in cloth boards, extra gilt, 1s. 6d.

[A large reduction to purchasers of quantities.]

Psalms and Hymns adapted to the

Services of the Church of England; with a Supplement of additional Hymns, and Indices. By the Rev. W. J. HALL, M.A. 8vo., 5s. 6d.; 18mo., 3s.; 24mo., 1s. 6d.; cloth limp, 1s. 3d.; 32mo., 1s.; cloth limp, 8d.

Selection of Psalms and Hymns; with

Accompanying Tunes selected and arranged by JOHN FOSTER, of Her Majesty's Chapels Royal. By the Rev. W. J. HALL, M.A. Crown 8vo. 2s. 6d. The Tunes only, 1s. Also an Edition of the Tunes for the Organ. 7s. 6d.

Waterloo Place, London

2. The Holy Scriptures.

The Greek Testament. With a Critically
Revised Text; a Digest of Various Readings; Marginal References to Verbal and Idiomatic Usage; Prolegomena; and a Critical and Exegetical Commentary. For the use of Theological Students and Ministers. By HENRY ALFORD, D.D., late Dean of Canterbury. New Edition. 4 Volumes. 8vo. 102s.

The Volumes are sold separately, as follows:—

Vol. I.—The Four Gospels. 28s.
Vol. II.—Acts to 2 Corinthians. 24s.
Vol. III.—Galatians to Philemon. 18s.
Vol. IV.—Hebrews to Revelation. 32s.

The New Testament for English
Readers: containing the Authorized Version, with a revised English Text; Marginal References; and a Critical and Explanatory Commentary. By HENRY ALFORD, D.D., late Dean of Canterbury. New Edition. 2 Volumes, or 4 Parts. 8vo. 54s. 6d.

The Volumes are sold separately, as follows:—

Vol. 1, Part I.—The Three first Gospels. 12s.
Vol. 1, Part II.—St. John and the Acts. 10s. 6d.
Vol. 2, Part I.—The Epistles of St. Paul. 16s.
Vol. 2, Part II.—Hebrews to Revelation. 16s.

and at Oxford and Cambridge

The Holy Bible; with Notes and Introductions.
By CHR. WORDSWORTH, D.D., Bishop of Lincoln. New Edition. 6 Vols. Imperial 8vo. 120s.

The Volumes are sold separately, as follows :—
Vol. I.—The Pentateuch. 25s.
Vol. II.—Joshua to Samuel. 15s.
Vol. III.—Kings to Esther. 15s.
Vol. IV.—Job to Song of Solomon. 25s.
Vol. V.—Isaiah to Ezekiel. 25s.
Vol. VI.—Daniel, Minor Prophets, and Index. 15s.

The New Testament of our Lord and Saviour
JESUS CHRIST, in the original Greek; with Notes, Introductions, and Indices. By CHR. WORDSWORTH, D.D., Bishop of Lincoln. New Edition. 2 Vols. Imperial 8vo. 60s.

The Volumes are sold separately, as follows :—
Vol. I.—Gospels and Acts. 23s.
Vol. II.—Epistles, Apocalypse, and Index. 37s.

Notes on the Greek Testament.
The Gospel according to S. Luke. By the Rev. ARTHUR CARR, M.A., Assistant-Master at Wellington College, late Fellow of Oriel College, Oxford. Crown 8vo. 6s.

"*It is a most useful and scholarly work, well adapted to the higher classes of public schools and the students at our colleges.*"—STANDARD.

"*The most useful and scholarly commentary, in a short compass, on the Gospel of S. Luke, in Greek, that has hitherto appeared.*"—HOUR.

"*The notes are brief, scholarly, and based on the best authorities. . . . The introduction will be found to be of especial value to the young student, informing him, as it does, of the Greek manuscripts which form the basis of the Greek text, and giving a most thorough and comprehensive account of S. Luke's life and the style of his writing.*"—SCHOOL BOARD CHRONICLE.

"*Grammatical peculiarities are brought into the foreground, and contrasted with classical usages; questions of various reading are carefully noted; historical and archæological information is supplied plentifully when needful to illustrate a passage; the drift of a narrative or discourse and the sequence of the thoughts is traced out and carefully analysed; in short, the Gospel is treated as we treat a classical author, and the student is here supplied with an* apparatus criticus *superior in kind and completeness to any we have ever seen afforded to him for the purpose elsewhere. A very clever and taking book.*"—LITERARY CHURCHMAN.

"*Admirably adapted for the use of those who begin the study of the New Testament in the original after having acquired a fair acquaintance with classical Greek.*"—SCOTSMAN.

The Psalms. Translated from the Hebrew.
With Notes, chiefly Exegetical. By WILLIAM KAY, D.D., Rector of Great Leghs, late Principal of Bishop's College, Calcutta. Third Edition. 8vo. 12s. 6d.

"*Like a sound Churchman, he reverences Scripture, upholding its authority against sceptics; and he does not denounce such as differ from him in opinion with a dogmatism unhappily too common at the present day. Hence, readers will be disposed to consider his conclusions worthy of attention; or perhaps to adopt them without inquiry. It is superfluous to say that the translation is better and more accurate on the whole than our received one, or that it often reproduces the sense of the original happily.*"—ATHENÆUM.

"*Dr. Kay has profound reverence for Divine truth, and exhibits considerable reading, with the power to make use of it.*"—BRITISH QUARTERLY REVIEW.

"*The execution of the work is careful and scholarly.*"—UNION REVIEW.

"*To mention the name of Dr. Kay is enough to secure respectful attention to his new translation of the Psalms. It is enriched with exegetical notes containing a wealth of sound learning, closely occasionally, perhaps too closely condensed. Good care is taken of the student not learned in Hebrew; we hope the Doctor's example will prevent any abuse of this consideration, and stimulate those who profit by it to follow him into the very text of the ancient Revelation.*"—JOHN BULL.

Ecclesiastes: the Authorized Version, with
a running Commentary and Paraphrase. By the Rev. THOS. PELHAM DALE, M.A., Rector of St. Vedast with St. Michael City of London, and late Fellow of Sidney Sussex College, Cambridge. 8vo. 7s. 6d.

Daniel the Prophet: Nine Lectures
delivered in the Divinity School of the University of Oxford. With copious Notes. By the Rev. E. B. PUSEY, D.D., Regius Professor of Hebrew, Canon of Christ Church, Oxford. Third Edition. 8vo. 10s. 6d.

Commentary on the Minor Prophets;
with Introductions to the several Books. By the Rev. E. B. PUSEY, D.D., Regius Professor of Hebrew, Canon of Christ Church, Oxford. 4to. 31s. 6d.

Parts I., II., III., IV., V., 5s. each. Part VI., 6s.

and at Oxford and Cambridge

Ruling Ideas in Early Ages and their
Relation to Old Testament Faith. Lectures delivered to Graduates of the University of Oxford. By J. B. MOZLEY, D.D., Regius Professor of Divinity in the University of Oxford, and Canon of Christ Church. Second Edition. 8vo. 10s. 6d.

"*Has all the same marks of a powerful and original mind which we observed in the volume of University Sermons. Indeed, as a continuous study of the rudimentary conditions of human thought, even as developed under the immediate guidance of a Divine Teacher, this volume has a higher and less fragmentary intellectual interest than the last.*"—SPECTATOR.

A Companion to the Old Testament;
being a Plain Commentary on Scripture History, down to the Birth of our Lord. Small 8vo. 3s. 6d.

Also in 2 Parts:

Part I.—The Creation of the World to the Reign of Saul.
Part II.—The Reign of Saul to the Birth of Our Lord.

Small 8vo. 2s. each.

[Especially adapted for use in Training Colleges and Schools.]

"*A very compact summary of the Old Testament narrative, put together so as to explain the connection and bearing of its contents, and written in a very good tone; with a final chapter on the history of the Jews between the Old and New Testaments. It will be found very useful for its purpose. It does not confine itself to merely chronological difficulties, but comments briefly upon the religious bearing of the text also.*"—GUARDIAN.

"*A most admirable Companion to the Old Testament, being far the most concise yet complete commentary on Old Testament history with which we have met. Here are combined orthodoxy and learning, an intelligent and at the same time interesting summary of the leading facts of the sacred story. It should be a text-book in every school, and its value is immensely enhanced by the copious and complete index.*"—JOHN BULL.

"*This will be found a very valuable aid to the right understanding of the Bible. It throws the whole Scripture narrative into one from the creation downwards, the author thus condensing Prideaux, Shuckford, and Russell, and in the most reverential manner bringing to his aid the writings of all modern annotators and chronologists. The book is one that should have a wide circulation amongst teachers and students of all denominations.*"—BOOKSELLER.

"*The handbook before us is so full and satisfactory, considering its compass, and sets forth the history of the old covenant with such conscientious minuteness, that it cannot fail to prove a godsend to candidates for examination in the Rudimenta Religionis as well as in the corresponding school at Cambridge. . . . Enough has been said to express our value of this useful work, which cannot fail to win its way into our schools, colleges, and universities.*"—ENGLISH CHURCHMAN.

Waterloo Place, London

A Key to the Narrative of the Four
Gospels. By the Rev. JOHN PILKINGTON NORRIS, B.D., Canon of Bristol, and Examining Chaplain to the Bishop of Manchester. New Edition. Small 8vo. 2s. 6d. Also a Cheap Edition, 1s. 6d.

Forming a Volume of "Keys to Christian Knowledge."

"*This is very much the best book of its kind we have seen. The only fault is its shortness, which prevents its going into the details which would support and illustrate its statements, and which, in the process of illustrating them, would fix them upon the minds and memories of its readers. It is, however, a great improvement upon any book of its kind we know. It bears all the marks of being the condensed work of a real scholar, and of a divine too. The bulk of the book is taken up with a 'Life of Christ,' compiled from the Four Gospels, so as to exhibit its steps and stages and salient points.*"—LITERARY CHURCHMAN.

"*This book is no ordinary compendium, no mere 'cram-book;' still less is it an ordinary reading-book for schools; but the schoolmaster, the Sunday-school teacher, and the seeker after a comprehensive knowledge of Divine truth will find it worthy of its name. Canon Norris writes simply, reverently, without great display of learning, giving the result of much careful study in a short compass, and adorning the subject by the tenderness and honesty with which he treats it. We hope that this little book will have a very wide circulation, and that it will be studied; and we can promise that those who take it up will not readily put it down again.*"—RECORD.

"*This is a golden little volume. . . . Its design is exceedingly modest. Canon Norris writes primarily to help 'younger students' in studying the Gospels. But this unpretending volume is one which all students may study with advantage. It is an admirable manual for those who take Bible Classes through the Gospels. Closely sifted in style, so that all is clear and weighty; full of unostentatious learning, and pregnant with suggestion; deeply reverent in spirit, and altogether Evangelical in spirit; Canon Norris's book supplies a real want, and ought to be welcomed by all earnest and devout students of the Holy Gospels.*"—LONDON QUARTERLY REVIEW.

A Key to the Narrative of the Acts of
the Apostles. By the Rev. JOHN PILKINGTON NORRIS, B.D., Canon of Bristol, and Examining Chaplain to the Bishop of Manchester. New Edition. Small 8vo. 2s. 6d. Also a Cheap Edition, 1s. 6d.

Forming a Volume of "Keys to Christian Knowledge."

"*The book is one which we can heartily recommend.*"—SPECTATOR.

"*Few books have ever given us more unmixed pleasure than this.*"—LITERARY CHURCHMAN.

"*This is a sequel to Canon Norris's 'Key to the Gospels,' which was published two years ago, and which has become a general favourite with those who wish to grasp the leading features of the life and work of Christ. The sketch of the Acts of the Apostles is done in the same style; there is the same reverent spirit and quiet enthusiasm running through it, and the same instinct for seizing the leading points in the narrative.*"—RECORD.

and at Oxford and Cambridge

A Devotional Commentary on the

Gospel Narrative. By the Rev. ISAAC WILLIAMS, B.D., formerly Fellow of Trinity College, Oxford. New Edition. 8 Vols. Crown 8vo. 5s. each. Sold separately. Or the Eight Volumes may be had in a Box, 45s.

THOUGHTS ON THE STUDY OF THE HOLY GOSPELS.

Characteristic Differences in the Four Gospels—Our Lord's Manifestations of Himself—The Rule of Scriptural Interpretation furnished by our Lord—Analogies of the Gospel—Mention of Angels in the Gospels—Places of our Lord's Abode and Ministry—Our Lord's mode of dealing with His Apostles—Conclusion.

A HARMONY OF THE FOUR EVANGELISTS.

Our Lord's Nativity—Our Lord's Ministry (second year)—Our Lord's Ministry (third year)—The Holy Week—Our Lord's Passion—Our Lord's Resurrection.

OUR LORD'S NATIVITY.

The Birth at Bethlehem—The Baptism in Jordan—The First Passover.

OUR LORD'S MINISTRY (Second Year).

The Second Passover—Christ with the Twelve—The Twelve sent forth.

OUR LORD'S MINISTRY (Third Year).

Teaching in Galilee—Teaching at Jerusalem—Last Journey from Galilee to Jerusalem.

THE HOLY WEEK.

The Approach to Jerusalem—The Teaching in the Temple—The Discourse on the Mount of Olives—The Last Supper.

OUR LORD'S PASSION.

The Hour of Darkness—The Agony—The Apprehension—The Condemnation—The Day of Sorrows—The Hall of Judgment—The Crucifixion—The Sepulture.

OUR LORD'S RESURRECTION.

The Day of Days—The Grave Visited—Christ appearing—The going to Emmaus—The Forty Days—The Apostles assembled—The Lake in Galilee—The Mountain in Galilee—The Return from Galilee.

"*There is not a better companion to be found for the season than the beautiful 'Devotional Commentary on the Gospel Narrative,' by the Rev. Isaac Williams. A rich mine for devotional and theological study.*"—GUARDIAN.

"*So infinite are the depths and so innumerable the beauties of Scripture, and more particularly of the Gospels, that there is some difficulty in describing the manifold excellences of Williams' exquisite Commentary. Deriving its profound appreciation of Scripture from the writings of the early Fathers, it is only what every student knows must be true to say, that it extracts a whole wealth of meaning from each sentence, each apparently faint allusion, each word in the text.*"—CHURCH REVIEW.

"*Stands absolutely alone in our English literature; there is, we should say, no chance of its being superseded by any better book of its kind; and its merits are of the very highest order.*"—LITERARY CHURCHMAN.

Waterloo Place, London

WILLIAMS' DEVOTIONAL COMMENTARY—*Continued.*

"This is, in the truest sense of the word, a 'Devotional Commentary' on the Gospel narrative, opening out everywhere, as it does, the spiritual beauties and blessedness of the Divine message; but it is something more than this, it meets difficulties almost by anticipation, and throws the light of learning over some of the very darkest passages in the New Testament."—ROCK.

"It would be difficult to select a more useful present, at a small cost, than this series would be to a young man on his first entering into Holy Orders, and many, no doubt, will avail themselves of the republication of these useful volumes for this purpose. There is an abundance of sermon material to be drawn from any one of them."— CHURCH TIMES.

Female Characters of Holy Scripture.
A Series of Sermons. By the Rev. ISAAC WILLIAMS, B.D., formerly Fellow of Trinity College, Oxford. New Edition. Crown 8vo. 5s.

CONTENTS.

Eve—Sarah—Lot's Wife—Rebekah—Leah and Rachel—Miriam—Rahab—Deborah—Ruth—Hannah—The Witch of Endor—Bathsheba—Rizpah—The Queen of Sheba—The Widow of Zarephath—Jezebel—The Shunammite—Esther—Elizabeth—Anna—The Woman of Samaria—Joanna—The Woman with the Issue of Blood—The Woman of Canaan—Martha—Mary—Salome—The Wife of Pilate—Dorcas—The Blessed Virgin.

The Characters of the Old Testament.
A Series of Sermons. By the Rev. ISAAC WILLIAMS, B.D., formerly Fellow of Trinity College, Oxford. New Edition. Crown 8vo. 5s.

CONTENTS.

Adam—Abel and Cain—Noah—Abraham—Lot—Jacob and Esau—Joseph—Moses—Aaron—Pharaoh—Korah, Dathan, and Abiram—Balaam—Joshua—Samson—Samuel—Saul—David—Solomon—Elijah—Ahab—Elisha—Hezekiah—Josiah—Jeremiah—Ezekiel—Daniel—Joel—Job—Isaiah—The Antichrist.

The Apocalypse. With Notes and Reflections.
By the Rev ISAAC WILLIAMS, B.D., formerly Fellow of Trinity College, Oxford. New Edition. Crown 8vo. 5s.

𝔄𝔫𝔡 𝔞𝔱 𝔒𝔵𝔣𝔬𝔯𝔡 𝔞𝔫𝔡 ℭ𝔞𝔪𝔟𝔯𝔦𝔡𝔤𝔢

Beginning of the Book of Genesis,
with Notes and Reflections. By the Rev. ISAAC WILLIAMS, B.D., formerly Fellow of Trinity College, Oxford. Small 8vo. 7s. 6d.

Ecclesiastes for English Readers. The
Book called by the Jews Koheleth. Newly translated, with Introduction, Analysis, and Notes. By the Rev. W. H. B. PROBY, M.A., formerly Tyrwhitt Hebrew Scholar in the University of Cambridge. 8vo. 4s. 6d.

The Ten Canticles of the Old Testa-
ment Canon, namely, the Songs of Moses (First and Second), Deborah, Hannah, Isaiah (First, Second, and Third), Hezekiah, Jonah, and Habakkuk. Newly translated, with Notes and Remarks on their Drift and Use. By the Rev. W. H. B. PROBY, M.A., formerly Tyrwhitt Hebrew Scholar in the University of Cambridge. 8vo. 5s.

Genesis. With Notes. By the Rev. G. V.
GARLAND, M.A., late Vicar of Aslacton, Norfolk. [The Hebrew Text, with Literal Translation.] Parts I. to XXXIV. 8vo. In paper cover, 6d. each.

Devotional Commentary on the Gospel
according to St. Matthew. Translated from the French of Quesnel. Crown 8vo. 7s. 6d.

The Acts of the Deacons; being a
Commentary, Critical and Practical, upon the Notices of St. Stephen and St. Philip the Evangelist, contained in the Acts of the Apostles. By EDWARD MEYRICK GOULBURN, D.D., Dean of Norwich. Second Edition. Small 8vo. 6s.

The Holy Scriptures

The Mystery of Christ: being an Examination of the Doctrine contained in the First Three Chapters of the Epistle of Paul the Apostle to the Ephesians. By GEORGE STAUNTON BARROW, M.A., Vicar of Stowmarket. Crown 8vo. 7s. 6d.

A Key to the Knowledge and Use of the Holy Bible. By the Rev. JOHN HENRY BLUNT, M.A., F.S.A., Editor of the "Dictionary of Theology," &c. &c. New Edition. Small 8vo. 2s. 6d. Also a Cheap Edition, 1s. 6d. Forming a Volume of "Keys to Christian Knowledge."

"*Another of Mr. Blunt's useful and workmanlike compilations, which will be most acceptable as a household book, or in schools and colleges. It is a capital book too for schoolmasters and pupil teachers. Its subject is arranged under the heads of—I. The Literary History of the Bible. II. Old Testament Writers and Writings. III. New Testament ditto. IV. Revelation and Inspiration. V. Objects of the Bible. VI. Interpretation of ditto. VII. The Bible a guide to Faith. VIII. The Apocrypha. IX. The Apocryphal Books associated with the New Testament. Lastly, there is a serviceable appendix of peculiar Bible words and their meanings.*"—LITERARY CHURCHMAN.

"*We have much pleasure in recommending a capital handbook by the learned Editor of 'The Annotated Book of Common Prayer.'*"—CHURCH TIMES.

"*Merits commendation, for the lucid and orderly arrangement in which it presents a considerable amount of valuable and interesting matter.*"—RECORD.

The Inspiration of Holy Scripture, its Nature and Proof. Eight Discourses preached before the University of Dublin. By WILLIAM LEE, D.D., Archdeacon of Dublin. Fourth Edition. 8vo. 15s.

On the Inspiration of the Bible. Five Lectures delivered at Westminster Abbey. By CHR. WORDSWORTH, D.D., Bishop of Lincoln. Eighth Edition. Small 8vo. 1s. 6d., or in paper cover, 1s.

Syntax and Synonyms of the Greek Testament. By the Rev. WILLIAM WEBSTER, M.A., late Fellow of Queen's College, Cambridge. 8vo. 9s.

and at Oxford and Cambridge

Bible Readings for Family Prayer.
By the Rev. W. H. RIDLEY, M.A., Rector of Hambleden. Crown 8vo.
   Old Testament—Genesis and Exodus. 2s.
   The Four Gospels, 3s. 6d.
      St. Matthew and St. Mark. 2s.
      St. Luke and St. John. 2s.
   The Acts of the Apostles, 2s.

A Complete Concordance to the Old
and the New Testament; or, a Dictionary, and Alphabetical Index to the Bible, in two Parts. To which is added, a Concordance to the Apocrypha. By ALEXANDER CRUDEN, M.A. With a Life of the Author, by ALEXANDER CHALMERS, F.S.A., and a Portrait. Fourteenth Edition. 4to. 21s.

Waterloo Place, London

3. Devotional Works

Library of Spiritual Works for English Catholics.

Elegantly printed with red borders, on extra superfine toned paper. Small 8vo. 5s. each.

OF THE IMITATION OF CHRIST. In 4 Books. By THOMAS À KEMPIS. A New Translation.

THE CHRISTIAN YEAR: Thoughts in Verse for the Sundays and Holydays throughout the Year.

THE SPIRITUAL COMBAT; together with the Supplement and the Path of Paradise. By LAURENCE SCUPOLI. A New Translation.

THE DEVOUT LIFE. By SAINT FRANCIS OF SALES, Bishop and Prince of Geneva. A New Translation.

The Volumes can also be had in the following extra bindings:—

	s.	d.
Morocco, stiff or limp	9	0
Morocco, thick bevelled sides, Old Style	12	0
Morocco, limp, with flap edges	11	6
Morocco, best, stiff or limp	16	0
Morocco, best, thick bevelled sides, Old Style	19	6
Russia, limp	11	6
Russia, limp, with flap edges	13	6

Most of the volumes in the above styles may be had illustrated with a beautiful selection of Photographs from Fra Angelico, 4s. 6d. extra.

Cheap Editions, 32mo, *cloth limp*, 6d. *each, or cloth extra, red edges*, 1s. *each.*

Of the Imitation of Christ.	The Hidden Life of the Soul.
The Spiritual Combat.	Spiritual Letters of Saint Francis of Sales.
The Christian Year.	

[Other Volumes are in preparation.]

and at Oxford and Cambridge

The Child Samuel. A Practical and
Devotional Commentary on the Birth and Childhood of the Prophet Samuel, as recorded in 1 Sam. i., ii. 1-27, iii. Designed as a Help to Meditation on the Holy Scriptures for Children and Young Persons. By EDWARD MEYRICK GOULBURN, D.D., Dean of Norwich. Small 8vo. 5s.

The Gospel of the Childhood: a Practical
and Devotional Commentary on the Single Incident of our Blessed Lord's Childhood (St. Luke ii. 41 to the end); designed as a Help to Meditation on the Holy Scriptures, for Children and Young Persons. By EDWARD MEYRICK GOULBUEN, D.D., Dean of Norwich. Second Edition. Square crown 8vo. 5s.

Thoughts on Personal Religion; being
a Treatise on the Christian Life in its Two Chief Elements, Devotion and Practice. By EDWARD MEYRICK GOULBURN, D.D., Dean of Norwich. New Edition. Small 8vo. 6s. 6d. Also a Cheap Edition, 3s. 6d. Presentation Edition, elegantly printed on Toned Paper. Two vols. Small 8vo. 10s. 6d.

The Pursuit of Holiness: a Sequel to
"Thoughts on Personal Religion," intended to carry the Reader somewhat farther onward in the Spiritual Life. By EDWARD MEYRICK GOULBURN, D.D. Fourth Edition. Small 8vo. 5s. Also a Cheap Edition, 3s. 6d.

Short Devotional Forms, for Morning,
Night, and Midnight, and for the Third, Sixth, Ninth Hours and Eventide of each Day of the Week. Arranged to meet the Exigencies of a Busy Life. By EDWARD MEYRICK GOULBURN, D.D. Fourth Edition. 32mo. 1s. 6d.

Devotional Works

The Star of Childhood: a First Book of Prayers and Instruction for Children. Compiled by a Priest. Edited by the Rev. T. T. CARTER, M.A., Rector of Clewer, Berks. With Illustrations reduced from Engravings by FRA ANGELICO. Third Edition. Square 16mo. 2s. 6d.

The Way of Life: a Book of Prayers and Instruction for the Young at School, with a Preparation for Confirmation. Compiled by a Priest. Edited by the Rev. T. T. CARTER, M.A. Second Edition. 18mo. 1s. 6d.

The Path of Holiness: a First Book of Prayers, with the Service of the Holy Communion, for the Young. Compiled by a Priest. Edited by the Rev. T. T. CARTER, M.A. With Illustrations. Third Edition. Crown 16mo. 1s. 6d.; cloth limp, 1s.

The Treasury of Devotion: a Manual of Prayers for General and Daily Use. Compiled by a Priest. Edited by the Rev. T. T. CARTER, M.A. New Edition, in Large Type. Crown 8vo. 5s.; in morocco limp, 10s. 6d.

A Smaller Edition. 18mo. 2s. 6d.; limp cloth, 2s., or bound with the Book of Common Prayer, 3s. 6d.

The Guide to Heaven: a Book of Prayers for every Want. (For the Working Classes.) Compiled by a Priest. Edited by the Rev. T. T. CARTER, M.A. New Edition. 18mo. 1s. 6d.; cloth limp, 1s.

An Edition in Large Type. Crown 8vo. 1s. 6d.; cloth limp, 1s.

Meditations on the Life and Mysteries of Our Lord and Saviour Jesus Christ. From the French. By the Compiler of "The Treasury of Devotion." Edited by the Rev. T. T. CARTER, M.A. Crown 8vo.

Vol. I.—The Hidden Life of Our Lord. 3s. 6d.
Vol. II.—The Public Life of Our Lord. 2 Parts. 5s. each.
Vol. III.—The Suffering Life and the Glorified Life of Our Lord. 3s. 6d.

and at Oxford and Cambridge

Prayers and Meditations for the Holy Communion.

By JOSEPHINE FLETCHER. With a Preface by C. J. ELLICOTT, D.D., Lord Bishop of Gloucester and Bristol. With rubrics and borders in red. New Edition. Royal 32mo. 2s. 6d.

An Edition without the red rubrics. 32mo. Cloth limp. 1s.

"*Devout beauty is the special character of this new manual, and it ought to be a favourite. Rarely has it happened to us to meet with so remarkable a combination of thorough practicalness with that almost poetic warmth which is the highest flower of genuine devotion.*"—LITERARY CHURCHMAN.

The Bishop recommends it to the newly confirmed, to the tender-hearted and the devout, as having been compiled by a youthful person, and as being marked by a peculiar 'freshness.' Having looked through the volume, we take pleasure in seconding the recommendations of the good Bishop. We know of no more suitable manual for the newly confirmed, and nothing more likely to engage the sympathies of youthful hearts. There is a union of the deepest spirit of devotion, a rich expression of experimental life, with a due recognition of the objects of faith, such as is not always to be found, but which characterises this manual in an eminent degree."—CHURCH REVIEW.

"*Among the supply of Eucharistic Manuals, one deserves special attention and commendation. 'Prayers and Meditations' merits the Bishop of Gloucester's epithets of 'warm, devout, and fresh.' And it is thoroughly English Church besides.*"—GUARDIAN.

"*We are by no means surprised that Bishop Ellicott should have been so much struck with this little work, on accidentally seeing it in manuscript, as to urge its publication, and to preface it with his commendation. The devotion which it breathes is truly fervent, and the language attractive, and as proceeding from a young person the work is altogether not a little striking.*"—RECORD.

Words to Take with Us.

A Manual of Daily and Occasional Prayers, for Private and Common Use. With Plain Instructions and Counsels on Prayer. By W. E. SCUDAMORE, M.A., Rector of Ditchingham, and formerly Fellow of S. John's College, Cambridge. Fourth Edition, revised. Small 8vo. 2s. 6d.

"*One of the best manuals of daily and occasional prayer we have seen. At once orthodox and practical, sufficiently personal, and yet not perplexingly minute in its details, it is calculated to be of inestimable value in many a household.*"—JOHN BULL.

"*We are again pleased to see an old friend on the editorial table, in a third edition of Mr. Scudamore's well-known Manual of Prayers. The special proper collects for each day of the week, as well as those for the several seasons of the Christian year, have been most judiciously selected. The compiler moreover, while recognizing the full benefits to be derived from the Book of Common Prayer, has not feared to draw largely from the equally invaluable writings of ancient Catholicity.*"—CHURCH REVIEW.

The Words of the Son of God, taken
from the Four Gospels, and arranged for Daily Meditation throughout the Year. By ELEANOR PLUMPTRE. Crown 8vo. 7s. 6d.

The Hour of Prayer; being a Manual of
Devotion for the Use of Families and Schools. With a Preface by the Rev. W. E. SCUDAMORE, M.A., Rector of Ditchingham, and formerly Fellow of S. John's College, Cambridge. Crown 8vo. 3s. 6d.

Family Prayers. Compiled from various
Sources (chiefly from Bishop Hamilton's Manual), and arranged on the Liturgical Principle. By EDWARD MEYRICK GOULBURN, D.D., Dean of Norwich. New Edition. Large type. Crown 8vo. 3s. 6d. Cheap Edition. 16mo. 1s.

Manual of Family Devotions, arranged
from the Book of Common Prayer. By the Hon. AUGUSTUS DUNCOMBE, D.D., Dean of York. Printed in red and black. Small 8vo. 3s. 6d.

Household Prayer, from Ancient and
Authorized Sources: with Morning and Evening Readings for a Month. By the Rev. P. G. MEDD, M.A., Rector of North Cerney, Gloucestershire; Canon of St. Albans; late Senior Fellow of University College, Oxford; and Rector of Barnes. Small 8vo. 4s. 6d.

A Book of Family Prayer. Compiled
by WALTER FARQUHAR HOOK, D.D., F.R.S., late Dean of Chichester. Eighth Edition, with Rubrics in Red. 18mo. 2s.

Aids to Prayer; or, Thoughts on the
Practice of Devotion. With Forms of Prayer for Private Use. By DANIEL MOORE, M.A., Chaplain in Ordinary to the Queen, and Vicar of Holy Trinity, Paddington. Second Edition. Square 32mo. 2s. 6d.

and at Oxford and Cambridge

A Manual of Private Devotions. Compiled principally from the works of Jeremy Taylor and Bishop Andrewes. Small 8vo. 2s.

Self-Renunciation. From the French. With an Introduction by the Rev. T. T. CARTER, M.A., Rector of Clewer, Berks. Crown 8vo. 6s.

Also a Cheap Edition. Small 8vo. 3s. 6d.

"It is excessively difficult to review or criticise, in detail, a book of this kind, and yet its abounding merits, its practicalness, its searching good sense and thoroughness, and its frequent beauty, too, make us wish to do something more than announce its publication. . . . . The style is eminently clear, free from redundance and prolixity."—LITERARY CHURCHMAN.

"Few save Religious and those brought into immediate contact with them are, in all probability, acquainted with the French treatise of Guilloré, a portion of which is now, for the first time we believe, done into English. . . . . Hence the suitableness of such a book as this for those who, in the midst of their families, are endeavouring to advance in the spiritual life. Hundreds of devout souls living in the world have been encouraged and helped by such books as Dr. Neale's 'Sermons preached in a Religious House.' For such the present work will be found appropriate, while for Religious themselves it will be invaluable."—CHURCH TIMES.

Spiritual Guidance. With an Introduction by the Rev. T. T. CARTER, M.A., Rector of Clewer, Berks. Crown 8vo. 6s.

EXTRACT FROM PREFACE.

["The special object of the volume is to supply practical advice in matters of conscience, such as may be generally applicable. While it offers, as it is hoped, much valuable help to Directors, it is full of suggestions, which may be useful to any one in private. It thus fulfils a double purpose, which is not, as far as I am aware, otherwise provided for, at least, not in so full and direct a manner."]

"As a work intended for general use, it will be found to contain much valuable help, and may be profitably studied by any one who is desiring to make progress in spiritual life. Much of the contents of this little book will be found more or less applicable to all persons amid the ordinary difficulties and trials of life, and a help to the training of the mind in habits of self-discipline."—CHURCH TIMES.

The Virgin's Lamp: Prayers and Devout Exercises for English Sisters. By the Rev. J. M. NEALE, D.D., late Warden of Sackville College, East Grinsted. Small 8vo. 3s. 6d.

Waterloo Place, London

Voices of Comfort. Edited by the Rev.
THOMAS VINCENT FOSBERY, M.A., sometime Vicar of St. Giles's, Reading. Third Edition. Crown 8vo. 7s. 6d.

[This Volume, of prose and poetry, original and selected, aims at revealing the fountains of hope and joy which underlie the griefs and sorrows of life.
It is so divided as to afford readings for a month. The key-note of each day is given by the title prefixed to it, such as: 'The Power of the Cross of Christ, Day 6. Conflicts of the Soul, Day 17. The Communion of Saints, Day 20. The Comforter, Day 22. The Light of Hope, Day 25. The Coming of Christ, Day 28.' Each day begins with passages of Holy Scripture. These are followed by articles in prose, which are succeeded by one or more short prayers. After these are Poems or passages of poetry, and then very brief extracts in prose or verse close the section. The book is meant to meet, not merely cases of bereavement or physical suffering, but 'to minister specially to the hidden troubles of the heart, as they are silently weaving their dark threads into the web of the seemingly brightest life.']

Hymns and Poems for the Sick and
Suffering. In connexion with the Service for the Visitation of the Sick. Selected from various Authors. Edited by the Rev. THOMAS VINCENT FOSBERY, M.A., sometime Vicar of St. Giles's, Reading. New Edition. Small 8vo. 3s. 6d.

[This Volume contains 233 separate pieces; of which about 90 are by writers who lived prior to the eighteenth century; the rest are modern, and some of these original. Amongst the names of the writers (between 70 and 80 in number) occur those of Sir J. Beaumont; Sir T. Brown; F. Davison; Elizabeth of Bohemia; P. Fletcher; G. Herbert; Dean Hickes; Bishop Ken; Norris; Quarles; Sandys; Bishop J. Taylor; Henry Vaughan; and Sir H. Wotton. And of modern writers :—Mrs. Barrett Browning; Bishop Wilberforce; S. T. Coleridge; Sir R. Grant; Miss E. Taylor; W. Wordsworth; Archbishop Trench; Rev. Messrs. Chandler, Keble, Lyte, Monsell, and Moultrie.]

The Christian Year: Thoughts in Verse
for the Sundays and Holy Days throughout the Year. Elegantly printed with red borders. 16mo. 2s. 6d. Cheap edition, without the red borders, cloth limp, 1s.; or in paper cover, 6d.

Forming a Volume of "Rivington's Devotional Series."

Also New Editions, forming Volumes of the "Library of Spiritual Works for English Catholics." Small 8vo. 5s. 32mo., cloth limp, 6d.; cloth extra, 1s. [See page 17.]

Private Devotions for School-boys;
with Rules of Conduct. By WILLIAM HENRY, Third Lord Lyttelton. New Edition. 32mo. 6d.

and at Oxford and Cambridge

Our Work for Christ among His Suffering People. A Book for Hospital Nurses. By M. A. MORRELL. Small 8vo. 2s. 6d.

"*The thoroughly sensible advice contained in this book cannot fail to be of the highest possible use; indeed, the whole work is so eminently practical, and deserves such hearty recognition, that we cordially recommend it, with the hope that it may find its way into the hands of all who minister to the sick within our hospital wards. The prayers at the end of the book seem exactly suited to their purpose, dealing as they do with the trials and necessities of a nurse's daily life.*"—JOHN BULL.

"*It should be in the hands of every sick-nurse who desires to fulfil her duties from the highest and holiest motives.*"—CHURCH BELLS.

"*Contains excellent advice on the subject of nursing, with the aim of raising its lowliest duties to a standard of high and holy motives.*"—GRAPHIC.

"*This excellent little book is intended for a limited class of readers, but the practical lessons it teaches on how to sanctify the labour of nursing, and how to overcome its difficulties, may be read with profit by those who are called on to nurse as amateurs in private homes, as well as by those who have adopted the occupation as a profession.*"—AUNT JUDY'S MAGAZINE.

From Morning to Evening: a Book for Invalids. From the French of M. l'Abbé Henri Perreyve. Translated and adapted by an Associate of the Sisterhood of S. John Baptist, Clewer. New Edition. Crown 8vo. 5s.

Consoling Thoughts in Sickness. Edited by HENRY BAILEY, B.D. Small 8vo. 1s. 6d.; or in paper cover, 1s.

A Manual for the Sick; with other Devotions. By LANCELOT ANDREWES, D.D., sometime Lord Bishop of Winchester. Edited with a Preface by H. P. LIDDON, D.D., Canon of St. Paul's. With Portrait. Third Edition. Large type. 24mo. 2s. 6d.

Sickness; its Trials and Blessings. Fine Edition. Small 8vo. 3s. 6d. Cheap Edition, 1s. 6d.; or in paper cover, 1s.

Help and Comfort for the Sick Poor. By the same Author. New Edition. Small 8vo. 1s.

Waterloo Place, London

Devotional Works

Prayers for the Sick and Dying. By the same Author. Fourth Edition. Small 8vo. 1s. 6d.

Consolatio; or, Comfort for the Afflicted. Edited by the Rev. C. E. KENNAWAY. With a Preface by SAMUEL WILBERFORCE, D.D., late Lord Bishop of Winchester. New Edition. Small 8vo. 3s. 6d.

The Armoury of Prayer. A Book of Devotion. Compiled by BERDMORE COMPTON, Vicar of All Saints', Margaret Street. 18mo. 3s. 6d.

"*It has a marked individuality of its own, and will no doubt meet with a certain number of persons—chiefly men, it is probable—to whose spiritual wants it is fitted above others. Those—and their number is far larger than is generally borne in mind—will find here a manual rich and abundant in its material for devotion, but remarkably modern in its tone—fitted to express the feelings and to interpret the aspirations of a cultured dweller in towns; and it is emphatically a book of and for the times.*"—LITERARY CHURCHMAN.

"*The great characteristic of the book is its thorough reality. It puts into the mouth of the worshipper words which express, without exaggeration, what an earnest English Christian would feel and desire. The language is neither a reproduction of foreign or mediæval sentiment nor an affected reproduction of archaic forms, but good English of the Bible and Prayer Book type.... We could not wish the book to be different, and on the whole we heartily recommend it as one of the best we know.*"—CHURCH BELLS.

The Light of the Conscience. By the Author of "The Hidden Life of the Soul," &c. With an Introduction by the Rev. T. T. CARTER, M.A., Rector of Clewer, Berks. Crown 8vo. 5s.

"*It is a book of counsels for those who wish to lead a pious and godly life, and may fill up a gap that has been felt since the external devotional habits of the advanced portion of the present generation have so much altered from those of the last, that the books of counsel previously in use are not deemed applicable to those who follow the full teachings of the extreme ritualistic party, for this book deals with the most 'advanced' customs.*"—GUARDIAN.

"*It consists of four-and-thirty short chapters or readings, every one of them full of quiet, sensible, practical advice, and directions upon some one point of Christian living or Christian feeling. It is a very beautiful little book, and it is a most thoroughly Christian little book, and it is, moreover, what many good books fall short of being, namely, a very wise little book. Its calm, gentle sagacity is most striking.*"—LITERARY CHURCHMAN.

and at Oxford and Cambridge

The English Poems of George Herbert,

together with his Collection of Proverbs, entitled JACULA PRUDENTUM. With red borders. 16mo. 2s. 6d.

Forming a Volume of "Rivington's Devotional Series."

"*This beautiful little volume will be found specially convenient as a pocket manual. The 'Jacula Prudentum,' or proverbs, deserve to be more widely known than they are at present. In many copies of George Herbert's writings these quaint sayings have been unfortunately omitted.*"—ROCK.

"*George Herbert is too much a household name to require any introduction. It will be sufficient to say that Messrs. Rivington have published a most compact and convenient edition of the poems and proverbs of this illustrious English divine.*"—ENGLISH CHURCHMAN.

"*An exceedingly pretty edition, the most attractive form we have yet seen from this delightful author, as a gift-book.*"—UNION REVIEW.

"*A very beautiful edition of the quaint old English bard. All lovers of the 'Holy' Herbert will be grateful to Messrs. Rivington for the care and pains they have bestowed in supplying them with this and withal convenient copy of poems so well known and so deservedly prized.*"—LONDON QUARTERLY REVIEW.

"*A very tasteful little book, and will doubtless be acceptable to many.*"—RECORD.

"*We commend this little book heartily to our readers. It contains Herbert's English poems and the 'Jacula Prudentum,' in a very neat volume, which does much credit to the publishers; it will, we hope, meet with extensive circulation as a choice gift-book at a moderate price.*"—CHRISTIAN OBSERVER.

A Short and Plain Instruction for the

better Understanding of the Lord's Supper; to which is annexed the Office of the Holy Communion, with proper Helps and Directions. By the Right Rev. THOMAS WILSON, D.D., sometime Lord Bishop of Sodor and Man. Complete Edition, in large type, with rubrics and borders in red. 16mo. 2s. 6d.

Also a Cheap Edition, without the red borders, 1s.; or in paper cover, 6d.

Forming a Volume of "Rivington's Devotional Series."

"*The Messrs. Rivington have published a new and unabridged edition of that deservedly popular work, Bishop Wilson on the Lord's Supper. The edition is here presented in three forms, suited to the various members of the household.*"—PUBLIC OPINION.

"*We cannot withhold the expression of our admiration of the style and elegance in which this work is got up.*"—PRESS AND ST. JAMES' CHRONICLE.

"*A departed Author being dead yet speaketh in a way which will never be out of date; Bishop Wilson on the Lord's Supper, published by Messrs. Rivington, in bindings to suit all tastes and pockets.*"—CHURCH REVIEW.

Of the Imitation of Christ. By

Thomas à Kempis. With Red borders. 16mo. 2s. 6d.

Also a Cheap Edition, without the red borders, 1s.; or in paper cover, 6d.

Forming a Volume of "Rivington's Devotional Series."

Also a New Translation, forming a Volume of the "Library of Spiritual Works for English Catholics." Small 8vo. 5s. 32mo., cloth limp, 6d.; cloth extra, 1s. [See page 17.]

Introduction to the Devout Life.

From the French of Saint Francis of Sales, Bishop and Prince of Geneva. A New Translation. With red borders. 16mo. 2s. 6d.

Forming a Volume of "Rivington's Devotional Series."

Also a New Translation, forming a Volume of the "Library of Spiritual Works for English Catholics." Small 8vo. 5s. [See page 17.]

The Rule and Exercises of Holy Living.

By the Right Rev. JEREMY TAYLOR, D.D., sometime Bishop of Down and Connor, and Dromore. With red borders. 16mo. 2s. 6d.

Also a Cheap Edition, without the red borders, 1s.

Forming a Volume of "Rivington's Devotional Series."

The Rule and Exercises of Holy Dying.

By the Right Rev. JEREMY TAYLOR, D.D., sometime Bishop of Down and Connor, and Dromore. With red borders. 16mo. 2s. 6d.

Also a Cheap Edition, without the red borders, 1s.

The 'HOLY LIVING' and the 'HOLY DYING' may be had bound together in one Volume, 5s.; or without the red borders, 2s. 6d.

Forming a Volume of "Rivington's Devotional Series."

and at Oxford and Cambridge

The Spirit of S. Francis de Sales, Bishop

and Prince of Geneva. Translated from the French by the Author of "The Life of S. Francis de Sales," "A Dominican Artist," &c., &c. Crown 8vo. 6s.

"*S. Francis de Sales, as shown to us by the Bishop of Belley, was clearly as bright and lively a companion as many a sinner of witty reputation. He was a student of human nature on the highest grounds, but he used his knowledge for amusement as well as edification. Naturally we learn this from one of his male friends rather than from his female adorers. This friend is Jean-Pierre Camus, Bishop of Belley, author, we are told, of two hundred books—one only however still known to fame, the Spirit of S. Francis de Sales, which has fairly earned him the title of the ecclesiastical Boswell.*"—SATURDAY REVIEW.

"*An admirable translation of Bishop Camus' well-known collection of that good man's sayings and opinions. As a whole, we can imagine no more delightful companion than 'The Spirit of S. Francis de Sales,' nor, we may add, a more useful one.*"—PEOPLE'S MAGAZINE.

The Hidden Life of the Soul. By the

Author of "A Dominican Artist," "Life of Bossuet," &c., &c. New Edition. Small 8vo. 2s. 6d.

Also a Cheap Edition, forming a Volume of the "Library of Spiritual Works for English Catholics." 32mo. Cloth limp, 6d.; cloth extra, 1s. [See page 17.]

"*It well deserves the character given it of being 'earnest and sober,' and not 'sensational.'*"—GUARDIAN.

"*From the French of Jean Nicolas Grou, a pious Priest, whose works teach resignation to the Divine will. He loved, we are told, to inculcate simplicity, freedom from all affectation and unreality, the patience and humility which are too surely grounded in self-knowledge to be surprised at a fall, but withal so allied to confidence in God as to make recovery easy and sure. This is the spirit of the volume which is intended to furnish advice to those who would cultivate a quiet, meek, and childlike spirit.*"—PUBLIC OPINION.

"*There is a wonderful charm about these readings—so calm, so true, so thoroughly Christian. We do not know where they would come amiss. As materials for a consecutive series of meditations for the faithful at a series of early celebrations they would be excellent, or for private reading during Advent or Lent.*"—LITERARY CHURCHMAN.

A Practical Treatise concerning Evil

Thoughts: wherein their Nature, Origin, and Effect are distinctly considered and explained, with many Useful Rules for restraining and suppressing such Thoughts; suited to the various conditions of Life, and the several tempers of Mankind, more especially of melancholy Persons. By WILLIAM CHILCOT, M.A. New Edition. With red borders. 16mo. 2s. 6d.

Forming a Volume of "Rivington's Devotional Series."

Waterloo Place, London

Ancient Hymns. From the Roman
Breviary. For Domestic Use every Morning and Evening of the Week, and on the Holy Days of the Church. To which are added, Original Hymns, principally of Commemoration and Thanksgiving for Christ's Holy Ordinances. By RICHARD MANT, D.D., sometime Lord Bishop of Down and Connor. New Edition. Small 8vo. 5s.

"*Real poetry wedded to words that breathe the purest and the sweetest spirit of Christian devotion. The translations from the old Latin Hymnal are close and faithful renderings.*"—STANDARD.

"*As a Hymn writer Bishop Mant deservedly occupies a prominent place in the esteem of Churchmen, and we doubt not that many will be the readers who will welcome this new edition of his translations and original compositions.*"—ENGLISH CHURCHMAN.

"*A new edition of Bishop Mant's 'Ancient Hymns from the Roman Breviary' forms a handsome little volume, and it is interesting to compare some of these translations with the more modern ones of our own day.*

While we have no hesitation in awarding the palm to the latter, the former are an evidence of the earliest germs of that yearning of the devout mind for something better than Tate and Brady, and which is now so richly supplied."—CHURCH TIMES.

"*This valuable manual will be of great assistance to all compilers of Hymn Books. The translations are graceful, clear, and forcible, and the original hymns deserve the highest praise. Bishop Mant has caught the very spirit of true psalmody, his metre flows musically, and there is a tuneful ring in his verses which especially adapts them for congregational singing.*"—ROCK.

The Mysteries of Mount Calvary.
Translated from the Latin of Antonio de Guevara. Edited by the Rev. ORBY SHIPLEY, M.A. Square crown 8vo. 3s. 6d.

Counsels on Holiness of Life.
Translated from the Spanish of "The Sinner's Guide" by Luis de Granada. Edited by the Rev. ORBY SHIPLEY, M.A. Square crown 8vo. 5s.

Preparation for Death.
Translated from the Italian of Alfonso, Bishop of S. Agatha. Edited by the Rev. ORBY SHIPLEY, M.A. Square crown 8vo. 5s.

Examination of Conscience upon Special
Subjects. Translated and abridged from the French of Tronson. Edited by the Rev. ORBY SHIPLEY, M.A. Square crown 8vo. 5s.

---

and at Oxford and Cambridge

Morning Notes of Praise. A Series of
Meditations upon the Morning Psalms. Dedicated to the Countess of Cottenham. By LADY CHARLOTTE-MARIA PEPYS. New Edition. Small 8vo. 2s. 6d.

Quiet Moments; a Four Weeks' Course
of Thoughts and Meditations before Evening Prayer and at Sunset. By LADY CHARLOTTE-MARIA PEPYS. New Edition. Small 8vo. 2s. 6d.

Vita et Doctrina Jesu Christi; or,
Meditations on the Life of our Lord. By AVANCINI. In the Original Latin. Adapted to the use of the Church of England by a CLERGYMAN. 18mo. 2s. 6d.

Faith and Life: Readings for the greater
Holy Days, and the Sundays from Advent to Trinity. Compiled from Ancient Writers. By WILLIAM BRIGHT, D.D., Canon of Christ Church, and Regius Professor of Ecclesiastical History in the University of Oxford. Second Edition. Small 8vo. 5s.

Christian Watchfulness, in the Prospect of Sickness, Mourning, and Death. By JOHN JAMES, D.D., sometime Canon of Peterborough. New Edition. 12mo. 3s.

Spiritual Life. By JOHN JAMES, D.D.,
sometime Canon of Peterborough. 12mo. 5s.

Waterloo Place, London

A Manual of Devotion, chiefly for the
use of Schoolboys. By the Rev. WILLIAM BAKER, D.D., Head Master of Merchant Taylors' School. With Preface by J. R. WOODFORD, D.D., Lord Bishop of Ely. Crown 16mo. 2s. 6d. Also a Cheap Edition. Cloth limp. 1s. 6d.

A Companion to the Lord's Supper.
By the Plain Man's Friend. Fifth Edition. 18mo. 8d.

The Good Shepherd; or, Meditations
for the Clergy upon the Example and Teaching of Christ. By the Rev. W. E. HEYGATE, M.A., Rector of Brighstone. Second Edition, revised. Small 8vo. 3s.

CONTENTS.

Thoughts on Meditation—Devotions Preparatory to Ordination—Early Life—Temptation—Fasting—Prayer—Divine Scripture—Retirement—Frequent Communion—Faith—Hope—Love—Preaching—Catechizing—Private Explanation—Intercession—Bringing Christians to Holy Communion—Preparation of those about to Communicate—Jesus absolving Sinners—Jesus celebrating the Eucharist—Care of Children—Care of the Sick and Afflicted—The Healing of Schism—Treatment of the Worldly—Treatment of Penitents—Care of God's House—Fear and Fearlessness of Offence—Bearing Reproach—Bearing Praise—Seeking out Sinners—Sorrow over Sinners—Consoling the Sorrowful—Rebuke—Silence—Disappointment—Compassion—Refusing those who suppose Godliness to be Gain—Peace-giving—Poverty—Opportunities of Speech—With Christ or Without—Watchfulness—In what to Glory—The Salt which has lost its Savour—Hard Cases—Weariness—Falling Back—Consideration for Others—Love of Pre-eminence—The Cross my Strength—The Will of God—The Fruit of Humiliation—The Praise of the World the Condemnation of God—Jesus rejoicing—Work while it is Day—Meeting again—The Reward. Further Prayers suitable to the Clergy—Prayer for the Flock—A General Prayer—Celebration of the Holy Eucharist—Preaching—Visitation.

Twenty-one Prayers, composed from the
Psalms, for the Sick and Afflicted. With Hints on the Visitation of the Sick. By the Rev. JAMES SLADE, M.A., Vicar of Bolton. Seventh Edition. 12mo. 3s. 6d.

and at Oxford and Cambridge

4. Parish Work.

The Book of Church Law. Being an
Exposition of the Legal Rights and Duties of the Clergy and Laity of the Church of England. By the Rev. JOHN HENRY BLUNT, M.A., F.S.A. Revised by WALTER G. F. PHILLIMORE, D.C.L., Barrister-at-Law, and Chancellor of the Diocese of Lincoln. Second Edition, revised. Crown 8vo. 7s. 6d.

CONTENTS.

BOOK I.—THE CHURCH AND ITS LAWS.—The Constitutional Status of the Church of England—The Law of the Church of England—The Administration of Church Law.

BOOK II.—THE MINISTRATIONS OF THE CHURCH.—Holy Baptism—Confirmation—The Holy Communion—Divine Service in General—Holy Matrimony—The Churching of Women—The Visitation of the Sick—The Practice of Confession—The Burial of the Dead.

BOOK III.—THE PAROCHIAL CLERGY.—Holy Orders—Licensed Curates—The Cure of Souls.

BOOK IV.—PAROCHIAL LAY OFFICERS.—Churchwardens—Church Trustees—Parish Clerks, Sextons and Beadles—Vestries.

BOOK V.—CHURCHES AND CHURCHYARDS.—The Acquisition of Churches and Churchyards as Ecclesiastical Property—Churches and Ecclesiastical Persons—Churches and Secular Persons.

BOOK VI.—THE ENDOWMENTS OF THE PAROCHIAL CLERGY.—Incomes—Parsonage Houses—The Sequestration of Benefices.

APPENDIX.—The Canons of 1603 and 1865—The Church Discipline Act of 1840—The Benefices Resignation Act of 1871—The Ecclesiastical Dilapidations Act of 1871—The Sequestration Act of 1871—The Public Worship Regulation Act of 1874—Index.

"*We have tested this work on various points of a crucial character, and have found it very accurate and full in its information. It embodies the results of the most recent Acts of the Legislature on the clerical profession and the rights of the laity.*"—STANDARD.

"*Already in our leading columns we have directed attention to Messrs. Blunt and Phillimore's 'Book of Church Law,' as an excellent manual for ordinary use. It is a book which should stand on every clergyman's shelves ready for use when any legal matter arises about which its possessor is in doubt. . . . It is to be hoped that the authorities at our Theological Colleges sufficiently recognize the value of a little legal knowledge on the part of the clergy to recommend this book to their students. It would serve admirably as the text-book for a set of lectures.*"—CHURCH TIMES.

Waterloo Place, London

The Bishopric of Souls. By ROBERT WILSON EVANS, B.D., late Vicar of Heversham and Archdeacon of Westmoreland. With an Introductory Memoir by EDWARD BICKERSTETH, D.D., Dean of Lichfield. With Portrait. Fifth Edition. Small 8vo. 5s. 6d.

Twenty-One Years in S. George's Mission. An account of its Origin, Progress, and Work of Charity. With an Appendix. By C. F. LOWDER, M.A., Vicar of S. Peter's, London Docks. Crown 8vo. 6s.

Directorium Pastorale. The Principles and Practice of Pastoral Work in the Church of England. By the Rev. JOHN HENRY BLUNT, M.A., F.S.A., Editor of "The Annotated Book of Common Prayer," &c., &c. Third Edition, revised. Crown 8vo. 7s. 6d.

"This is the third edition of a work which has become deservedly popular as the best extant exposition of the principles and practice of the pastoral work in the Church of England. Its hints and suggestions are based on practical experience, and it is further recommended by the majority of our Bishops at the ordination of priests and deacons."—STANDARD.

"Its practical usefulness to the parochial clergy is proved by the acceptance it has already received at their hands, and no faithful parish priest, who is working in real earnest for the extension of spiritual instruction amongst all classes of his flock, will rise from the perusal of its pages without having obtained some valuable hints as to the best mode of bringing home our Church's system to the hearts of his people."—NATIONAL CHURCH.

Ars Pastoria. By FRANK PARNELL, M.A., Rector of Oxtead, near Godstone. Second Edition. Small 8vo. 2s.

Instructions for the Use of Candidates for Holy Orders, and of the Parochial Clergy; with Acts of Parliament relating to the same, and Forms proposed to be used. By CHRISTOPHER HODGSON, M.A., Secretary to the Governors of Queen Anne's Bounty. Ninth Edition. 8vo. 16s.

and at Oxford and Cambridge

Flowers and Festivals; or, Directions

for the Floral Decoration of Churches. By W. A BARRETT, Mus. Bac., Oxon., of St. Paul's Cathedral. With Coloured Illustrations. Second Edition. Square crown 8vo. 5s.

The Chorister's Guide. By W. A. BAR-

RETT, Mus. Bac., Oxon., of St. Paul's Cathedral. Second Edition. Crown 8vo. 2s. 6d.

"... One of the most useful books of instructions for choristers—and, we may add, choral singers generally—that has ever emanated from the musical press.... Mr. Barrett's teaching is not only conveyed to his readers with the consciousness of being master of his subject, but he employs words terse and clear, so that his meaning may be promptly caught by the neophyte...."—ATHENÆUM.

"A nicely graduated, clear, and excellent introduction to the duties of a chorister."—STANDARD.

"It seems clear and precise enough to serve its end."—EXAMINER.

"A useful manual for giving boys such a practical and technical knowledge of music as shall enable them to sing both with confidence and precision."—CHURCH HERALD.

"In this little volume we have a manual long called for by the requirements of church music. In a series of thirty-two lessons it gives, with an admirable conciseness, and an equally observable completeness, all that is necessary a chorister should be taught out of a book, and a great deal calculated to have a value as bearing indirectly upon his actual practice in singing."—MUSICAL STANDARD.

"We can highly recommend the present able manual."—EDUCATIONAL TIMES.

"A very useful manual, not only for choristers, or rather those who may aim at becoming choristers, but for others, who wish to enter upon the study of music."—ROCK.

"The work will be found of singular utility by those who have to instruct choirs."—CHURCH TIMES.

"A most grateful contribution to the agencies for improving our Services. It is characterised by all that clearness in combination with conciseness of style which has made 'Flowers and Festivals' so universally admired."—TORONTO HERALD.

Church Organs: their Position and Con-

struction. With an Appendix containing some Account of the Mediæval Organ Case still existing at Old Radnor, South Wales. By FREDERICK HEATHCOTE SUTTON, M.A., Vicar of Theddingworth. With Illustrations. Folio. 6s. 6d.

Notes on Church Organs: their Position

and the Materials used in their Construction. By C. K. K. BISHOP. With Illustrations. Small 4to. 6s.

Waterloo Place, London

Stones of the Temple; or, Lessons
from the Fabric and Furniture of the Church. By WALTER FIELD, M.A., F.S.A., Vicar of Godmersham. With numerous Illustrations. New Edition. Crown 8vo. 7s. 6d.

"*Any one who wishes for simple information on the subjects of Church architecture and furniture, cannot do better than consult 'Stones of the Temple.' Mr. Field modestly disclaims any intention of supplanting the existing regular treatises, but his book shows an amount of research, and a knowledge of what he is talking about, which make it practically useful as well as pleasant. The woodcuts are numerous, and some of them very pretty.*"—GRAPHIC.

"*A very charming book, by the Rev. Walter Field, who was for years Secretary of one of the leading Church Societies. Mr. Field has a loving reverence for the beauty of the* domus mansionalis Dei, *as the old law books called the Parish Church. . . . Thoroughly sound in Church feeling, Mr. Field has chosen the medium of a tale to embody real incidents illustrative of the various portions of his subject. There is no attempt at elaboration of the narrative, which, indeed, is rather a string of anecdotes than a story, but each chapter brings home to the mind its own lesson, and each is illustrated with some very interesting engravings. . . . The work will properly command a hearty reception from Churchmen. The footnotes are occasionally most valuable, but are always pertinent, and the text is sure to be popular with young folks for Sunday reading.*"—STANDARD.

"*Mr. Field's chapters on brasses, chancel screens, crosses, encaustic tiles, mural paintings, porches and pavements, are agreeably written, and people with a turn for Ritualism will no doubt find them edifying. The illustrations of Church architecture and Church ornaments are very attractive.*"—PALL MALL GAZETTE.

"'*Stones of the Temple' is a grave book, the result of antiquarian, or rather ecclesiological, tastes and of devotional feelings. We can recommend it to young people of both sexes, and it will not disappoint the most learned among them. . . . Mr. Field has brought together, from well-known authorities, a considerable mass of archæological information, which will interest the readers he especially addresses.*"—ATHENÆUM.

"*Very appropriate as a Christmas present, is an elegant and instructive book. . . . A full and clear account of the meaning and history of the several parts of the fabric and of the furniture of the Church. It is illustrated with a number of carefully drawn pictures, sometimes of entire churches, sometimes of remarkable monuments, windows, or wall paintings. We may add that the style of the commentary, which is cast in the form of a dialogue between a parson and some of his parishioners, and hangs together by a slight thread of story, is quiet and sensible, and free from exaggeration or intolerance.*"—GUARDIAN.

A Handy Book on the Ecclesiastical
Dilapidations Act, 1871. With the Amendment Act, 1872. By EDWARD G. BRUTON, F.R.I.B.A., Diocesan Surveyor, Oxford. With Analytical Index and Precedent Forms. Second Edition. Crown 8vo. 5s.

and at Oxford and Cambridge

The Church Builder: a Quarterly Journal
of Church Extension in England and Wales. Published in connexion with "The Incorporated Church Building Society." 14 Annual Volumes. With Illustrations. Crown 8vo. 1s. 6d.
> New Series. Enlarged. Volumes for 1876 and 1877. 3s. each.

Priest and Parish. By the Rev. HARRY JONES, M.A., Rector of St. George's-in-the-East, London. Square crown 8vo. 6s. 6d.

List of Charities, General and Diocesan,
for the Relief of the Clergy, their Widows and Families. New Edition. Small 8vo. 3s.

Waterloo Place, London

5. The Church and Doctrine.

The Holy Catholic Church; its Divine
Ideal, Ministry, and Institutions. A short Treatise. With a Catechism on each Chapter, forming a Course of Methodical Instruction on the subject. By EDWARD MEYRICK GOULBURN, D.D., Dean of Norwich. Second Edition. Crown 8vo. 6s. 6d.

CONTENTS.

What the Church is, and when and how it was founded—Duty of the Church towards those who hold to the Apostles' doctrine, in separation from the Apostles' fellowship—The Unity of the Church, and its Disruption—The Survey of Zion's towers, bulwarks, and palaces—The Institution of the Ministry, and its relation to the Church—The Holy Eucharist at its successive stages—On the powers of the Church in Council—The Church presenting, exhibiting, and defending the Truth—The Church guiding into and illustrating the Truth—On the Prayer-Book as a Commentary on the Bible—Index.

"*Dr. Goulburn has conferred a great boon on the Church of England by the treatise before us, which vindicates her claim as a branch of the Catholic Church on the allegiance of her children, setting forth as he does, with singular precision and power, the grounds of her title-deeds, and the Christian character of her doctrine and discipline.*"—STANDARD.

"*His present book would have been used for an educational book even if he had not invited men to make that use of it by appending a catechism to each particular chapter, and thus founding a course of methodical instruction upon his text. We have not yet come across any better book for giving to Dissenters or to such inquirers as hold fast to Holy Scripture. It is, we need scarcely say, steeped in Scripturalness, and full of bright and suggestive interpretations of particular texts.*"—ENGLISH CHURCHMAN.

"*Must prove highly useful, not only to young persons, but to the very large class, both Churchmen and Dissenters, who are painfully ignorant of what the Catholic Church really is, and of the peculiar and fixed character of her institutions.*"—ROCK.

"*The catechetical questions and answers at the end of each chapter will be useful both for teachers and learners, and the side-notes at the head of the paragraphs are very handy.*"—CHURCH TIMES.

"*It contains a great deal of instructive matter, especially in the catechisms —or, as they might be called, dialogues —and is instinct with a spirit at once temperate and uncompromising. It is a good book for all who wish to understand, neither blindly asserting it nor being half ashamed of it, the position of a loyal member of the English Church.*"—GUARDIAN.

and at Oxford and Cambridge

Dictionary of Doctrinal and Historical Theology.

By Various Writers. Edited by the Rev. JOHN HENRY BLUNT, M.A., F.S.A., Editor of the "Annotated Book of Common Prayer," &c., &c. Second Edition. Imperial 8vo. 42s.; or in half-morocco, 52s. 6d.

"*Taken as a whole the articles are the work of practised writers, and well-informed and solid theologians. . . . We know no book of its size and bulk which supplies the information here given at all; far less which supplies it in an arrangement so accessible, with a completenes of information so thorough, and with an ability in the treatment of profound subjects so great. Dr. Hook's most useful volume is a work of high calibre, but it is the work of a single mind. We have here a wider range of thought from a greater variety of sides. We have here also the work of men who evidently know what they write about, and are somewhat more profound (to say the least) than the writers of the current Dictionaries of Sects and Heresies.*"—GUARDIAN.

"*Thus it will be obvious that it takes a very much wider range than any undertaking of the same kind in our language; and that to those of our clergy who have not the fortune to spend in books, and would not have the leisure to use them if they possessed them, it will be the most serviceable and reliable substitute for a large library we can think of. And in many cases, while keeping strictly within its province as a Dictionary, it contrives to be marvellously suggestive of thought and reflections, which a serious-minded man will take with him and ponder over for his own elaboration and future use. We trust most sincerely that the book may be largely used. For a present to a Clergyman on his ordination, or from a parishioner to his pastor, it would be most appropriate. It may indeed be called 'a box of tools for a working clergyman.'*"—LITERARY CHURCHMAN.

"*Seldom has an English work of equal magnitude been so permeated with Catholic instincts, and at the same time seldom has a work on theology been kept so free from the drift of rhetorical incrustation. Of course, it is not meant that all these remarks apply in their full extent to every article. In a great Dictionary there are compositions, as in a great house there are vessels, of various kinds. Some of these at a future day may be replaced by others more substantial in their build, more proportionate in their outline, and more elaborate in their detail. But admitting all this, the whole remains a home to which the student will constantly recur, sure to find spacious chambers, substantial furniture, and (which is most important) no stinted light.*"—CHURCH REVIEW.

"*Within the sphere it has marked out for itself, no equally useful book of reference exists in English for the elucidation of theological problems. . . . Entries which display much care, research, and judgment in compilation, and which will make the task of the parish priest who is brought face to face with any of the practical questions which they involve far easier than has been hitherto. The very fact that the utterances are here and there somewhat more guarded and hesitating than quite accords with our judgment, is a gain in so far as it protects the work from the charge of inculcating extreme views, and will thus secure its admission in many places where moderation is accounted the crowning grace.*"—CHURCH TIMES.

"*It will be found of admirable service to all students of theology, as advancing and maintaining the Church's views on all subjects as fall within the range of fair argument and inquiry. It is not often that a work of so comprehensive and so profound a nature is marked to the very end by so many signs of wide and careful research, sound criticism, and well-founded and well-expressed belief.*"—STANDARD.

Waterloo Place, London

Dictionary of Sects, Heresies, Ecclesiastical Parties and Schools of Religious Thought.
By Various Writers. Edited by the Rev. JOHN HENRY BLUNT, M.A., F.S.A., Editor of the "Dictionary of Doctrinal and Historical Theology," the "Annotated Book of Common Prayer," &c., &c. Imperial 8vo. 36s.; or in half-morocco, 48s.

"*Taken as a whole, we doubt not that the Dictionary will prove a useful work of reference; and it may claim to give in reasonable compass a mass of information respecting many religious schools knowledge of which could previously only be acquired from amid a host of literature. The articles are written with great fairness, and in many cases display careful scholarly work.*"—ATHENÆUM.

"*A very comprehensive and bold undertaking, and is certainly executed with a sufficient amount of ability and knowledge to entitle the book to rank very high in point of utility.*"—GUARDIAN.

"*That this is a work of some learning and research is a fact which soon becomes obvious to the reader.*"—SPECTATOR.

"*A whole library is condensed into this admirable volume. All authorities are named, and an invaluable index is supplied.*"—NOTES AND QUERIES.

"*We have tested it rigidly, and in almost every instance we have been satisfied with the account given under the name of sects, heresy, or ecclesiastical party.*"—JOHN BULL.

"*After all deductions, it is the fullest and most trustworthy book of the kind that we possess. The quantity of information it presents in a convenient and accessible form is enormous, and having once appeared, it becomes indispensable to the theological student.*"—CHURCH TIMES.

"*It has considerable value as a copious work of reference, more especially since a list of authorities is in most cases supplied.*"—EXAMINER.

The Doctrine of the Church of England,
as stated in Ecclesiastical Documents set forth by Authority of Church and State, in the Reformation Period between 1536 and 1662. Edited by the Rev. JOHN HENRY BLUNT, M.A., F.S.A., Editor of the "Dictionary of Doctrinal and Historical Theology," the "Annotated Book of Common Prayer," &c. &c. 8vo. 7s. 6d.

The Orthodox Doctrine of the Church
of England explained in a Commentary on the Thirty-Nine Articles. By the Rev. T. I. BALL. With an Introduction by the Rev. W. J. E. BENNETT, M.A., Vicar of Frome-Selwood. Crown 8vo. 7s. 6d.

and at Oxford and Cambridge

Thirty-two Years of the Church of
England, 1842-1875: The Charges of Archdeacon SINCLAIR. Edited by WILLIAM SINCLAIR, M.A., Prebendary of Chichester, Rector of Pulborough, late Vicar of S. George's, Leeds. With a Preface by ARCHIBALD CAMPBELL TAIT, D.D., Archbishop of Canterbury, and a Historical Introduction by ROBERT CHARLES JENKINS, M.A., Hon. Canon of Canterbury, Rector and Vicar of Lyminge. 8vo. 12s. 6d.

The Principal Ecclesiastical Judg-
ments delivered in the Court of Arches, 1867-1875. By the Right Hon. Sir ROBERT PHILLIMORE, D.C.L. 8vo. 12s.

The Holy Angels: Their Nature and
Employments, as recorded in the Word of God. Small 8vo. 6s.

Dogmatic Faith: an Inquiry into the
Relation subsisting between Revelation and Dogma. Being the Bampton Lectures for 1867. By EDWARD GARBETT, M.A., Incumbent of Christ Church, Surbiton. New Edition. Crown 8vo. 5s.

Prophecies and the Prophetic Spirit
in the Christian Era: an Historical Essay. By JOHN J. IGN. VON DÖLLINGER, D.D., D.C.L. Translated, with Introduction, Notes, and Appendices, by the Rev. ALFRED PLUMMER, M.A., Master of University College, Durham, late Fellow of Trinity College, Oxford. 8vo. 10s. 6d.

Lectures on the Reunion of the
Churches. By JOHN J. IGN. VON DÖLLINGER, D.D., D.C.L. Authorized Translation, with Preface by HENRY NUTCOMBE OXENHAM, M.A., late Scholar of Balliol College, Oxford. Crown 8vo. 5s.

Waterloo Place, London

Apostolical Succession in the Church

of England. By the Rev. ARTHUR W. HADDAN, B.D., late Rector of Barton-on-the-Heath. 8vo. 12*s.*

"*Thoroughly well written, clear and forcible in style, and fair in tone. It cannot but render valuable service in placing the claims of the Church in their true light before the English public.*"—GUARDIAN.

"*Among the many standard theological works devoted to this important subject Mr. Haddan's will hold a high place.*"—STANDARD.

"*We should be glad to see the volume widely circulated and generally read.*"—JOHN BULL.

"*A weighty and valuable treatise, and we hope that the study of its sound and well-reasoned pages will do much to fix the importance, and the full meaning of the doctrine in question, in the minds of Church people.* . . ."

We hope that our extracts will lead our readers to study Mr. Haddan for themselves."—LITERARY CHURCHMAN.

"*This is not only a very able and carefully written treatise upon the doctrine of Apostolical Succession, but it is also a calm yet noble vindication of the validity of the Anglican Orders: it well sustains the brilliant reputation which Mr. Haddan left behind him at Oxford, and it supplements his other profound historical researches in ecclesiastical matters. This book will remain for a long time the classic work upon English Orders.*"—CHURCH REVIEW.

"*A very temperate, but a very well reasoned book.*"—WESTMINSTER REVIEW.

The Civil Power in its Relations to the

Church; considered with Special Reference to the Court of Final Ecclesiastical Appeal in England. By the Rev. JAMES WAYLAND JOYCE, M.A., Prebendary of Hereford, and Examining Chaplain to the Bishop of Hereford. 8vo. 10*s.* 6*d.*

Defence of the English Ordinal, with

some Observations upon Spiritual Jurisdiction and the Power of the Keys. By the Rev. W. R. CHURTON, M.A., Fellow of King's College, Cambridge, and Honorary Canon of Rochester Cathedral. 8vo. 3*s.*

The Religion, Discipline, and Rites of

the Church of England. Written at the Instance of Edward Hyde, Earl of Clarendon. By JOHN COSIN, sometime Bishop of Durham. Now first published in English. By the Rev. FREDERICK MEYRICK, M.A. Small 8vo. 1*s.*

and at Oxford and Cambridge

Eight Lectures on the Miracles; being the Bampton Lectures for 1865. By J. B. MOZLEY, D.D., Regius Professor of Divinity, and Canon of Christ Church, Oxford. Third Edition. Crown 8vo. 7s. 6d.

"*There is great brightness and beauty in many of the images in which the author condenses the issues of his arguments. And many passages are marked by that peculiar kind of eloquence which comes with the force of close and vigorous thinking; passages which slime-like steal through their very temper, and which are instinct with a controlled energy, that melts away all ruggedness of language. There can be no question that, in the deeper qualities of a scientific theology, the book is thoroughly worthy of the highest reputation which had been gained by Mr. Mozley's previous writings.*"—CONTEMPORARY REVIEW.

"*Mr. Mozley's Bampton Lectures are an example, and a very fine one, of a mode of theological writing which is characteristic of the Church of England, and almost peculiar to it. The distinguishing features, a combination of intense seriousness with a self-restrained, severe calmness, and of very vigorous and wide-ranging reasoning on the realities of the case. . . . . Mr. Mozley's book belongs to that class of writings of which Butler may be taken as the type. It is strong, genuine argument about difficult matters, fairly facing what is difficult, fairly trying to grapple, not with what appears the gist and strong point of a question, but with what really and at bottom is the knot of it.*"—TIMES.

The Happiness of the Blessed considered as to the Particulars of their State: their Recognition of each other in that State: and its Differences of Degrees. To which are added Musings on the Church and her Services. By RICHARD MANT, D.D., sometime Lord Bishop of Down and Connor. New Edition. Small 8vo. 3s. 6d.

"*A welcome republication of a treatise once highly valued, and which can never lose its value. Many of our readers already know the fulness and discrimination with which the author treats his subject, which must be one of the most delightful topics of meditation to all whose hearts are where the only true treasure is, and particularly to those who are entering upon the evening of life.*"—CHURCH REVIEW.

"*The value of this book needs not to be referred to, its standard character having been for many years past established. The edition in which it reappears has evidently been carefully prepared, and will be the means of making it more generally known.*"—BELL'S MESSENGER.

"*All recognise the authority of the command to set the affections on things above, and such works as the one now before us will be found helpful towards this good end. We are, therefore, sincerely glad that Messrs. Rivington have brought out a new edition of Bishop Mant's valuable treatise.*"—RECORD.

"*This beautiful and devotional treatise, which it is impossible to read without feeling a more deepened interest in the eternal blessedness which awaits the true servants of our God, concludes very appropriately with 'Musings on the Church and her Services,' which we cordially recommend to our readers.*"—ROCK.

Waterloo Place, London

Out of the Body. A Scriptural Inquiry.
By the Rev. JAMES S. POLLOCK, M.A., Incumbent of S. Alban's, Birmingham. Crown 8vo. 5s.

CONTENTS.

Introduction—Scope of the Inquiry—The Presentiment—The Anticipation—The Departure—The Life of the Body—The Life of the Spirit—Dream-Life—The Spirit-World—Spirit-Groups—Helping one another—Limits of Communication—Spiritual Manifestations.

"We have read this book with interest... We esteem the honesty with which it is evidently written, and we admire the courage which the author has shown in searching the Bible for evidences as to the destination of departed spirits, and in accepting such evidences as he has found."—BIRMINGHAM MORNING NEWS.

"The writer discusses with considerable ability, and in a devout and reverent frame of mind."—SPIRITUAL MAGAZINE.

"This is a curious, thoughtful, and interesting little book, in which the author endeavours to ascertain and to define the relations of living men as regards their communication with the spirits of those whom we call dead, as authorised by the words and teaching of Holy Scripture.... Will be very welcome to a host of readers on either side of the disputed ground, and cannot fail to be of lasting interest and profit to all candid students."—STANDARD.

The Origin and Development of Religious Belief. By the Rev. S. BARING-GOULD, M.A., Author of "Curious Myths of the Middle Ages," &c. New Edition. Two Parts. Crown 8vo. 6s. each. Sold separately.

Part I. MONOTHEISM and POLYTHEISM.
Part II. CHRISTIANITY.

"The ability which Mr. Baring-Gould displays in the treatment of a topic which branches out in so many directions, and requires such precise handling, is apparent. His pages abound with the results of large reading and calm reflection. The man of culture, thought, philosophic cast, is mirrored in the entire argument. The book is sound and healthy in tone. It excites the reader's interest, and brightens the path of inquiry opened to his view. The language, too, is appropriate, neat, lucid, often happy, sometimes wonderfully terse and vigorous."—ATHENÆUM.

"Mr. Baring-Gould has undertaken a great and ambitious work. And no one can deny that he possesses some eminent qualifications for this great work. He has a wealth of erudition of the most varied description, especially in those particular regions of mediæval legend and Teutonic mythology which are certain to make large contributions to the purpose he has in hand. It is a contribution to religious thought of very high value."—GUARDIAN.

"Mr. Baring-Gould's work, from the importance of its subject and the lucid force of its expositions, as well as from the closeness of argument and copiousness of illustration with which its comprehensive views are treated, is entitled to attentive study, and will repay the reader by amusement and instruction."—MORNING POST.

"Our space warns us that we are attempting in vain to compress into a few columns the contents of four hundred pages of a work which has had few equals for brilliancy, learning, and point in this department of literature. We therefore conclude by recommending the volume itself to all students of mind and theology."—CHURCH TIMES.

and at 𝔒𝔵𝔣𝔬𝔯𝔡 and 𝔒𝔞𝔪𝔟𝔯𝔦𝔡𝔤𝔢

Our Mother Church: being Simple Talk
on High Topics. By ANNE MERCIER. New Edition. Small 8vo. 3s. 6d.

"*We have rarely come across a book dealing with an old subject in a healthier and, as far as may be, more original manner, while yet thoroughly practical. It is intended for and admirably adapted to the use of girls. Thoroughly reverent in its tone, and bearing in every page marks of learned research, it is yet easy of comprehension, and explains ecclesiastical terms with the accuracy of a lexicon without the accompanying dulness. It is to be hoped that the book will attain to the large circulation it justly merits.*"—JOHN BULL.

"*We have never seen a book for girls of its class which commends itself to us more particularly. The author, who is the wife of an earnest parish priest of the Anglican school, near London, calls her work 'simple talk on great subjects,' and calls it by a name that describes it almost as completely as we could do in a longer notice than we can spare the volume. Here are the headings of the chapters:—*

'The Primitive Church,' 'Primitive Places and Modes of Worship,' 'The Early English Church,' 'The Monastic Orders,' 'The Friars,' 'A Review of Church History,' 'The Prayer Book,' (four chapters), 'Symbolism,' 'Church Architecture,' 'Windows and Bells,' 'Church Music,' 'Church Work.' *No one can fail to comprehend the beautifully simple, devout, and appropriate language in which Mrs. Mercier embodies what she has to say; and for the facts with which she deals she has taken good care to have their accuracy assured.*"—STANDARD.

"*The plan of this pleasant-looking book is excellent. It is a kind of Mrs. Markham on the Church of England, written especially for girls, and we shall not be surprised to find it become a favourite in schools. It is really a conversational hand-book to the English Church's history, doctrine, and ritual, compiled by a very diligent reader from some of the best modern Anglican sources.*"—ENGLISH CHURCHMAN.

A Selection from the Spiritual Letters
of S. Francis de Sales, Bishop and Prince of Geneva. Translated by the Author of "Life of S. Francis de Sales," "A Dominican Artist," &c. &c. Crown 8vo. 6s.

"*It is a collection of epistolary correspondence of rare interest and excellence. With those who have read the Life, there cannot but have been a strong desire to know more of so beautiful a character.*"—CHURCH HERALD.

"*A few months back we had the pleasure of welcoming the Life of S. Francis de Sales. Here is the promised sequel:—the 'Selection from his Spiritual Letters' then announced:—*

and a great boon it will be to many. The Letters are addressed to people of all sorts:—to men and to women:— to laity and to ecclesiastics, to people living in the world, or at court, and to the inmates of Religious Houses. We hope that with our readers it may be totally needless to urge such a volume on their notice."—LITERARY CHURCHMAN.

Also a Cheap Edition, forming a Volume of the "Library of Spiritual Works for English Catholics." 32mo., cloth limp, 6d.; cloth extra, 1s. [See page 17.]

Spiritual Letters to Men. By Archbishop Fénelon. By the Author of "Life of Fénelon," "Life of S. Francis de Sales," &c., &c. Crown 8vo. 6s.

"*Clergy and laity alike will welcome this volume. Fénelon's religious counsels have always seemed to us to present the most remarkable combination of high principle and practical common-sense, and now in this English dress it is really wonderful how little of the aroma of their original expression has evaporated. Elder clergy will delight in comparing their own experiences with Fénelon's ways of treating the several classes of cases here taken in hand. To younger clergy it will be quite a series of specimen examples how to deal with that which is daily becoming a larger and larger department of the practical work of any really efficient clergyman, and laymen will find it so straightforward and intelligible, so utterly free from technicality, and so entirely sympathetic with a layman's position, that we hope it will be largely bought and read among them. A more useful work has rarely been done than giving these letters to English readers.*"—Church Quarterly Review.

"*This volume should take a place amongst the most precious of the Christian classics.*"—Nonconformist.

"*One of those renderings which by faithfulness to their original, and the idiomatic beauty of their style, are real works of art in their way. It is not too much to say that these Letters read as if they had been first written in English, and that by some masterhand. . . . Of the whole book it would be difficult to speak too highly.*"—Literary Churchman.

"*Those who have the 'Life of Fénelon' by this author will not omit to add his 'Spiritual Letters.' They are unique for their delicacy and tenderness of sentiment, their subtle analysis of character, and deep insight into the human heart.*"—Church Eclectic (New York).

Spiritual Letters to Women. By Archbishop Fénelon. By the Author of "Life of Fénelon," "Life of S. Francis de Sales," &c., &c. Crown 8vo. 6s.

"*As for the 'Spiritual Letters,' they cannot be read too often, and each time we take them up we see new beauties in them. The time to read them is in the early morning, when they seem to breathe the very atmosphere of heaven, and have all the fragrance of fresh spiritual thought about them, as the flowers carry on their bosom the early dew. A stillness of devotion and wrapt contemplation of God and of heavenly things characterizes every page.*"—Irish Ecclesiastical Gazette.

"*Writing such as this will do more to commend religion than all the vain dogmatic thunder in which so many of its professors indulge; whilst the sweet and tender piety which runs through every page will impress the reader with the highest conceivable respect for the character of the author.*"—Morning Advertiser.

"*This is an exceedingly well-got-up edition, admirably translated, of Fénelon's celebrated 'Spiritual Letters.' The translation is by the author of the valuable Lives of Fénelon and Bossuet, and forms a very suitable companion to the previous work. Of the Letters themselves, there is no need to speak. The judgment to be formed of them depends so much on the point of view from which they are regarded; but any one will be ready to admit the beauty of their thoughts, the grace of their tone, and the nobility of their sentiments.*"—Examiner.

---

and at Oxford and Cambridge

The Thirty-nine Articles of the Church

of England explained in a Series of Lectures. By the Rev. R. W. JELF, D.D., late Canon of Christ Church, Oxford, and sometime Principal of King's College, London. Edited by the Rev. J. R. KING, M.A., Vicar of St. Peter's-in-the-East, Oxford, and formerly Fellow and Tutor of Merton College. 8vo. 15*s*.

St. John Chrysostom's Liturgy.

Translated by H. C. ROMANOFF, Author of "Sketches of the Rites and Customs of the Greco-Russian Church," &c. With Illustrations. Square crown 8vo. 4*s*. 6*d*.

Letters from Rome on the Council.

By QUIRINUS. Reprinted from the "Allgemeine Zeitung." Authorized Translation. Crown 8vo. 12*s*.

The Pope and the Council. By JANUS.

Authorized Translation from the German. Fourth Edition. Crown 8vo. 7*s*. 6*d*.

6. Sermons.

Some Elements of Religion. Lent
Lectures. By HENRY PARRY LIDDON, D.D., D.C.L., Canon of St. Paul's, and Ireland Professor of Exegesis in the University of Oxford. Second Edition. Crown 8vo. 5s.

CONTENTS.

The Idea of Religion—God, the Object of Religion—The Subject of Religion, the Soul—The Obstacle to Religion, Sin—Prayer, the Characteristic action of Religion—The Mediator, the Guarantee of Religious Life.

The Divinity of our Lord and Saviour
Jesus Christ. Being the Bampton Lectures for 1866. By HENRY PARRY LIDDON, D.D., D.C.L., Canon of St. Paul's, and Ireland Professor of Exegesis in the University of Oxford. Seventh Edition. Crown 8vo. 5s.

Sermons Preached before the University
of Oxford. By HENRY PARRY LIDDON, D.D., D.C.L., Canon of St. Paul's, and Ireland Professor of Exegesis in the University of Oxford. Sixth Edition. Crown 8vo. 5s.

CONTENTS.

God and the Soul—The Law of Progress—The Honour of Humanity—The Freedom of the Spirit—Immortality—Humility and Action—The Conflict of Faith with undue Exaltation of Intellect—Lessons of the Holy Manger—The Divine Victim—The Risen Life—Our Lord's Ascension, the Church's Gain—Faith in a Holy Ghost—The Divine Indwelling a motive to Holiness.

and at Oxford and Cambridge

The Life of Justification. A Series of
Lectures delivered in Substance at All Saints', Margaret Street. By the Rev. GEORGE BODY, B.A., Rector of Kirkby Misperton. Fourth Edition. Crown 8vo. 4s. 6d.

CONTENTS.

Justification the Want of Humility—Christ our Justification—Union with Christ the Condition of Justification—Conversion and Justification—The Life of Justification—The Progress and End of Justification.

"*On the whole we have rarely met with a more clear, intelligible and persuasive statement of the truth as regards the important topics on which the volume treats. Sermon II. in particular, will strike every one by its eloquence and beauty, but we scarcely like to specify it, lest in praising it we should seem to disparage the other portions of this admirable little work.*"—CHURCH TIMES.

"*These discourses show that their author's position is due to something more and higher than mere fluency, gesticulation, and flexibility of voice. He appears as having drunk deeply at the fountain of St. Augustine, and as understanding how to translate the burning words of that mighty genius into the current language of to-day.*"—UNION REVIEW.

"*There is real power in these sermons:—power, real power, and plenty of it. . . . There is such a moral veraciousness about him, such a profound and over-mastering belief that Christ has proved a bonâ-fide cure for unholiness, and such an intensity of eagerness to lead others to seek and profit by that means of attaining the true sanctity which alone can enter Heaven—that we wonder not at the crowds which hang upon his preaching, nor at the success of his fervid appeals to the human conscience. If any one doubts our verdict, let him buy this volume. No one will regret its perusal.*"—LITERARY CHURCHMAN.

The Life of Temptation. A Course of
Lectures delivered in Substance at St. Peter's, Eaton Square; also at All Saints', Margaret Street. By the Rev. GEORGE BODY, B.A., Rector of Kirkby Misperton. Fourth Edition. Crown 8vo. 4s. 6d.

CONTENTS.

The Leading into Temptation—The Rationale of Temptation—Why we are Tempted—Safety in Temptation—With Jesus in Temptation—The End of Temptation.

"*Regeneration and conversion seem here to occupy their proper places in the Christian economy, and the general subject of temptation is worked out with considerable ability.*"—CHURCH TIMES.

"*This is another volume of simple, earnest, soul-stirring words, dealing with the mysteries of Christian experience.*"—LONDON QUARTERLY REVIEW.

"*A collection of sermons, pious, earnest, and eloquent.*"—ENGLISH CHURCHMAN.

Waterloo Place, London

Sermons on the Epistles and Gospels

for the Sundays and Holy Days throughout the Year. By the Rev. ISAAC WILLIAMS, B.D., Author of a "Devotional Commentary on the Gospel Narrative." New Edition. 2 Vols. Crown 8vo. 5s. each. Sold separately.

CONTENTS OF VOL. I.

The King of Salem—The Scriptures bearing Witness—The Church bearing Witness—The Spirit bearing Witness—The Adoption of Sons—Love strong as Death—The Love which passeth Knowledge—Of such is the Kingdom of Heaven—The Spirit of Adoption—The Old and the New Man—The Day Star in the Heart—Obedience the best Sacrifice—The Meekness and Gentleness of Christ — The Faith that overcometh the World—Our Refuge in Public Troubles—Light and Safety in Love—The Great Manifestation—Perseverance found in Humility—Bringing forth Fruit with Patience—The most excellent Gift—The Call to Repentance—The accepted Time—Perseverance in Prayer—The Unclean Spirit returning—The Penitent refreshed—Our Life in the Knowledge of God—The Mind of Christ—The Triumph of the Cross—The Man of Sorrows—The Great Sacrifice—The Memorial of the Great Sacrifice—The Fulfilment—Buried with Christ—The Power of Christ risen—Walking in Newness of Life—Belief in the Resurrection of Christ—The Faith that overcometh the World—Following the Lamb of God—A little while—The Giver of all Good—Requisites of effectual Prayer—Ascending with Christ—The Days of Expectation—They shall walk with Me in White—The Holy Spirit and Baptism—Let all Things be done in order.

CONTENTS OF VOL. II.

The Door opened in Heaven—Love the mark of God's Children—The Gospel a Feast of Love—The Lost Sheep—Mercy the best preparation for Judgment—The peaceable ordering of the World—Brotherly Love and the Life in Christ—The Bread which God giveth—By their Fruits ye shall know them—Looking forward, or Divine Covetousness—The Day of Visitation—The Prayer of the Penitent—Weakness of Faith—Love the fulfilling of the Law—Thankfulness the Life of the Regenerate—My Beloved is Mine and I am His—The Knowledge which is Life Eternal—The Sabbath of Christ found in Meekness—Christ is on the Right Hand of God—The Forgiveness of Sins—Love and Joy in the Spirit—The Warfare and the Armour of Saints—The Love of Christians—The Earthly and Heavenly Citizenship—Mutual Intercessions—Gleanings after Harvest—Bringing unto Christ—Slowness in believing—Grace not given in Vain—The Refiner's Fire—The Lost Crown—Faith in the Incarnation—Value of an Inspired Gospel—The severe and social Virtues—Go and do thou likewise—Joy at hearing the Bridegroom's Voice—The Strength of God in Man's Weakness—Hidden with Christ in God—Do good, hoping for nothing again—The good exchange—War in Heaven—Healing and Peace—The Sacrament of Union—They which shall be accounted Worthy.

and at Oxford and Cambridge

Parochial and Plain Sermons. By JOHN HENRY NEWMAN, B.D., formerly Vicar of St. Mary's, Oxford. Edited by the Rev. W. J. COPELAND, B.D., Rector of Farnham, Essex. New Edition. 8 Vols. Crown 8vo. 5s. each. Sold separately.

CONTENTS OF VOL. I.

Holiness necessary for Future Blessedness— The Immortality of the Soul— Knowledge of God's Will without Obedience— Secret Truths— Self-denial the Test of Religious Earnestness— The Spiritual Mind— Sins of Ignorance and Weakness— God's Commandments not grievous— The Religious use of exalted Feelings— Profession without Practice— Profession without Hypocrisy— Profession without Ostentation— Promising without Doing— Religious Emotion— Religious Faith Rational— The Christian Mysteries— The Self-wise Inquirer— Obedience the Remedy for Religious Perplexity— Times of Private Prayer— Forms of Private Prayer— The Resurrection of the Body— Witnesses of the Resurrection— Christian Reverence— The Religion of the Day— Scripture a Record of Human Sorrow— Christian Manhood.

CONTENTS OF VOL. II.

The World's Benefactors— Faith without Sight— The Incarnation— Martyrdom— Love of Relations and Friends— The Mind of Little Children— Ceremonies of the Church— The Glory of the Christian Church— His Conversion viewed in Reference to His Office— Secrecy and Suddenness of Divine Visitations— Divine Decrees— The Reverence due to Her— Christ, a Quickening Spirit— Saving Knowledge— Self-contemplation— Religious Cowardice— The Gospel Witnesses— Mysteries in Religion— The Indwelling Spirit— The Kingdom of the Saints— The Gospel, a Trust committed to us— Tolerance of Religious Error— Rebuking Sin— The Christian Ministry— Human Responsibility— Guilelessness— The Danger of Riches— The Powers of Nature— The Danger of Accomplishments— Christian Zeal— Use of Saints' Days.

CONTENTS OF VOL. III.

Abraham and Lot— Wilfulness of Israel in rejecting Samuel— Saul— Early years of David— Jeroboam— Faith and Obedience— Christian Repentance— Contracted Views in Religion— A particular Providence as revealed in the Gospel— Tears of Christ at the Grave of Lazarus— Bodily Suffering— The Humiliation of the Eternal Son— Jewish Zeal a Pattern to Christians— Submission to Church Authority— Contest between Truth and Falsehood in the Church— The Church Visible and Invisible— The Visible Church an Encouragement to Faith— The Gift of the Spirit— Regenerating Baptism— Infant Baptism— The Daily Service— The Good Part of Mary— Religious Worship a Remedy for Excitements— Intercession— The Intermediate State.

CONTENTS OF VOL. IV.

The Strictness of the Law of Christ— Obedience without Love, as instanced in the Character of Balaam— Moral Consequences of Single Sins— Acceptance of Religious Privileges compulsory— Reliance on Religious Observances— The Individuality of the Soul— Chastisement amid Mercy— Peace and Joy amid Chastisement— The State of Grace— The Visible Church for the sake of the Elect— The Communion of Saints— The Church a

NEWMAN'S PAROCHIAL AND PLAIN SERMONS—*Continued.*

Home for the Lonely—The Invisible World—The Greatness and Littleness of Human Life—Moral Effects of Communion with God—Christ Hidden from the World—Christ Manifested in Remembrance—The Gainsaying of Korah—The Mysteriousness of our Present Being—The Ventures of Faith—Faith and Love—Watching—Keeping Fast and Festival.

CONTENTS OF VOL V.

Worship, a Preparation for Christ's Coming—Reverence, a Belief in God's Presence—Unreal Words—Shrinking from Christ's Coming—Equanimity—Remembrance of past Mercies—The Mystery of Godliness—The State of Innocence—Christian Sympathy—Righteousness not of us, but in us—The Law of the Spirit—The New Works of the Gospel—The State of Salvation—Transgressions and Infirmities—Sins of Infirmity—Sincerity and Hypocrisy—The Testimony of Conscience—Many called, few chosen—Present Blessings—Endurance, the Christian's portion—Affliction a School of Comfort—The thought of God, the stay of the Soul—Love the one thing needful—The Power of the Will.

CONTENTS OF VOL. VI.

Fasting, a Source of Trial—Life, the Season of Repentance—Apostolic Abstinence, a Pattern for Christians—Christ's Privations, a Meditation for Christians—Christ the Son of God made Man—The Incarnate Son, a Sufferer and Sacrifice—The Cross of Christ the Measure of the World—Difficulty of realizing Sacred Privileges—The Gospel Sign addressed to Faith—The Spiritual Presence of Christ in the Church—The Eucharistic Presence—Faith the Title for Justification—Judaism of the present day—The Fellowship of the Apostles—Rising with Christ—Warfare the Condition of Victory—Waiting for Christ—Subjection of the Reason and Feelings to the Revealed Word—The Gospel Palaces—The Visible Temple—Offerings for the Sanctuary—The Weapons of Saints—Faith without Demonstration—The Mystery of the Holy Trinity—Peace in Believing.

CONTENTS OF VOL. VII.

The Lapse of Time—Religion, a Weariness to the Natural Man—The World our Enemy—The Praise of Men—Temporal Advantages—The Season of Epiphany—The Duty of Self-denial—The Yoke of Christ—Moses the Type of Christ—The Crucifixion—Attendance on Holy Communion—The Gospel Feast—Love of Religion, a new Nature—Religion pleasant to the Religious—Mental Prayer—Infant Baptism—The Unity of the Church—Steadfastness in the Old Paths.

CONTENTS OF VOL. VIII.

Reverence in Worship—Divine Calls—The Trial of Saul—The Call of David—Curiosity a Temptation to Sin—Miracles no remedy for Unbelief—Josiah, a Pattern for the Ignorant—Inward Witness to the Truth of the Gospel—Jeremiah, a Lesson for the Disappointed—Endurance of the World's Censure—Doing Glory to God in Pursuits of the World—Vanity of Human Glory—Truth hidden when not sought after—Obedience to God the Way to Faith in Christ—Sudden Conversions—The Shepherd of our Souls—Religious Joy—Ignorance of Evil.

and at Oxford and Cambridge

Lectures on the Doctrine of Justification.
By JOHN HENRY NEWMAN, B.D., sometime Fellow of Oriel College, Oxford. New Edition. Crown 8vo. 5s.

CONTENTS.

Faith considered as the Instrument of Justification—Love considered as the Formal Cause of Justification—Primary Sense of the term Justification—Secondary Senses of the term Justification—Misuse of the term Just or Righteous—On the Gift of Righteousness—The Characteristics of the Gift of Righteousness—Righteousness viewed as a Gift and as a Quality—Righteousness the Fruit of our Lord's Resurrection—The Office of Justifying Faith—The Nature of Justifying Faith—Faith viewed relatively to Rites and Works—On preaching the Gospel—Appendix.

Sermons Bearing upon Subjects of the Day.
By JOHN HENRY NEWMAN, B.D., sometime Fellow of Oriel College, Oxford. Edited by the Rev. W. J. COPELAND, B.D., Rector of Farnham, Essex. New Edition. Crown 8vo. 5s.

CONTENTS.

The Work of the Christian—Saintliness not forfeited by the Penitent—Our Lord's Last Supper and His First—Dangers to the Penitent—The Three Offices of Christ—Faith and Experience—Faith and the World—The Church and the World—Indulgence in Religious Privileges—Connection between Personal and Public Improvement—Christian Nobleness—Joshua, a Type of Christ and His Followers—Elisha, a Type of Christ and His Followers—The Christian Church a continuation of the Jewish—The Principle of continuity between the Jewish and Christian Churches—The Christian Church an Imperial Power—Sanctity the Token of the Christian Empire—Condition of the Members of the Christian Empire—The Apostolical Christian—Wisdom and Innocence—Invisible Presence of Christ—Outward and Inward Notes of the Church—Grounds for Steadfastness in our Religious Profession—Elijah the Prophet of the Latter Days—Feasting in Captivity—The Parting of Friends.

Fifteen Sermons preached before the
University of Oxford, between A.D. 1826 and 1843. By JOHN HENRY NEWMAN, B.D., sometime Fellow of Oriel College, Oxford. New Edition. Crown 8vo. 5s.

CONTENTS.

The Philosophical Temper first enjoined by the Gospel—The Influence of Natural and Revealed Religion respectively—Evangelical Sanctity the Perfection of Natural Virtue—The Usurpations of Reason—Personal Influence, the means of Propagating the Truth—Our Justice, as a Principle of Divine Governance—Contest between Faith and Light—Human Responsibility, as Independent of Circumstances—Wilfulness the Sin of Saul—Faith and Reason, contrasted as Habits of Mind—The Nature of Faith in Relation to Reason—Love the Safeguard of Faith against Superstition—Implicit and Explicit Reason—Wisdom, as contrasted with Faith and with Bigotry—The Theory of Developments in Religious Doctrine.

Sermons preached before the University of Oxford, and on various occasions. By J. B. MOZLEY, D.D., Regius Professor of Divinity, Oxford, and Canon of Christ Church. Third Edition. Crown 8vo. 7s. 6d.

CONTENTS.

The Roman Council—The Pharisees—Eternal Life—The Reversal of Human Judgment—War—Nature—The Work of the Spirit on the Natural Man—The Atonement—Our Duty to Equals—The Peaceful Temper—The Strength of Wishes—The unspoken Judgment of Mankind—The true test of Spiritual Birth—Ascension Day—Gratitude—The Principle of Emulation—Religion the First Choice—The Influence of Dogmatic Teaching on Education.

"*There are sermons in it which, for penetrating insight into the mysteries and anomalies of human character, its power of holding together strange opposites, its capacity for combination, for disguise, and unconscious transformation, are as wonderful, it may almost be said as terrible, in their revelations and suggestions as are to be found anywhere. There are four sermons, one on the 'Pharisees,' one on 'Eternal Life,' one on the 'Reversal of Human Judgment,' the fourth on the 'Unspoken Judgment of Mankind,' which must almost make an epoch in the thought and history of any one who reads them and really takes in what they say. There is in them a kind of Shakspearian mixture of subtlety of remark with boldness and directness of phrase, and with a grave, pathetic irony, which is not often characteristic of such compositions.*"—TIMES.

"*These are unusually remarkable sermons. They are addressed to educated, reflective, and, in some cases, philosophical readers, and they exhibit, by turns or in combination, high philosophical power, a piercing appreciation of human motives, vivid conceptions, and a great power of clothing those conceptions in the language of trenchant aphorism, or lofty, earnest poetry.*"—GUARDIAN.

"*A new gleam of religious genius. . . . Keen simplicity and reality in the way of putting things is characteristic of these sermons of Dr. Mozley's, but not less characteristic of them—and this is what shows that the Christian faith has in him appealed to a certain original faculty of the kind which we call 'genius'—is the instinctive sympathy which he seems to have with the subtler shades of Christ's teaching, so as to make it suddenly seem new to us, as well as more wonderful than ever.*"—SPECTATOR.

"*The volume possesses intrinsic merits so remarkable as to be almost unique. . . . There is scarcely a sermon in it which does not possess eloquence, in a very true sense, of a high order. But it is the eloquence not so much of language as of thought. It is the eloquence of concentration, of vigorous grasp, of delicate irony, of deep but subdued pathos, of subtle delicacy of touch, of broad strong sense; it impresses the mind rather than strikes the ear. We cannot help feeling, as we read, not only that the preacher means what he says, but that he has taken pains to think out his meaning, and has applied to the process the whole energy and resources of no common intellect.*" — SATURDAY REVIEW.

anb at 𝔒xforb anb Cambridge

Sermons Preached in the Temporary
Chapel of Keble College, Oxford, 1870—1876. Crown 8vo. 6s.

CONTENTS.

The Service of God the Principle of Daily Life—The Costliness of Acceptable Offerings—The Hearing of Sermons—The Missionary Character of all Christian Lives—The Revelation of the Son as well in Nature as in the Incarnation—The New Chapel—The Secret of Spiritual Strength—The Preparation of Lent—The Spirit of the Daily Services: I. The Spiritual Sacrifice of the Universal Priesthood. II. Offering to God of His Own—The Life of Love—The Resurrection—Redeeming the Time—The Devotional Study of Holy Scripture—Conversion—Conversation—Enthusiasm—Growth in the Knowledge of God—The Imitation of Christ—Manliness—Truth—Saints' Days—Eternity—Life.

"There is a healthy, manly, and moderate tone in the sermons, which may well allay any anxiety with regard to the character of the teaching at Keble. Although this volume was primarily intended for members and friends of the College, it may be read with profit by any one, and more especially by young men, to whom it will show that the spiritual life does not demand the close air and tender nursing of a conservatory, and is perfectly compatible with the open-air, work-a-day life, which the large majority of mankind must of necessity lead."—CHURCH BELLS.

"If ever young men require spiritual strength, it is when they are first set as undergraduates to battle with the temptations which a University offers. The pulpit-teaching of Keble College has been adapted, with great skill and earnestness, to meet that want, and the result is a volume which no young man, be he cleric or layman, can peruse without being roused and stirred in heart and conscience.... We would notice especially the noble sermon on 'The Secret of Spiritual Strength' as deserving an attentive perusal. The volume is a valuable one."—CHURCH QUARTERLY REVIEW.

Farewell Counsels of a Pastor to his
Flock, on Topics of the Day. By EDWARD MEYRICK GOULBURN, D.D., Dean of Norwich. Third Edition. Small 8vo. 4s.

CONTENTS.

Absolution—Ritualism—The Doctrine of the Eucharist—The Atonement—The Stability of an Orthodox Faith—The Stability of Personal Religion—On Preaching Christ Crucified—The Responsibility of Hearers.

Warnings of the Holy Week, &c. Being
a Course of Parochial Lectures for the Week before Easter and the Easter Festivals. By the Rev. W. ADAMS, M.A., Author of "Sacred Allegories," &c. Seventh Edition. Small 8vo. 4s. 6d.

CONTENTS.

The Warning given at Bethany—The Warning of the Day of Excitement—The Warning of the Day of Chastisement—The Warning of the Fig Tree—The Warning of Judas—The Warning of Pilate—The Warning of the Day of Rest—The Signs of Our Lord's Presence—The Remedy for Anxious Thoughts—Comfort under Despondency.

Waterloo Place, London

The Catholic Sacrifice. Sermons Preached

at All Saints, Margaret Street. By the Rev. BERDMORE COMPTON, M.A., Vicar of All Saints, Margaret Street. Crown 8vo. 5s.

CONTENTS.

The Eucharistic Life—The Sacrifice of Sweet Savour—The Pure Offering—The Catholic Oblation—The Sacrificial Feast—The Preparation for the Eucharist—The Introductory Office—The Canon—Degrees of Apprehension—The Fascination of Christ Crucified—The Shewbread—Consecration of Worship and Work—Water, Blood, Wine—The Blood of Sprinkling—The Mystery of Sacraments—The Oblation of Gethsemane—Offertory and Tribute Money.

The Sayings of the Great Forty Days,

between the Resurrection and Ascension, regarded as the Outlines of the Kingdom of God. In Five Discourses. With an Examination of Dr. Newman's Theory of Development. By GEORGE MOBERLY, D.C.L., Bishop of Salisbury. Fifth Edition. Crown 8vo. 5s.

Plain Sermons, preached at Brighstone.

By GEORGE MOBERLY, D.C.L., Bishop of Salisbury. Third Edition. Crown 8vo. 5s.

CONTENTS.

Except a Man be Born again—The Lord with the Doctors—The Draw-Net—I will lay me down in Peace—Ye have not so learned Christ—Trinity Sunday—My Flesh is Meat indeed—The Corn of Wheat dying and multiplied—The Seed Corn springing to new Life—I am the Way, the Truth, and the Life—The Ruler of the Sea—Stewards of the Mysteries of God—Ephphatha—The Widow of Nain—Josiah's Discovery of the Law—The Invisible World: Angels—Prayers, especially Daily Prayers—They all with one consent began to make excuse—Ascension Day—The Comforter—The Tokens of the Spirit—Elijah's Warning, Fathers and Children—Thou shalt see them no more for ever—Baskets full of Fragments—Harvest—The Marriage Supper of the Lamb—The Last Judgment.

Sermons preached at Winchester College.

By GEORGE MOBERLY, D.C.L., Bishop of Salisbury. 2 Vols. Small 8vo. 6s. 6d. each. Sold separately.

---

and at Oxford and Cambridge

Sermons. By HENRY MELVILL, B.D., late
Canon of St. Paul's, and Chaplain in Ordinary to the Queen. New Edition. 2 Vols. Crown 8vo. 5s. each. Sold separately.

CONTENTS OF VOL. I.

The First Prophecy—Christ the Minister of the Church—The Impossibility of Creature-Merit—The Humiliation of the Man Christ Jesus—The Doctrine of the Resurrection viewed in connection with that of the Soul's Immortality—The Power of Wickedness and Righteousness to reproduce themselves—The Power of Religion to strengthen the Human Intellect—The Provision made by God for the Poor—St. Paul, a Tent-Maker—The Advantages of a state of Expectation—Truth as it is in Jesus—The Difficulties of Scripture.

CONTENTS OF VOL. II.

Jacob's Vision and Vow—The continued Agency of the Father and the Son—The Resurrection of Dry Bones—Protestantism and Popery—Christianity a Sword—The Death of Moses—The Ascension of Christ—The Spirit upon the Waters—The Proportion of Grace to Trial—Pleading before the Mountains—Heaven—God's Way in the Sanctuary.

"Every one who can remember the days when Canon Melvill was the preacher of the day, will be glad to see these four-and-twenty of his sermons so nicely reproduced. His Sermons were all the result of real study and genuine reading, with far more theology in them than those of many who make much more profession of theology. There are sermons here which we can personally remember; it has been a pleasure to us to be reminded of them, and we are glad to see them brought before the present generation. We hope that they may be studied, for they deserve it thoroughly."—LITERARY CHURCHMAN.

"The Sermons of Canon Melvill, now republished in two handy volumes, need only to be mentioned to be sure of a hearty welcome. Sound learning, well-weighed words, calm and keen logic, and solemn devoutness, mark the whole series of masterly discourses, which embrace some of the chief doctrines of the Church, and set them forth in clear and Scriptural strength."—STANDARD.

"It would be easy to quote portions of exceeding beauty and power. It was not, however, the charm of style, nor wealth of words, both which Canon Melvill possessed in so great abundance, that he relied on to win souls; but the power and spirit of Him Who said, ' I if I be lifted up, will draw all men to Me.'"—RECORD.

"Messrs. Rivington have published very opportunely, at a time when Churchmen are thinking with satisfaction of the new blood infused into the Chapter of St. Paul's, Sermons by Henry Melvill, who in his day was as celebrated as a preacher as is Canon Liddon now. The sermons are not only couched in elegant language, but are replete with matter which the younger clergy would do well to study."—JOHN BULL.

"Few preachers have had more admirers than the Rev. Henry Melvill, and the new edition of his Sermons, in two volumes, will doubtless find plenty of purchasers. The Sermons abound in thought, and the thoughts are couched in English which is at once elegant in construction and easy to read."—CHURCH TIMES.

. . . . "As they are models of their particular style of oratory, they will be valuable helps to young preachers."—UNION REVIEW.

"Henry Melvill's intellect was large, his imagination brilliant, his ardour intense, and his style strong, fervid, and picturesque. Often he seemed to glow with the inspiration of a prophet."—AMERICAN QUARTERLY CHURCH REVIEW.

Waterloo Place, London

Sermons on Certain of the Less

Prominent Facts and References in Sacred Story. By HENRY MELVILL, B.D., late Canon of St. Paul's, and Chaplain in Ordinary to the Queen. New Edition. 2 Vols. Crown 8vo. 5*s.* each. Sold separately.

CONTENTS OF VOL. I.

The Faith of Joseph on his Death-bed—Angels as Remembrancers—The Burning of the Magical Books—The Parting Hymn—Cæsar's Household—The Sleepless Night—The Well of Bethlehem—The Thirst of Christ—The second Delivery of the Lord's Prayer—Peculiarities in the Miracle in the Coasts of Decapolis—The Latter Rain—The Lowly Errand—Nehemiah before Artaxerxes—Jabez.

CONTENTS OF VOL. II.

The Young Man in the Linen Cloth—The Fire on the Shore—The Finding the Guest-Chamber—The Spectre's Sermon a truism—Various Opinions—The Misrepresentations of Eve—Seeking, after Finding—The Bird's Nest—Angels our Guardians in trifles—The appearance of failure—Simon the Cyrenian—The power of the Eye—Pilate's Wife—Examination of Cain.

"*We are glad to see this new edition of what we have always considered to be Melvill's best sermons, because in them we have his best thoughts. . . . Many of these sermons are the strongest arguments yet adduced for internal evidence of the veracity of the Scriptural narratives.*"—STANDARD.

"*Polished, classical, and winning, these sermons bear the marks of literary labour. A study of them will aid the modern preacher to refine and polish his discourses, and to add to the vigour which is now the fashion, the graces of chastened eloquence and winning rhetoric.*"—ENGLISH CHURCHMAN.

"*The sermons of the lamented Melvill are too well known to require any commendation from us. We have here all the power of rhetoric, and the grace and beauty of style, for which the author has been distinguished, and which have contributed to render him a model to preachers, and given him a representative position in the history of the English pulpit.*"—WEEKLY REVIEW.

'*Unusually interesting . . . . No one can read these sermons without deriving instruction from them, without being compelled to acknowledge that new light has been cast for him on numerous passages of Scripture, which he must henceforth read with greater intelligence and greater interest than before.*"—EDINBURGH COURANT.

"*For skill in developing the significance of the less prominent facts of Holy Scripture' no one could compete with the late Canon Melvill, four volumes of whose discourses—two of them occupied entirely with his sermons on subjects of this class—are before us. His preaching was unique. He selected for the most part texts that are not frequently treated, and when he chose those of a more ordinary character, he generally presented them in a new light, and elicited from them some truth which would not have suggested itself to any other preacher. He was singularly ingenious in some of his conceptions, and wonderfully forcible and impressive in his mode of developing and applying them.*"—NONCONFORMIST.

"*The publishers of these well-known, almost classic sermons, have conferred a boon on all lovers of our pulpit literature by this beautiful, portable edition of some of the most brilliant and original discourses that have been delivered to this generation.*"—BRITISH QUARTERLY REVIEW.

and at 𝔒xford and 𝔈ambridge

Selection from the Sermons preached

during the Latter Years of his Life, in the Parish Church of Barnes, and in the Cathedral of St. Paul's. By HENRY MELVILL, B.D., late Canon of St. Paul's, and Chaplain in Ordinary to the Queen. New Edition. 2 Vols. Crown 8vo. 5s. each. Sold separately.

CONTENTS OF VOL. I.

The Parity of the consequences of Adam's Transgression and Christ's Death—The Song of Simeon—The Days of Old—Omissions of Scripture—The Madman in Sport—Peace, Peace, when there is no Peace—A very lovely Song—This is that King Ahaz—Ariel—New Wine and Old Bottles—Demas—Michael and the Devil—The Folly of Excessive Labour—St. Paul at Philippi—Believing a Lie—The Prodigal Son—The Foolishness of Preaching—Knowledge and Sorrow—The Unjust Steward—The Man born blind.

CONTENTS OF VOL. II.

Rejoicing as in Spoil — Satan a Copyist — The binding the Tares into Bundles — Two walking together—Agreeing with the Adversary—God speaking to Moses—Hoping in Mercy—Faith as a Grain of Mustard Seed—Mary's Recompense—War in Heaven—Glory into Shame—The Last Judgment—Man like to Vanity—God so Loved the World—Saul—And what shall this Man do?—The Sickness and Death of Elisha—Abiding in our Callings—Trinity Sunday.

"*The main characteristics of Canon Melvill's sermons are these—they are not polemical; the* odium theologicum *is nowhere to be found in them, and nowhere is the spirit of true Christian charity and love absent from them. This will widen their usefulness, for they will on this account make a ready way amongst all sects and creeds of professing Christians. Again, these sermons are eminently practical and devotional in their tone and aim. The truths here proclaimed pierce the heart to its very core, so true is the preacher's aim, so vigorous is the force with which he shoots the convictions of his own heart into the hearts of his hearers.*"—STANDARD.

"*There are in the sermons before us all Melvill's wonted grace of diction, strength of reasoning, and aptness of illustration.*"—WEEKLY REVIEW.

"*Two other volumes of the late Canon Melvill's sermons contain forty discourses preached by him in his later years, and they are prefaced by a short memoir of one of the worthiest and most impressive preachers of recent times.*"—EXAMINER.

"*Many years have now elapsed since we first heard Henry Melvill. But we can still recall the text, the sermon, the deep impression made upon us by the impassioned eloquence of the great preacher. It was our first, and very profitable experience of what influence there resides in the faithful preaching of the Gospel of the Lord Jesus Christ. For while it was impossible to be indifferent to the messenger, yet the message was brought home by him to the heart and to the conscience. It is pleasant in these, the latest sermons delivered by Mr. Melvill, to find the same faithful utterance.*"—CHRISTIAN OBSERVER.

Lectures delivered at St. Margaret's,

Lothbury. By the Rev. HENRY MELVILL, B.D., late Canon of St. Paul's, and Chaplain in Ordinary to the Queen. New Edition. Crown 8vo. 5s.

CONTENTS.

The Return of the Dispossessed Spirit—Honey from the Rock—Easter—The Witness in Oneself—The Apocrypha—A Man a Hiding-place—The Hundredfold Recompense—The Life more than Meat—Isaiah's Vision—St. John the Baptist—Building the Tombs of the Prophets—Manifestation of the Sons of God—St. Paul's Determination—The Song of Moses and the Lamb—The Divine Longsuffering—Sowing the Seed—The Great Multitude—The Kinsman Redeemer—St. Barnabas—Spiritual Decline.

"*We receive with welcome a new edition of these well-known and deservedly popular lectures. The time for criticising them has passed, the time for reading them will not pass for many years.*"—NONCONFORMIST.

"*The admirers of the late Canon Melvill will rejoice to see his well-known Lothbury Lectures republished in such a handy, cheap, and excellent edition. Canon Melvill's sermons are still well worthy of study. They are elegant, yet exact; scholarly, yet popular; full of searching logic, yet easy to understand; always earnest and devout, marked by freshness and interest, and written in language of indued and chastened eloquence. They will be found useful and readable by all sects and creeds.*" — GLASGOW HERALD.

"*Canon Melvill was known in his day as one of the most brilliant pulpit orators in the English Church, and of the many volumes of his sermons that have appeared, there is not one which is more likely to justify the estimate in which he has been held than this, furnishing as it does abundant proof of his wide learning, rare expository power, and exuberant splendour of language.*"—SCOTSMAN.

The Reconciliation of Reason and

Faith. Being Sermons on Faith, Evil, Sin and Suffering, Immortality, God, Science, Prayer, and other Subjects. By REGINALD E. MOLYNEUX, M.A. Crown 8vo. 4s.

The Soul in its Probation: Sermons

Preached at the Church of S. Alban the Martyr, Holborn, on the Sundays in Lent, 1873. By the Rev. F. N. OXENHAM, M.A. 8vo. 5s.

The Christian Character; Six Sermons

preached in Lent. By JOHN JACKSON, D.D., Bishop of London. Seventh Edition. Small 8vo. 3s. 6d.

---

and at Oxford and Cambridge

Sermons on Special Occasions.

By DANIEL MOORE, M.A., Chaplain in Ordinary to the Queen, and Vicar of Holy Trinity, Paddington. Crown 8vo. 7s. 6d.

CONTENTS.

The Words of Christ imperishable—The Gospel Welcome—The Conversion of St. Paul—The Christian's Mission—Business and Godliness—Soberness and Watchfulness—The Joy of the Disciples at the Resurrection—The Saviour's Ascension—Jesus in the Midst—The Moral Attractions of the Cross—The Gospel Workmen—The Work of the Holy Spirit—The Doctrine of the Holy Trinity—The Law of Moral Recompenses—The Goodness of King Joash—The Tenderness of Christ—Christ our Example in Youth—Jacob in Life and in Death—The Spiritual Mind—Britain's Obligations to the Gospel—The Throne in Mourning—Prayer and Providence—The Unsearchableness of God.

The Age and the Gospel; Four Sermons

preached before the University of Cambridge, at the Hulsean Lecture, 1864. With a Discourse on Final Retribution. By DANIEL MOORE, M.A., Chaplain in Ordinary to the Queen, and Vicar of Holy Trinity, Paddington. Crown 8vo. 5s.

The Mystery of the Temptation: a

Course of Lectures. By the Rev. W. H. HUTCHINGS, M.A., Sub-Warden of the House of Mercy, Clewer. Crown 8vo. 4s. 6d.

CONTENTS.

The Entrance into the Temptation—The Fast—The Personality of Satan—The First Temptation—The Second Temptation—The Third Temptation—The End of the Temptation.

"*We can mention with unmixed praise a series of lectures on 'The Mystery of the Temptation,' by Mr. Hutchings of Clewer. They are deeply thoughtful, full, and well written, in a style which, from its calmness and dignity, befits the subject.*"—GUARDIAN.

"*This book is one of the refreshing proofs still occasionally met with that the traditional culture and refinement of the Anglican clergy is not quite exhausted, nor its exhaustion implied, by the endless and vulgar controversies that fill the columns of religious newspapers. The sober earnestness that has always been a characteristically Anglican virtue has not failed in a preacher like Mr. Hutchings.*"—ACADEMY.

"*Students of Scripture will find in 'The Mystery of the Temptation' sound reasoning, the evidences of close study, and the spirit of reverence and fervent faith.*"—MORNING POST.

"*This is a volume of lectures which will repay serious study. They are earnest to the last degree.*"—LITERARY CHURCHMAN.

"*Very good indeed.*"—NEW YORK CHURCH JOURNAL.

The Religion of the Christ: its Historic and Literary Development considered as an Evidence of its Origin. Being the Bampton Lectures for 1874. By the Rev. STANLEY LEATHES, M.A., Minister of St. Philip's, Regent Street, and Professor of Hebrew, King's College, London. Second Edition. Crown 8vo. 7s. 6d.

"*These lectures are a noble contribution to the evidences of the Christian faith.*"—BRITISH QUARTERLY REVIEW.

"*Admirably adapted to meet some of the foremost objections which are now being brought against 'the divine authority of the Holy Scriptures.' We earnestly recommend our readers to buy the book for themselves.*"—LITERARY CHURCHMAN.

"*A volume which ought to take its place beside the best standard works on the evidences of Christianity—a kind of literature in which the Church of England is peculiarly rich.*"—SCOTSMAN.

"*His Bampton Lectures are perhaps the most suggestive and elaborate of all his productions, and would of themselves win for him a high position as a writer on Christian evidence.*"—FREEMAN.

"*The preface, in which Mr. Leathes sums up the arguments in his lucid way, which are more elaborately drawn out in the Lectures, is one of the finest specimens of clear, candid, temperate reasoning in modern literature.*"—NEW YORK INDEPENDENT.

"*With thoughtful minds it will carry great weight.*"—NEW YORK CHURCHMAN.

The Witness of the Old Testament to Christ. Being the Boyle Lectures for the year 1868. By the Rev. STANLEY LEATHES, M.A., Minister of St. Philip's, Regent Street, and Professor of Hebrew, King's College, London. 8vo. 9s.

The Witness of St. Paul to Christ. Being the Boyle Lectures for 1869. With an Appendix on the Credibility of the Acts, in Reply to the Recent Strictures of Dr. Davidson. By the Rev. STANLEY LEATHES, M.A., Minister of St. Philip's, Regent Street, and Professor of Hebrew, King's College, London. 8vo. 10s. 6d.

The Witness of St. John to Christ. Being the Boyle Lectures for 1870. With an Appendix on the Authorship and Integrity of St. John's Gospel, and the Unity of the Johannine Writings. By the Rev. STANLEY LEATHES, M.A., Minister of St. Philip's, Regent Street, and Professor of Hebrew, King's College, London. 8vo. 10s. 6d.

and at Oxford and Cambridge

The Doctrine of the Cross: specially in its relation to the Troubles of Life. Sermons preached during Lent in the Parish Church of New Windsor by HENRY J. ELLISON, M.A. (sometime Vicar of Windsor), Honorary Chaplain to the Queen, Honorary Canon of Christ Church, and Rector of Haseley, Oxon. Small 8vo. 2s. 6d.

The Permanence of Christianity. Considered in Eight Lectures preached before the University of Oxford, in the year 1872, on the Foundation of the late Rev. John Bampton, M.A. By JOHN RICHARD TURNER EATON, M.A., late Fellow and Tutor of Merton College, Rector of Lapworth, Warwickshire. 8vo. 12s.

Short Sermons on the Psalms in their Order. Preached in a Village Church. By W. J. STRACEY, M.A., Rector of Oxnead, and Vicar of Buxton, Norfolk, formerly Fellow of Magdalen College, Cambridge. Crown 8vo.

Vol. I.—Psalms I—XXV. 5s.
Vol. II.—Psalms XXVI—LI. 5s.

Pleadings for Christ. Being Sermons, Doctrinal and Practical, preached in St. Andrew's Church, Liverpool. By WILLIAM LEFROY, M.A., Incumbent. Crown 8vo. 6s.

The Way of Holiness in Married Life. A Course of Sermons preached in Lent. By the Rev. HENRY J. ELLISON, M.A., Hon. Canon of Christ Church, and Vicar of New Windsor, Berks. Second Edition. Small 8vo. 2s. 6d.

Waterloo Place, London

Sermons Preached in the Parish Church of Barnes, 1871 to 1876. By PETER GOLDSMITH MEDD, M.A., Rector of North Cerney, Canon of St. Albans, and Examining Chaplain to the Bishop; late Senior Fellow of University College, Oxford, and Rector of Barnes. Crown 8vo. 7s. 6d.

CONTENTS.

Thankfulness for God's Mercies—Subjection to the Civil Power—Christ's Prophecy of the End—God's Purpose of Love in Creation—The Introduction of Evil into the Creation—Christian Love—Christianity a Religion of Self-Denial—The Nature of Sin—The Consequences of Sin (No. 1)—The Consequences of Sin (No. 2)—The Remedy of Sin (No. 1)—The Remedy of Sin (No. 2)—With Christ in Paradise—The Remedy of Sin (No. 3)—The Remedy of Sin (No. 4)—Christ the Resurrection and the Life—The Hope of the Resurrection—The Three Resurrections—The Hope of the Christian—The Publican's Prayer—The Conflict of Flesh and Spirit—Christian Unity—The Duty of Forgiveness—Present Salvation—The Marks of the Children of God—Against Religious Narrowness—The Necessity of Meditation on Religious Subjects—The Need of Effort in the Christian Life—Bodily Works of Mercy—The Athanasian Creed—Conscious Religion—The Comfort of the Christian Faith—Appendix.

" *The special merit of his volume is its thoughtfulness; and as Mr. Medd writes in a very condensed style, the thirty-two sermons which he has given us contain a great deal more of valuable matter than many books of much larger bulk. . . . We believe that many of our readers, among the clergy as well as the laity, will thank us for having drawn their attention to the excellences of the volume before us.*"—GUARDIAN.

" *Mr. Medd's sermons are well worthy of publication . . . they are above the average of such compositions, and form an instructive volume.*"—CHURCH TIMES.

" *They range over a wide circle of subjects, theological and practical; but are always full, vigorous, and energetic, yet with a sobriety of style and an elegance of treatment that must have charmed the hearer just as they win upon the reader. We do not often meet with a volume of discourses of such uniform excellence. Nothing hazardous is attempted; but in all that he attempts Mr. Medd entirely succeeds. The teaching is plain, direct, and effective; while the breadth of view and the liberality of sentiment are most refreshing in these days when the sermon is too often made a party manifesto. Professor Blackie would find in them both 'vigour' and 'grace.' And the reader will also find in them a considerable knowledge of the heart, an intelligent comprehension of the Christian system, much lucid exposition of Scriptural truth, and a forcible application of it to the human conscience.*"—SCOTTISH GUARDIAN.

." *Careful and practical expositions of Christian duties, doctrines, and responsibilities, written with much force of language, and brought home to the unlettered with considerable logical vigour.*"—STANDARD.

and at Oxford and Cambridge

The Last Three Sermons preached at Oxford by PHILIP N. SHUTTLEWORTH, D.D., sometime Lord Bishop of Chichester. Justification through Faith—The Merciful Character of the Gospel Covenant—The Sufficiency of Scripture a Rule of Faith. To which is added a Letter addressed in 1841 to a Young Clergyman, now a Priest in the Church of Rome. New Edition. Small 8vo. 2s. 6d.

Not Tradition but Scripture. By the late PHILIP NICHOLAS SHUTTLEWORTH, D.D., Warden of New College, Oxford, and Rector of Foxley, Wilts, afterwards Bishop of Chichester. Fourth Edition. Crown 8vo. 4s. 6d.

Faith and Practice: A Selection of Sermons Preached in St. Philip's Chapel, Regent Street. By the Rev. FRANCIS PIGOU, M.A., Vicar of Halifax, and Hon. Chaplain in Ordinary to the Queen. Small 8vo. 6s.

CONTENTS.

The Certainty of the Resurrection—Whitsunday—The Stilling of the Tempest—Practical Religion—The Memory of the Just—The Remembrance of Sin—The Danger of Relapse—Individual Influence—The use and abuse of God's gifts—Natural and Spiritual Instincts—Prayer—Preparation for Death.

7. Religious Education.

A Key to Christian Doctrine and Practice,

founded on the Church Catechism. By the Rev. JOHN HENRY BLUNT, M.A., F.S.A., Editor of "The Annotated Book of Common Prayer," &c. &c. Small 8vo. 2s. 6d.

Forming a Volume of "Keys to Christian Knowledge."

"*Of cheap and reliable text-books of this nature there has hitherto been a great want. We are often asked to recommend books for use in Church Sunday-schools, and we therefore take this opportunity of saying that we know of none more likely to be of service both to teachers and scholars than these 'Keys.'*" — CHURCHMAN'S SHILLING MAGAZINE.

"*This is another of Mr. Blunt's most useful manuals, with all the precision of a school book, yet diverging into matters of practical application so freely as to make it most serviceable, either as a teacher's suggestion book, or as an intelligent pupil's reading book.*"—LITERARY CHURCHMAN.

"*Will be very useful for the higher classes in Sunday-schools, or rather for the fuller instruction of the Sunday-school teachers themselves, where the parish priest is wise enough to devote a certain time regularly to their preparation for their voluntary task.*"—UNION REVIEW.

Household Theology: a Handbook of

Religious Information respecting the Holy Bible, the Prayer Book, the Church, the Ministry, Divine Worship, the Creeds, &c. &c. By the Rev. JOHN HENRY BLUNT, M.A., F.S.A., Editor of "The Annotated Book of Common Prayer," &c. &c. New Edition. Small 8vo. 3s. 6d.

CONTENTS.

The Bible—The Prayer Book—The Church—Table of Dates—Ministerial Offices—Divine Worship—The Creeds—A Practical Summary of Christian Doctrine—The Great Christian Writers of Early Times—Ancient and Modern Heresies and Sects—The Church Calendar—A short explanation of Words used in Church History and Theology—Index.

and at Oxford and Cambridge   c

Manuals of Religious Instruction.

Edited by JOHN PILKINGTON NORRIS, B.D., Canon of Bristol, and Examining Chaplain to the Bishop of Manchester.

3 Volumes. Small 8vo. 3*s.* 6*d.* each. Sold separately.

The Old Testament.
The New Testament.
The Prayer Book.

Or each Volume in Five Parts. 1*s.* each Part.

[These Manuals are intended to supply a five years' course of instruction for young people between the ages of thirteen and eighteen.

It will be seen that fifteen small graduated text-books are provided :—

Five on the Old Testament ;
Five on the New Testament ;
Five on the Catechism and Liturgy.

In preparing the last, the Editor has thought it best to spread the study of the Catechism over several years, rather than compress it into one.

This may give rise to what may appear some needless repetition. But the Lessons of our Catechism are of such paramount importance, that it seems desirable to keep it continually in our Pupils' hands, as the best key to the study of the Prayer Book.

There has been a grievous want of *definiteness* in our young people's knowledge of Church doctrine. Especially have the Diocesan Inspectors noticed it in our Pupil Teachers. It has arisen, doubtless, from their Teachers assuming that they had clear elementary ideas about religion, in which really they had never been grounded. It is therefore thought not too much to ask them to give one-third of their time to the study of the Prayer Book.

In the Old Testament and New Testament Manuals the greatest pains have been taken to give them such a character as shall render it impossible for them to supersede the Sacred Text. Two main objects the writers of the Old and New Testament Manuals have proposed to themselves; first, to stimulate interest; second, to supply a sort of running commentary on the inspired page. Especial pains have been taken to draw the reader's attention to the *spiritual* teaching of Holy Scripture, and to subordinate to this the merely historical interest.

The writer of the Old Testament Manual has made it his endeavour to help the reader to see our Lord Christ in Law, in Psalms, in Prophets.

The New Testament Manual is confined to the Gospels and Acts. It was found impossible to include any of the Epistles. But the Fourth Part of the Prayer Book Manual will in some measure supply this deficiency.

Although they were originally prepared with special regard to Pupil Teachers, they will be found adapted also for all students of a like age (from thirteen to eighteen) who have not access to many books.]

Waterloo Place, London

Rudiments of Theology. A First Book

for Students. By JOHN PILKINGTON NORRIS, B.D., Canon of Bristol, and Examining Chaplain to the Bishop of Manchester. Crown 8vo. 7s. 6d.

"*It is altogether a remarkable book. We have seldom seen clear, incisive reasoning, orthodox teaching, and wide-mindedness in such happy combination.*"—LITERARY CHURCHMAN.

"*A most useful book for theological students in the earlier part of their course. . . . The book is one for which the Church owes a debt of gratitude to Canon Norris, combining, as it does, orthodoxy and learning, and logical accuracy of definition with real charity. We heartily commend it.*"—JOHN BULL.

"*We can recommend this book to theological students as a useful and compendious manual. It is clear and well arranged. . . . We venture to believe that, on the whole, he is a very fair exponent of the teaching of the English Church, and that his book may be profitably used by those for whom it is chiefly intended—that is, candidates for ordination.*"—SPECTATOR.

"*This unpretending work supplies a real* desideratum. *. . . It seeks to lead us from the shifting sands of human systems to the solid ground of Divine revelation, wisely recognising as its most trustworthy interpreters those who came nearest to its times,* and directing the student's mind to 'what the early Fathers thought and wrote in the days when the Church's theologians had to hold their own against an adverse world.'"—GUARDIAN.

"*This work was prepared as a handbook for theological students. But it is to reach a far wider field. It is capable of doing a most important service among all classes. We have seldom, if ever, met a more satisfactory or a clearer presentation of the fundamental facts of theology than those given in these pages. . . . The author has the rare faculty—it amounts really to genius—of saying just the thing that ought to be said, and of presenting any truth in such a shape that the reader can easily take hold of it and make it his own. . . . We commend this work to Churchmen generally as one from which all can derive profit. To the Clergy it will serve as a model method of dogmatic teaching, and to the laity it will be a rich storehouse of information concerning the things to be believed. . . . The whole thing is so admirable in tone, arrangement, and style that it will, no doubt, become universally popular.*"—CHURCHMAN (NEW YORK).

The Young Churchman's Companion

to the Prayer Book. By the Rev. J. W. GEDGE, M.A., Winchester Diocesan Inspector of Schools for West Surrey and the Channel Islands. (Recommended by the late and present Lord Bishops of Winchester.)

Part I.—Morning and Evening Prayer and Litany.
Part II.—Baptismal and Confirmation Services.
Part III.—Holy Communion.

18mo., 1s. each Part; or in paper cover, 6d.

and at Oxford and Cambridge

A Catechism on Gospel History, in-
culcating Church Doctrine. By the Rev. SAMUEL KETTLE-
WELL, M.A., late Vicar of St. Mark's, Leeds. Third Edition.
Small 8vo. 3s. 6d.

"*To further the good and pious cus-* *to assist the Christian teacher.*"—Ex-
tom of parents giving religious instruc- TRACT FROM PREFACE.
tion to their own children, as well as

Catechesis; or, Christian Instruction
preparatory to Confirmation and First Communion. By
CHARLES WORDSWORTH, D.C.L., Bishop of St. Andrews.
New Edition. Small 8vo. 2s.

A Help to Catechizing. For the Use of
Clergymen, Schools, and Private Families. By JAMES BEAVEN,
D.D., formerly Professor of Divinity in the University of King's
College, Toronto. New Edition. 18mo. 2s.

Catechetical Exercises on the Apostles'
Creed; chiefly from Bp. Pearson. By EDWARD BICKER-
STETH, D.D., Dean of Lichfield. New Edition. 18mo. 2s.

Questions illustrating the Thirty-Nine
Articles of the Church of England, with Proofs from Holy
Scripture, and the Primitive Church. By EDWARD BICKER-
STETH, D.D., Dean of Lichfield. Sixth Edition. Small 8vo.
3s. 6d.

The Idle Word: Short Religious Essays
upon the Gift of Speech. By EDWARD MEYRICK GOULBURN,
D.D., Dean of Norwich. Fourth Edition. Small 8vo. 3s.

CONTENTS.

The Connexion of Speech with Reason—The Connexion of Speech with Reason
—The Heavenly Analogy of the Connexion of Speech with Reason
—An Idle Word Defined from the Decalogue—An Idle Word defined
from the Decalogue—What is an Idle Word?—Words of Business and
innocent Recreation not Idle—Speech the Instrument of Prophecy and
Sacrifice—Hints for the Guidance of Conversation—On Religious Conversation—Appendix.

A Manual of Confirmation, Comprising

—1. A General Account of the Ordinance. 2. The Baptismal Vow, and the English Order of Confirmation, with Short Notes, Critical and Devotional. 3. Meditations and Prayers on Passages of Holy Scripture, in connexion with the Ordinance. With a Pastoral Letter instructing Catechumens how to prepare themselves for their first Communion. By EDWARD MEYRICK GOULBURN, D.D., Dean of Norwich. Ninth Edition. Small 8vo. 1s. 6d.

Easy Lessons Addressed to Candidates

for Confirmation. By JOHN PILKINGTON NORRIS, B.D., Canon of Bristol, and sometime Vicar of St. George's, Brendon Hill. Small 8vo. 1s. 6d.

"*An admirable hand-book on confirmation. It is sound, scriptural, plain, and practical. It brings out only important points, and is not overloaded with unessential things. Besides, it has the rare merit of being adapted to persons of varying ages.*"—CHURCHMAN (NEW YORK).

"*Is so arranged as to convey the teaching of the Catechism to those who, from early disadvantages, are unable to commit it to memory. Earnest counsels are appended for the guidance of the confirmed in maturer years.*"—NATIONAL CHURCH.

"*The Canon aims in the first nine lessons to transfuse the substance of the Catechism into a form which such persons could readily apprehend; and in this he has entirely succeeded. His little book, however, is equally well adapted for better educated candidates, whose interest in the time-honoured formula so often repeated will probably be stimulated afresh by the novelty of the arrangement. Canon Norris's explanations are thoroughly clear, and it is needless to say that his teaching is sound and moderate.*"—SCOTTISH GUARDIAN.

"*A valuable little work, in which the principal points of the Church's teaching are clearly and fully set forth. The remarks on the Sacraments are exceedingly good, and although these 'Lessons' are primarily intended for those who are preparing for confirmation, they might with advantage be studied by those who, having passed this stage, are desirous of refreshing their memories respecting the doctrines they profess to believe.*"—ROCK.

and at 𝔒xford and ℭambridge

8. Allegories and Tales.

Allegories and Tales. By the Rev. W. E. HEYGATE, M.A., Rector of Brighstone. Crown 8vo. 5s.

"*It is eminently original, and every one of its sixty-three short allegories is a story that the dullest child will read and the intelligent child will understand and enjoy. Grave thought, kindly raillery, biting sarcasm, grim humour, sincere indignation, wise counsel, a broad charity, and other characteristics, run through the allegories, many of which are highly poetical and good models of that style of composition.*"—EDINBURGH COURANT.

"*Mr. Heygate's volume contains about sixty short tales or allegories, all rife with good teaching, plainly set forth, and written in a very engaging and attractive style. As a present for children this book would be at once acceptable and beneficial. It can be highly commended.*"—CHURCH HERALD.

"*There are both grace and precision about these 'Allegories and Tales,' which make them charming to read either for young or for old. The stories are some of them quaint, some of them picturesque, all of them pleasant; and the moral they inclose shines out soft and clear as through a crystal. This is a book that may be recommended for a present, not only for young people, but for those of larger growth.*"—ATHENÆUM.

"*The Rector of Brighstone has the gift of writing moral and spiritual lessons for the young in the most attractive fashion. His 'Allegories and Tales' are excellent specimens of stories, with a moral, in which the moral is not obtrusive and yet is not lost.*"—ENGLISH INDEPENDENT.

"*A book of very great beauty and power. Mr. Heygate is a thoughtful, earnest and able writer, on whom more than any one is fallen in a striking manner the mantle of the great author of 'Agathos.'*"—JOHN BULL.

Soimême; a Story of a Wilful Life. Small 8vo. 3s. 6d.

"*There is a very quiet, earnest tone in this story, which reconciles the reader to the lesson which it is intended to teach. It is essentially a story of character, and the heroine who is supposed to relate it is presented in a clearly defined and somewhat picturesque manner . . . To the thoughtful who are passing from youth to riper years, 'Soimême' will prove both attractive and useful.*"—PUBLIC OPINION.

"*A vein of lofty, moral, and deep religious feeling runs through the whole tale, and the author neither proses nor preaches.*"—STANDARD.

"*A very natural, unaffected, and simple little story for young people—one which they will not only read but enjoy.*"—MORNING HERALD.

"*The author promises to become a valuable accession to the ranks of our popular lady writers. 'Soimême' is a simple life-like story, charmingly told and gracefully written, and, what is better still, its tendencies are excellent. The lessons it teaches are of the highest order.*"—EUROPEAN MAIL.

"*There are many clever little bits of description, and excellent maxims worth remembering. The scenery is all charmingly described.*"—MONTHLY PACKET.

Waterloo Place, London

The First Chronicle of Æscendune.

A Tale of the Days of Saint Dunstan. By the Rev. A. D. CRAKE, B.A., Chaplain of All Saints' School, Bloxham, Author of the "History of the Church under the Roman Empire," &c. &c. Crown 8vo. 3s. 6d.

"*The volume will possess a strong interest, especially for the young, and be useful, too, for though in form a tale, it may be classed among 'the side-lights of history.'*"—STANDARD.

"*Altogether the book shows great thought and careful study of the manners and customs of those early Saxon times.*"—JOHN BULL.

"*We shall be glad when Mr. Crake takes up his pen once more, to give us a further instalment of the annals of the House of Æscendune.*"—CHURCH TIMES.

"*A very interesting and well-written story of Saxon times—the times of Dunstan and the hapless Edwy. The author has evidently taken great pains to examine into the real history of the period. We can scarcely imagine it possible that it should be anything else than a great favourite.*"—LITERARY CHURCHMAN.

"*It is one of the best historical tales for the young that has been published for a long time.*"—NONCONFORMIST.

"*Written with much spirit and a careful attention to the best authorities on the history of the period of which he treats.*"—NATIONAL CHURCH.

"*The facts upon which the Chronicle is based have been carefully brought together from a variety of sources, and great skill has been shown in the construction of the narrative. The aim of the author is certainly a good one, and his efforts have been attended with a considerable amount of success.*"—ROCK.

Alfgar the Dane, or the Second Chronicle of Æscendune.

A Tale. By the Rev. A. D. CRAKE, B.A., Chaplain of All Saints' School, Bloxham, Author of the "History of the Church under the Roman Empire," &c. &c. Crown 8vo. 3s. 6d.

"*Mr. Crake's 'Chronicles of Æscendune' have their second instalment in 'Alfgar the Dane,' a youth who is saved from the massacre on S. Brice's night to meet with many capital adventures.*"—GUARDIAN.

"*Sure to be excessively popular with boys, and we look forward with great interest to the Third Chronicle, which will tell of the Norman invasion.*"—CHURCH TIMES.

"*As in his former production, Mr. Crake seems to have taken great pains to be correct in his facts, and he has, we really believe, combined accuracy with liveliness. Schoolboys, not at Bloxham only, ought to be very grateful to him; though in thus speaking we by no means intend to imply that seniors will not find this little book both interesting and instructive. Its tone is as excellent as that of Mr. Crake's previous tale.*"—CHURCH QUARTERLY REVIEW.

"*Here, strung together with characters in harmony with the times, is a thoroughly well-written history of the later Danish invasions of England. . . . . As a tale his work is interesting; as a history it is of very considerable value.*"—NONCONFORMIST.

"*It is not often that a writer combines so completely the qualities which go to make up the historian and the novelist, but Mr. Crake has this happy conjunction of faculties in an eminent degree.*"—STANDARD.

and at 𝔒xford and 𝔒ambridge

Sacred Allegories. The Shadow of the
Cross—The Distant Hills—The Old Man's Home—The King's Messengers. By the Rev. WILLIAM ADAMS, M.A., late Fellow of Merton College, Oxford. New Edition. With numerous Illustrations. Small 8vo. 5s.

The Four Allegories may be had separately, with Illustrations. Small 8vo. 1s. each.

Semele; or, The Spirit of Beauty: a
Venetian Tale. By the Rev. J. D. MEREWEATHER, B.A. English Chaplain at Venice. Small 8vo. 3s. 6d.

The Hillford Confirmation. A Tale.
By M. C. PHILLPOTTS. New Edition. 16mo. 1s.

9. History and Biography.

Christian Biographies. By H. L. SIDNEY LEAR.
New and Uniform Editions. Eight Volumes. Crown 8vo. 3s. 6d. each. Sold separately. Or the Eight Volumes in a Box, 31s. 6d.

Bossuet and his Contemporaries.
Forming a Volume of "Christian Biographies." By H. L. SIDNEY LEAR. Crown 8vo. 3s. 6d.

"It contains so many interesting facts that it may be profitably read even by those who already know the man and the period."—SPECTATOR.

"Here is a clear and good work, the product of thorough industry and of honest mind."—NONCONFORMIST.

"All biography is delightful, and this story of Bossuet is eminently so."—NOTES AND QUERIES.

"Bossuet's daily life, his style of preaching, his association with the stirring political, social, and ecclesiastical events of his time, are presented in a simple but picturesque way."—DAILY NEWS.

"We are always glad to welcome a fresh work from the graceful pen of the author of 'A Dominican Artist.'"—SATURDAY REVIEW.

Fénelon, Archbishop of Cambrai.
A Biographical Sketch. Forming a Volume of "Christian Biographies." By H. L. SIDNEY LEAR. Crown 8vo. 3s. 6d.

"Those who know—and we may fairly ask, who does not?—the charming books which we have already had from the present writer, will need nothing more than the announcement of it to make them welcome this new account of the life of the saintly Fénelon."—CHURCH QUARTERLY REVIEW.

"The history of the Church offers few more attractive biographies than that of the great Archbishop, whom everybody appreciated save his king."—GUARDIAN.

"The delightful volume under notice will add much to the well-deserved reputation of its author."—CHURCH TIMES.

"The writer has found a subject which suits her genius, and she handles it with both skill and sympathy. . . . The account of his life at Cambrai is one of the most delightful narratives that we have ever read. It would be scarcely too much to extend the same praise to the whole book."—SPECTATOR.

"Fénelon is thoroughly readable, and is much more than a biographical sketch. There are nearly 500 pages, and there are very few which fail to give a reader something for glad or serious thought."—NOTES AND QUERIES.

"We doubt much whether the real man was ever so vividly portrayed or his portrait so elegantly framed as in this choice and readable book."—WATCHMAN.

"One of the great charms of this work consists in the letters scattered up and down its pages, some addressed to his royal pupil, and others to his friends. The sweet nature and singular fascination of the Archbishop shine forth conspicuously in these self-revelations, which breathe a truly religious spirit."—ENGLISH INDEPENDENT.

---

and at Oxford and Cambridge

A Christian Painter of the Nineteenth

Century; being the Life of Hippolyte Flandrin. Forming a Volume of "Christian Biographies." By H. L. SIDNEY LEAR. Crown 8vo. 3s. 6d.

"*This is a touching and instructive story of a life singularly full of nobility, affection, and grace, and it is worthily told.*"—SPECTATOR.

"*Sympathetic, popular, and free, almost to a fault, from technicalities. . . . The book is welcome as a not untimely memorial to a man who deserves to be held up as an example.*"—SATURDAY REVIEW.

"*The record of a life marked by exalted aims, and crowned by no small amount of honour and success, cannot but be welcome to earnest students of all kinds. . . . There are many fine pieces of criticism in this book,—utterances of Flandrin's which show the clear wit of the man, his candour, and self-balanced judgment. . . . We have written enough to show how interesting the book is*"—ATHENÆUM.

"*This is a charming addition to biographical literature.*"—NOTES AND QUERIES.

A Dominican Artist: A Sketch of the

Life of the Rev. Père Besson, of the Order of St. Dominic. Forming a Volume of "Christian Biographies." By H. L. SIDNEY LEAR. Crown 8vo. 3s. 6d.

"*The author of the Life of Père Besson writes with a grace and refinement of devotional feeling peculiarly suited to a subject-matter which suffers beyond most others from any coarseness of touch. It would be difficult to find 'the simplicity and purity of a holy life' more exquisitely illustrated than in Father Besson's career, both before and after his joining the Dominican Order under the auspices of Lacordaire. . . . Certainly we have never come across what could more strictly be termed in the truest sense 'the life of a beautiful soul.' The author has done well in presenting to English readers this singularly graceful biography, in which all who can appreciate genuine simplicity and nobleness of Christian character will find much to admire and little or nothing to condemn.*"—SATURDAY REVIEW.

"*It would indeed have been a deplorable omission had so exquisite a biography been by any neglect lost to English readers, and had a character so perfect in its simple and complete devotion been withheld from our admiration. . . . But we have dwelt too long already on this fascinating book, and must now leave it to our readers.*"—LITERARY CHURCHMAN.

"*A beautiful and most interesting sketch of the late Père Besson, an artist who forsook the easel for the altar.*"—CHURCH TIMES.

"*Whatever a reader may think of Père Besson's profession as a monk, no one will doubt his goodness; no one can fail to profit who will patiently read his life, as here written by a friend, whose sole defect is in being slightly unctuous.*"—ATHENÆUM.

"*The story of Père Besson's life is one of much interest, and told with simplicity, candour, and good feeling.*"—SPECTATOR.

"*We strongly recommend it to our readers. It is a charming biography, that will delight and edify both old and young.*"—WESTMINSTER GAZETTE.

The Life of Madame Louise de France,

Daughter of Louis XV., also known as the Mother Térèse de S. Augustin. Forming a Volume of "Christian Biographies." By H. L. SIDNEY LEAR. Crown 8vo. 3s. 6d.

"*Such a record of deep, earnest, self-sacrificing piety, beneath the surface of Parisian life, during what we all regard as the worst age of French godlessness, ought to teach us all a lesson of hope and faith, let appearances be what they may. Here, from out of the court and family of Louis XV. there issues this Madame Louise, whose life is set before us as a specimen of as calm and unworldly devotion—of a devotion, too, full of shrewd sense and practical administrative talent—as any we have ever met with.*"—LITERARY CHURCHMAN.

The Revival of Priestly Life in the

Seventeenth Century in France. CHARLES DE CONDREN— S. PHILIP NERI and CARDINAL DE BERULLE—S. VINCENT DE PAUL — SAINT SULPICE and JEAN JACQUES OLIER. Forming a Volume of "Christian Biographies." By H. L. SIDNEY LEAR. Crown 8vo. 3s. 6d.

"*A book the authorship of which will command the respect of all who can honour sterling worth. No Christian, to whatever denomination he may belong, can read without quick sympathy and emotion these touching sketches of the early Oratorians and the Lazarists.*"—STANDARD.

Life of S. Francis de Sales. Forming a

Volume of "Christian Biographies." By H. L. SIDNEY LEAR. Crown 8vo. 3s. 6d.

"*It is written with the delicacy, freshness, and absence of all affectation which characterized the former works by the same hand, and which render these books so very much more pleasant reading than are religious biographies in general. The character of S. Francis de Sales, Bishop of Geneva, is a charming one; a more simple, pure, and pious life it would be difficult to conceive. His unaffected humility, his freedom from dogmatism in an age when dogma was placed above religion, his freedom from bigotry in an age of persecution, were alike admirable.*"—STANDARD.

"*The author of 'A Dominican Artist,' in writing this new life of the wise and loving Bishop and Prince of Geneva, has aimed less at historical or ecclesiastical investigation than at a vivid and natural representation of the inner mind and life of the subject of his biography, as it can be traced in his own writings and in those of his most intimate and affectionate friends. The book is written with the grave and quiet grace which characterizes the productions of its author, and cannot fail to please those readers who can sympathize with all forms of goodness and devotion to noble purpose.*"—WESTMINSTER REVIEW.

"*A book which contains the record of a life as sweet, pure, and noble, as any man by divine help, granted to devout sincerity of soul, has been permitted to live upon earth. The example of this gentle but resolute and energetic spirit, wholly dedicated to the highest conceivable good, offering itself, with all the temporal uses of mental existence, to the service of infinite and eternal beneficence, is extremely touching. It is a book worthy of acceptance.*"—DAILY NEWS.

and at Oxford and Cambridge

Henri Perreyve. By A. Gratry, Prêtre

de l'Oratoire, Professeur de Morale Evangélique à la Sorbonne, et Membre de l'Académie Française. Translated, by special permission. With Portrait. Forming a Volume of "Christian Biographies." By H. L. Sidney Lear. Crown 8vo. 3s. 6d.

"*A most touching and powerful piece of biography, interspersed with profound reflections on personal religion, and on the prospects of Christianity.*"—Church Review.

"*The works of the translator of Henri Perreyve form, for the most part, a series of saintly biographies which have obtained a larger share of popularity than is generally accorded to books of this description. . . . The description of his last days will probably be read with greater interest than any other part of the book; presenting as it does an example of fortitude under suffering, and resignation, when cut off so soon after entering upon a much-coveted and useful career, of rare occurrence in this age of self-assertion. This is, in fact, the essential teaching of the entire volume.*"—Morning Post.

"*Those who take a pleasure in reading a beautiful account of a beautiful character would do well to procure the Life of 'Henri Perreyve.' . . . We would especially recommend the book for the perusal of English priests, who may learn many a holy lesson from the devoted spirit in which the subject of the memoir gave himself up to the duties of his sacred office, and to the cultivation of the graces with which he was endowed.*"—Church Times.

"*It is easy to see that Henri Perreyve, Professor of Moral Theology at the Sorbonne, was a Roman Catholic priest of no ordinary type. With comparatively little ·of what Protestants call superstition, with great courage and sincerity, with a nature singularly guileless and noble, his priestly vocation, although pursued, according to his biographer, with unbridled zeal, did not stifle his human sympathies and aspirations. He could not believe that his faith compelled him 'to renounce sense and reason,' or that a priest was not free to speak, act, and think like other men. Indeed, the Abbé Gratry makes a kind of apology for his friend's free-speaking in this respect, and endeavours to explain it. Perreyve was the beloved disciple of Lacordaire, who left him all his manuscripts, notes, and papers, and he himself attained the position of a great pulpit orator.*"—Pall Mall Gazette.

The Last Days of Père Gratry. By Père

Adolphe Perraud, of the Oratory, and Professor of La Sorbonne. Translated by Special permission. By the Author of "Life of S. Francis de Sales," &c. Crown 8vo. 3s. 6d.

Walter Kerr Hamilton, Bishop of Salis-

bury. A Sketch by Henry Parry Liddon, D.D., Canon of St. Paul's, and Ireland Professor of Exegesis in the University of Oxford. Second Edition. 8vo. 2s. 6d.

Waterloo Place, London

Life of S. Vincent de Paul. With Introduction by the Rev. R. F. WILSON, M.A., Prebendary of Salisbury and Vicar of Rownhams, and Chaplain to the Bishop of Salisbury. Crown 8vo. 9s.

"*A most readable volume, illustrating plans and arrangements, which from the circumstances of the day are invested with peculiar interest.*"—ENGLISH CHURCHMAN.

"*All will be pleased at reading the present admirably written narrative, in which we do not know whether to admire more the candour and earnestness of the writer or his plain, sensible, and agreeable style.*"—WEEKLY REGISTER.

"*We trust that this deeply interesting and beautifully written biography will be extensively circulated in England.*"—CHURCH HERALD.

"*We heartily recommend the introduction to the study of all concerned with ordinations.*"—GUARDIAN.

"*We are glad that S. Vincent de Paul, one of the most remarkable men produced by the Gallican Church, has at last found a competent English biographer. The volume before us has evidently been written with conscientious care and scrupulous industry. It is based on the best authorities, which have been compared with praiseworthy diligence; its style is clear, elegant, and unambitious; and it shows a fine appreciation of the life and character of the man whom it commemorates.*"—SCOTTISH GUARDIAN.

"*Mr. Wilson has done his work admirably and evidently con amore, and he completely proves the thesis with which he starts, viz., that in the life of the Saint there is a homeliness and simplicity, and a general absence of the miraculous or the more ascetic type of saintliness.*"—JOHN BULL.

John Wesley's Place in Church History
determined, with the aid of Facts and Documents unknown to, or unnoticed by, his Biographers. With a New and Authentic Portrait. By R. DENNY URLIN, of the Middle Temple, Barrister-at-Law, &c. Small 8vo. 5s. 6d.

A History of the Holy Eastern Church.
The Patriarchate of Antioch. By the Rev. JOHN MASON NEALE, D.D., late Warden of Sackville College, East Grinsted. A Posthumous Fragment. Together with Memoirs of the Patriarchs of Antioch, by Constantius, Patriarch of Constantinople; translated from the Greek, and three Appendices. Edited, with an Introduction, by the Rev. GEORGE WILLIAMS, B.D., Vicar of Ringwood, late Fellow of King's College, Cambridge. 8vo. 10s. 6d.

and at Oxford and Cambridge

History of the Church under the Roman Empire,

A.D. 30-476. By the Rev. A. D. CRAKE, B.A., Chaplain of All Saints' School, Bloxham. Crown 8vo. 7s. 6d.

"*A compendious history of the Christian Church under the Roman Empire will be hailed with pleasure by all readers of ecclesiastical lore. . . . The author is quite free from the spirit of controversialism; wherever he refers to a prevalent practice of ancient times he gives his authority. In his statement of facts or opinions he is always accurate and concise, and his manual is doubtless destined to a lengthened period of popularity.*"—MORNING POST.

"*It is very well done. It gives a very comprehensive view of the progress of events, ecclesiastical and political, at the great centres of civilisation during the first five centuries of Christianity.*"—DAILY NEWS.

"*In his well-planned and carefully written volume of 500 pages Mr. Crake has supplied a well-known and long-felt want. Relying on all the highest and best authorities for his main facts and conclusions, and wisely making use of all modern research, Mr. Crake has spared neither time nor labour to make his work accurate, trustworthy, and intelligent.*"—STANDARD.

"*Really interesting, well suited to the needs of those for whom it was prepared, and its Church tone is unexceptionable.*"—CHURCH TIMES.

"*As a volume for students and the higher forms of our public schools it is admirably adapted.*"—CHURCH HERALD.

"*We cordially recommend it for schools for the young.*"—ENGLISH CHURCHMAN.

"*Mr. Crake gives us in a clear and concise form a narrative of the Church history during the period with which it is most important that the young should first be made acquainted. The different events appear to be described with a judicious regard to their relative importance, and the manual may be safely recommended.*"—JOHN BULL.

"*The facts are well marshalled, the literary style of the book is simple and good; while the principles enunciated throughout render it a volume which may be safely put into the hands of students. For the higher forms of grammar-schools it is exactly the book required. Never ponderous, and frequently very attractive and interesting, it is at once readable and edifying, and fills efficiently a vacant place in elementary historical literature. Furthermore its type is clear and bold, and it is well broken up into paragraphs.*"—UNION REVIEW.

"*It retells an oft-told tale in a singularly fresh and perspicuous style, rendering the book neither above the comprehension of an intelligent boy or girl of fourteen or upwards, nor beneath the attention of an educated man. We can imagine no better book as an addition to a parochial library, as a prize, or as a reading book in the upper forms of middle-class schools.*"—SCOTTISH GUARDIAN.

Church Memorials and Characteristics;

being a Church History of the six First Centuries. By the late WILLIAM ROBERTS, Esq., M.A., F.R.S. Edited by his Son, ARTHUR ROBERTS, M.A., Rector of Woodrising, Norfolk. 8vo. 7s. 6d.

Waterloo Place, London

A Key to the Knowledge of Church

History (Ancient). Edited by the Rev. JOHN HENRY BLUNT, M.A., F.S.A., Editor of "The Annotated Book of Common Prayer," &c. &c. Small 8vo. 2s. 6d. Also a Cheap Edition, 1s. 6d.

Forming a Volume of "Keys to Christian Knowledge."

"*It offers a short and condensed account of the origin, growth, and condition of the Church in all parts of the world, from A.D. 1 down to the end of the fifteenth century. Mr. Blunt's first object has been conciseness, and this has been admirably carried out, and to students of Church history this feature will readily recommend itself. As an elementary work 'A Key' will be specially valuable, inasmuch as it points out certain definite lines of thought, by which those who enjoy the opportunity may be guided in reading the statements of more elaborate histories. At the same time it is but fair to Mr. Blunt to remark that, for general readers, the little volume contains everything that could be consistently expected in a volume of its character. There are many notes, theological, scriptural, and historical, and the 'get up' of the book is specially commendable. As a text-book for the higher forms of schools the work will be acceptable to numerous teachers.*"—PUBLIC OPINION.

"*It contains some concise notes on Church History, compressed into a small compass, and we think it is likely to be useful as a book of reference.*"—JOHN BULL.

"*A very terse and reliable collection of the main facts and incidents connected with Church History.*"—ROCK.

A Key to the Knowledge of Church

History (Modern). Edited by the Rev. JOHN HENRY BLUNT, M.A., F.S.A., Editor of "The Annotated Book of Common Prayer," &c. &c. Small 8vo. 2s. 6d. Also a Cheap Edition, 1s. 6d.

Forming a Volume of "Keys to Christian Knowledge."

The Reformation of the Church of

England; its History, Principles, and Results. A.D. 1514-1547. By the Rev. JOHN HENRY BLUNT, M.A., F.S.A., Editor of "The Annotated Book of Common Prayer," &c. &c. Third Edition. 8vo. 16s.

Perranzabuloe, the Lost Church Found;

or, The Church of England not a New Church, but Ancient, Apostolical, and Independent, and a Protesting Church Nine Hundred Years before the Reformation. By the Rev. C. T. COLLINS TRELAWNY, M.A., late Rector of Timsbury, Somerset. New Edition. Crown 8vo. 3s. 6d.

---

and at Oxford and Cambridge

History of the English Institutions.
By PHILIP V. SMITH, M.A., Barrister-at-Law, Fellow of King's College, Cambridge. Crown 8vo. 3s. 6d.

Forming a Volume of "Historical Handbooks," edited by OSCAR BROWNING, M.A., Fellow of King's College, Cambridge.
[See RIVINGTON'S SCHOOL CATALOGUE.]

History of French Literature, adapted
from the French of M. Demogeot. By C. BRIDGE. Crown 8vo. 3s. 6d.

Forming a Volume of "Historical Handbooks," edited by OSCAR BROWNING, M.A., Fellow of King's College, Cambridge.
[See RIVINGTON'S SCHOOL CATALOGUE.]

The Roman Empire. From the Death
of Theodosius the Great to the Coronation of Charles the Great, A.D. 395 to A.D. 800. By A. M. CURTEIS, M.A., Assistant-Master at Sherborne School, late Fellow of Trinity College, Oxford. With Maps. Crown 8vo. 3s. 6d.

Forming a Volume of "Historical Handbooks," edited by OSCAR BROWNING, M.A., Fellow of King's College, Cambridge.
[See RIVINGTON'S SCHOOL CATALOGUE.]

History of Modern English Law. By
Sir ROLAND KNYVET WILSON, Bart., M.A., Barrister-at-Law, late Fellow of King's College, Cambridge. Crown 8vo. 3s. 6d.

Forming a Volume of "Historical Handbooks," edited by OSCAR BROWNING, M.A., Fellow of King's College, Cambridge.
[See RIVINGTON'S SCHOOL CATALOGUE.]

The Reign of Lewis XI. By P. F. Willert,
M.A., Fellow of Exeter College, Oxford. With Map. Crown 8vo. 3s. 6d.

Forming a Volume of "Historical Handbooks," edited by OSCAR BROWNING, M.A., Fellow of King's College, Cambridge.
[See RIVINGTON'S SCHOOL CATALOGUE.]

English History in the Fourteenth

Century. By CHARLES H. PEARSON, late Fellow of Oriel College, Oxford. Crown 8vo. 3s. 6d.

Forming a Volume of "Historical Handbooks," edited by OSCAR BROWNING, M.A., Fellow of King's College, Cambridge.

[See RIVINGTON'S SCHOOL CATALOGUE.]

Life of Robert Gray, Bishop of Cape

Town and Metropolitan of the Province of South Africa. Edited by his Son, the Rev. CHARLES GRAY, M.A., Vicar of Helmsley, York. With Portrait and Map. 2 Vols. 8vo. 32s.

"*We have noticed this work at great length; but not, we venture to think, at a length that exceeds its merits and its interest. It is, in fact, more than a biography; it is a valuable addition to the history of the nineteenth century. Mr. Keble more than once described Bishop Gray's struggles as 'like a bit out of the fourth century.'*"—GUARDIAN.

"*The two volumes contain nearly twelve hundred pages; but the life which is here written is that of no ordinary man, and we do not know that we could wish a page omitted. The compiler has judiciously kept himself in the background. His own opinions are rarely given; his work has been limited to arranging the events of a stirring and devoted life,*

and throughout, by a felicitous selection of letters, we have the Bishop himself before us. His actions are related almost without comment, while the reasons for his actions are given in his own words."—SATURDAY REVIEW.

"*There is a fascination in these volumes which few Churchmen will be able to resist.*"—JOHN BULL.

"*We welcome it as a worthy tribute to the memory of one who possessed the true apostolic spirit, was a faithful son of the Church, and a distinguished ornament of the Episcopate.*"—STANDARD.

"*Not only interesting as the record of a good man's life, but extremely valuable as materials for Church history.*"—CHURCH TIMES.

Life, Journals, and Letters of Henry

ALFORD, D.D., late Dean of Canterbury. Edited by his WIDOW. With Portrait and Illustrations. New Edition. Crown 8vo. 9s.

"*On the whole, Mrs. Alford has acquitted herself admirably. . . . Those who desire thoroughly to appreciate a valuable life and a beautiful character we refer to the volume itself.*"—TIMES.

"*It was a beautiful life he lived; and touchingly beautiful in its unadorned simplicity is the record given to us in this volume by his life-long companion, who from his early boyhood*

had shared his every thought."—GUARDIAN.

"*We have here the simple and loving record of a happy, industrious, and holy life. . . . To have known and valued Henry Alford will long be a source of heartfelt satisfaction to many others, besides those immediate friends whose names are linked with his in this beautiful and touching Life by his widow.*"—SATURDAY REVIEW.

---

and at 𝔒𝔵𝔣𝔬𝔯𝔡 and 𝔈𝔞𝔪𝔟𝔯𝔦𝔡𝔤𝔢

The Life of Alexander Lycurgus,
Archbishop of the Cyclades. By F. M. F. SKENE. With an Introduction by the BISHOP OF LINCOLN. Crown 8vo. 3s. 6d.; or in paper cover, 3s.

Historical Narratives. From the Russian.
By H. C. ROMANOFF, Author of "Sketches of the Rites and Customs of the Greco-Russian Church," &c. Crown 8vo. 6s.

Sketches of the Rites and Customs of
the Greco-Russian Church. By H. C. ROMANOFF. With an Introductory Notice by the Author of "The Heir of Redclyffe." Second Edition. Crown 8vo. 7s. 6d.

"*The volume before us is anything but a formal liturgical treatise. It might be more valuable to a few scholars if it were, but it would certainly fail to obtain perusal at the hands of the great majority of those whom the writer, not unreasonably, hopes to attract by the narrative style she has adopted. What she has set before us is a series of brief outlines, which, by their simple effort to clothe the information given us in a living garb, reminds us of a once-popular child's book which we remember a generation ago, called 'Sketches of Human Manners.'*"—CHURCH TIMES.

"*The twofold object of this work is 'to present the English with correct descriptions of the ceremonies of the Greco-Russian Church, and at the same time with pictures of domestic life in Russian homes, especially those of the clergy and the middle class of nobles;' and, beyond question, the author's labour has been so far successful that, whilst her Church scenes may be commended as a series of most dramatic and picturesque tableaux, her social sketches enable us to look at certain points beneath the surface of Russian life, and materially enlarge our knowledge of a country concerning which we have still a very great deal to learn.*"—ATHENÆUM.

Fables respecting the Popes of the
Middle Ages. A Contribution to Ecclesiastical History. By JOHN J. IGN. VON DÖLLINGER, D.D., D.C.L. Translated by the Rev. ALFRED PLUMMER, M.A., Master of University College, Durham, late Fellow of Trinity College, Oxford. 8vo. 14s.

Curious Myths of the Middle Ages.
By S. BARING-GOULD, M.A., Author of "Origin and Development of Religious Belief," &c. With Illustrations. New Edition. Crown 8vo. 6s.

Waterloo Place, London

A History of England. By the Rev.
J. FRANCK BRIGHT, M.A., Fellow of University College, and Historical Lecturer in Balliol, New, and University Colleges, Oxford; late Master of the Modern School in Marlborough College. With Numerous Maps and Plans. Crown 8vo.

PERIOD I.—FEUDAL MONARCHY. The Departure of the Romans, to Richard III. A.D. 449-1485. 4s. 6d.

PERIOD II.—PERSONAL MONARCHY : Henry VII. to James II. A.D. 1485-1688. 5s.

PERIOD III.—CONSTITUTIONAL MONARCHY. William and Mary, to the present time. A.D. 1689-1837. 7s. 6d.

Historical Biographies. Edited by the
Rev. M. CREIGHTON, M.A., late Fellow of Merton College, Oxford. With Maps. Small 8vo.

SIMON DE MONTFORT. 2s. 6d.

THE BLACK PRINCE. 2s. 6d.

SIR WALTER RALEGH. 3s.

A History of England for Children.
By GEORGE DAVYS, D.D., formerly Bishop of Peterborough. New Edition. 18mo. 1s. 6d.

The Annual Register: a Review of Public
Events at Home and Abroad, for the Years 1863 to 1877. New Series. 8vo. 18s. each.

---

and at Oxford and Cambridge

10. Miscellaneous.

The Authorship of the "De Imitatione Christi." With many interesting particulars about the Book. By SAMUEL KETTLEWELL, M.A., late Vicar of St. Mark's, Leeds. Containing Photographic Engravings of the "De Imitatione" written by Thomas à Kempis, 1441, and of two other MSS. 8vo. 14s.

Yesterday, To-Day, and for Ever: A Poem in Twelve Books. By E. H. BICKERSTETH, M.A., Vicar of Christ Church, Hampstead. Eleventh Edition. Small 8vo. 3s. 6d.

A Presentation Edition with red borders. Small 4to. 10s. 6d.

"*We should have noticed among its kind a very magnificent presentation edition of 'Yesterday, To-day, and For Ever,' by the Rev. E. H. Bickersteth. This blank-verse poem, in twelve books, has made its way into the religious world of England and America without much help from the critics. It is now made splendid for its admirers by morocco binding, broad margins, red lines, and beautiful photographs.*"—TIMES.

"*The most simple, the richest, and the most perfect sacred poem which recent days have produced.*"—MORNING ADVERTISER.

"*A poem worth reading, worthy of attentive study; full of noble thoughts, beautiful diction, and high imagination.*"—STANDARD.

"*In these light miscellany days there is a spiritual refreshment in the spectacle of a man girding up the loins of his mind to the task of producing a genuine epic. And it is true poetry. There is a definiteness, a crispness about it, which in these moist, viewy, hazy days is no less invigorating than novel.*"—EDINBURGH DAILY REVIEW.

"*Mr. Bickersteth writes like a man who cultivates at once reverence and earnestness of thought.*"—GUARDIAN.

The Two Brothers, and other Poems. By EDWARD HENRY BICKERSTETH, M.A., Vicar of Christ Church, Hampstead. Second Edition. Small 8vo. 6s.

Waterloo Place, London

The Knight of Intercession, and other
Poems. By the Rev. S. J. STONE, M.A., Pembroke College, Oxford. Fourth Edition. Crown 8vo. 6s.

A Year's Botany. Adapted to Home
Reading. By FRANCES ANNA KITCHENER. Illustrated by the Author. Crown 8vo. 5s.

CONTENTS.

General Description of Flowers—Flowers with Simple Pistils—Flowers with Compound Pistils—Flowers with Apocarpous Fruits—Flowers with Syncarpous Fruits—Stamens and Morphology of Branches—Fertilization—Seeds—Early Growth and Food of Plants—Wood, Stems, and Roots—Leaves—Classification—Umbellates, Composites, Spurges, and Pines—Some Monocotyledonous Families—Orchids—Appendix of Technical Terms—Index.

[See RIVINGTON'S SCHOOL CATALOGUE.]

An Easy Introduction to Chemistry.
For the Use of Schools. Edited by the Rev. ARTHUR RIGG, M.A., late Principal of the College, Chester; and WALTER T. GOOLDEN, B.A., late Science Scholar of Merton College, Oxford. New Edition, considerably altered and revised. With Illustrations. Crown 8vo. 2s. 6d.

[See RIVINGTON'S SCHOOL CATALOGUE.]

A Shadow of Dante. Being an Essay
towards studying Himself, his World, and his Pilgrimage. By MARIA FRANCESCA ROSSETTI. With Illustrations. Second Edition. Crown 8vo. 10s. 6d.

"*We find the volume furnished with useful diagrams of the Dantesque universe, of Hell, Purgatory, and the 'Rose of the Blessed,' and adorned with a beautiful group of the likenesses of the poet, and with symbolic figures (on the binding) in which the taste and execution of Mr. D. G. Rossetti will be recognised. The exposition appears to us remarkably well arranged and digested; the author's appreciation of Dante's religious sentiments and opinions is peculiarly hearty, and her style refreshingly independent and original.*"—PALL MALL GAZETTE.

"*The result has been a book which is not only delightful in itself to read, but is admirably adapted as an encouragement to those students who wish to obtain a preliminary survey of the land before they attempt to follow Dante through his long and arduous pilgrimage. Of all poets Dante stands most in need of such assistance as this book offers.*"—SATURDAY REVIEW.

---

and at Oxford and Cambridge

Hymns and other Verses. By WILLIAM BRIGHT, D.D., Canon of Christ Church, and Regius Professor of Ecclesiastical History in the University of Oxford. Second Edition. Small 8vo. 5s..

Parish Musings; or, Devotional Poems.
By JOHN S. B. MONSELL, LL.D., late Vicar of S. Nicholas, Guildford, and Rural Dean. New Edition. Small 8vo. 5s.
Also a Cheap Edition. Cloth limp, 1s. 6d.; or in paper cover, 1s.

Miscellaneous Poems. By HENRY FRANCIS LYTE, M.A. New Edition. Small 8vo. 5s.

The Elegies of Propertius. Translated into English Verse, by CHARLES ROBERT MOORE, M.A. Small 8vo. 2s. 6d.

The Iliad of Homer. Translated by J. G. CORDERY, late of Balliol College, Oxford, and now of H.M. Bengal Civil Service. Two Vols. 8vo. 16s.

English Nursery Rhymes. Translated into French. By JOHN ROBERTS, M.A., Fellow of Magdalen College, Cambridge. Square crown 8vo. 2s. 6d.

Immanuel: Thoughts for Christmas and other Seasons, with other Poems. By A. MIDDLEMORE MORGAN, M.A. Small 8vo. 6s.

A Dictionary of English Philosophical
Terms. By the Rev. FRANCIS GARDEN, M.A., Professor of Theology and Rhetoric at Queen's College, London, and Sub-Dean of Her Majesty's Chapels-Royal. Small 8vo. 4s. 6d.

At Home and Abroad; or, First Lessons
in Geography. By J. K. LAUGHTON, M.A., F.R.A.S., F.R.G.S., Mathematical Instructor and Lecturer in Meteorology at the Royal Naval College. Crown 8vo. 3s. 6d.

Mazzaroth; or, the Constellations. By
FRANCES ROLLESTON. Royal 8vo. 12s.

Darwinism tested by Language. By
FREDERIC BATEMAN, M.D., F.R.C.P., &c. With a Preface by EDWARD MEYRICK GOULBURN, D.D., Dean of Norwich. Crown 8vo. 6s.

Physical Facts and Scriptural Record;
or, Eighteen Propositions for Geologists. By the Rev. W. B. GALLOWAY, M.A., Vicar of St. Mark's, Regent's Park, Author of "Egypt's Record of Time," &c. 8vo. 10s. 6d.

Rivington's Devotional Series.

IN ELEGANT BINDINGS, SUITABLE FOR PRESENTS.

"TO many persons there is something repulsive in a devotional volume unbound, and Messrs. Rivington have now turned their attention to the binding of their Devotional Library in forms that, like the books themselves, are neat, handsome, good, and attractive."—*The Bookseller.*

The Christian Year.

16MO. ELEGANTLY PRINTED WITH RED BORDERS.

	£	s.	d.
CALF or MOROCCO *limp, blind tooled* .	0	5	0
THE SAME, ILLUSTRATED WITH STEEL ENGRAVINGS .	0	6	6
THE SAME, ILLUSTRATED WITH A CHOICE SELECTION OF PHOTOGRAPHS .	0	9	0
MOROCCO *superior* .	0	6	6
RUSSIA *limp, gilt cross* .	0	8	6
RUSSIA *limp, gilt lines and gilt cross*, ILLUSTRATED WITH A CHOICE SELECTION OF PHOTOGRAPHS .	0	12	6
TURKEY MOROCCO, *limp circuit* .	0	7	6
RUSSIA, *limp circuit* .	0	9	0

The Christian Year.

CHEAP EDITION, WITHOUT THE RED BORDERS.

	£	s.	d.
FRENCH ROAN, *red inlaid or gilt outline cross* .	0	1	6
THE SAME, ILLUSTRATED WITH STEEL ENGRAVINGS .	0	2	6
FRENCH MOROCCO, *gilt extra* .	0	2	0

The Imitation of Christ is also kept in the above-mentioned styles at the same prices.

The other Volumes of "The Devotional Series," viz.:—

Taylor's Holy Living | Wilson's Lord's Supper
Taylor's Holy Dying | De Sales' Devout Life
Herbert's English Poems and Proverbs

Can be had in a variety of elegant bindings.

Waterloo Place, London

Index.

	PAGE
ADAMS (WILLIAM), *Sacred Allegories*	72
———— *Warnings of the Holy Week*	54
A KEMPIS, *Imitation of Christ*	17, 27, 88
ALFORD (Dean), *Life, Journal, and Letters*	81
———— *Greek Testament*	7
———— *New Testament for English Readers*	7
ANDREWES (Bishop), *Manual for the Sick*	24
Angels, The Holy	40
Annotated Book of Common Prayer	2
———— *Compendious Edition*	1
Annual Register	83
Ascetic Library: edited by ORBY SHIPLEY:—	
Mysteries of Mount Calvary	29
Counsels on Holiness of Life	29
Preparation for Death	29
Examination of Conscience	29
Athanasian Creed, Recent Theories considered, by G. D. W. OMMANNEY	
———— "*Damnatory Clauses of*," by MALCOLM MACCOLL	5
———— *Athanasian Origin of*, by J. S. BREWER	5
AVANCINI, *Vita et Doctrina Jesu Christi*	30
BAKER'S (W.), *Manual of Devotion for Schoolboys*	31
BALL (T.) *On the XXXIX Articles*	39
Bampton Lectures for 1865, by J. B. MOZLEY	42
———— 1866, by H. P. LIDDON	47
———— 1867, by E. GARBETT	45
———— 1872, by J. R. T. EATON	62
———— 1874, by STANLEY LEATHES	61
BARING-GOULD (S.), *Origin and Development of Religious Belief*	43
———— *Curious Myths of the Middle Ages*	82
BARRETT (W. A.), *Flowers and Festivals*	34
———— *Chorister's Guide*	34
BARROW (G. S.), *The Mystery of Christ*	15
BATEMAN (FREDERIC), *Darwinism tested by Language*	87
BEAMONT (W. J.), and CAMPION (W. M.), *Prayer Book Interleaved*	3
BEAVEN (JAMES), *Help to Catechising*	68
BICKERSTETH (Dean), *Catechetical Exercises on the Apostles' Creed*	68
———— *Questions Illustrating the XXXIX Articles*	68
———— (E. H.), *Yesterday, To-day, and for Ever*	84
———— *The Two Brothers*	84

	PAGE
BISHOP (C. K. K.), *Notes on Church Organs*	34
BLUNT (J. H.), *Annotated Prayer Book*	2
——— *Compendious Edition*	1
——— *Dictionary of Theology*	38
——— *Sects, Heresies, &c.*	39
——— *Directorium Pastorale*	33
——— *Doctrine of the Church of England*	39
——— *Sacraments and Sacramental Ordinances*	4
——— *Household Theology*	65
——— *Key to Church Catechism*	65
——— *History (Ancient)*	79
——— *(Modern)*	79
——— *Holy Bible*	15
——— *Prayer Book*	4
——— *Reformation of the Church of England*	79
——— and PHILLIMORE (W. G. F.), *Book of Church Law*	32
BODY (GEORGE), *Life of Justification*	48
——— *Temptation*	48
Bossuet and his Contemporaries	73
BREWER (J. S.), *Athanasian Origin of the Athanasian Creed*	5
BRIDGE (C.), *History of French Literature*	80
BRIGHT (J. FRANCK), *English History*	83
BRIGHT (WILLIAM), *Faith and Life*	30
——— *Hymns and other Verses*	86
——— and MEDD (P. G.), *Liber Precum Publicarum*	2
BROWNING (OSCAR), *Historical Handbooks. See under "Historical."*	
BRUTON (E. G.), *Ecclesiastical Dilapidations Act*	35
CAMPION (W. M.), and BEAMONT (W. J.), *Prayer Book Interleaved*	3
CARR (ARTHUR), *Notes on S. Luke's Gospel*	8
Catechism on Gospel History, by S. KETTLEWELL	68
CHILCOT (WILLIAM), *Evil Thoughts*	28
Christian Biographies	73—76
——— *Painter of the Nineteenth Century*	74
——— *Year*	17, 23, 88
Church Builder	36
——— *Law, Book of*, by J. H. BLUNT and W. G. F. PHILLIMORE	32
——— *Organs*, by C. K. K. BISHOP	34
——— by F. H. SUTTON	34
CHURTON (W. R.), *Defence of the English Ordinal*	41
Clergy Charities, List of	36
Companion to the Old Testament	10
——— *Lord's Supper*, by the Plain Man's Friend	31
COMPTON (BERDMORE), *The Catholic Sacrifice*	55
——— *The Armoury of Prayer*	25
Consoling Thoughts in Sickness	24
CORDERY (J. G.), *Translation of Homer's Iliad*	86
COSIN (Bishop), *Religion of the Realm of England*	41
CRAKE (A. D.), *First Chronicle of Æscendune*	71
——— *Second* ———	71
——— *History of the Church under the Roman Empire*	78
CRUDEN (ALEXANDER), *Concordance to the Bible*	16
CURTEIS (A. M.), *History of the Roman Empire, A.D. 395-800*	80
DALE (T. P.), *Commentary on Ecclesiastes*	9

Waterloo Place, London

Index

	PAGE
Dante, *A Shadow of*, by M. F. ROSSETTI	85
DAVYS (Bishop), *History of England*	83
DENTON (W.), *Commentary on the Lord's Prayer*	5
Dictionary of Theology, edited by J. H. BLUNT	38
——— *Sects, Heresies, &c.* edited by J. H. BLUNT	39
DÖLLINGER (J. J. I. von), *Prophecies and the Prophetic Spirit*	40
——— *on Reunion*	40
——— *Fables respecting the Popes*	82
Dominican Artist, (A)	74
DUNCOMBE (Dean), *Family Devotions*	21
EATON (J. R. T.), *The Permanence of Christianity*	62
Ecclesiastes, Commentary on, by T. P. DALE	9
——— *for English Readers*, by W. H. B. PROBY	14
ELLISON (H. J.), *Doctrine of the Cross*	62
——— *Way of Holiness in Married Life*	62
EVANS (R. W.), *The Bishopric of Souls*	33
Fénelon, A Biographical Sketch	73
——— *Spiritual Letters to Men*	45
——— *Women*	45
FIELD (WALTER), *Stones of the Temple*	35
FLETCHER (JOSEPHINE), *Prayers and Meditations for Holy Communion*	20
FOSBERY (T. V.), *Hymns and Poems for the Sick and Suffering*	23
——— *Voices of Comfort*	23
From Morning to Evening	24
GALLOWAY (W. B.), *Physical Facts and Scriptural Record*	87
GARBETT (EDWARD), *Dogmatic Faith*	40
GARDEN (F.), *Dictionary of English Philosophical Terms*	87
GARLAND (G. V.), *Genesis, with Notes*	14
GEDGE (J. W.), *Young Churchman's Companion to the Prayer Book*	67
GOULBURN (Dean), *Acts of the Deacons*	14
——— *The Child Samuel*	18
——— *Commentary on the Communion Office*	4
——— *Farewell Counsels of a Pastor*	54
——— *Family Prayers*	21
——— *Gospel of the Childhood*	18
——— *Holy Catholic Church*	37
——— *Manual of Confirmation*	69
——— *Occasional Sermons*	54
——— *Pursuit of Holiness*	18
——— *Short Devotional Forms*	18
——— *The Idle Word*	68
——— *Thoughts on Personal Religion*	18
Gray, *Life of Bishop*	81
Gratry (Père), *Last Days of*, by PÈRE PERRAUD	75
——— *Life of Henri Perreyve*	76
Guide to Heaven, edited by T. T. CARTER	19
HADDAN (A. W.), *Apostolical Succession*	41
HALL (W. J.), *Psalms and Hymns*	6
——— *New Mitre Hymnal*	6
——— *Selection of Psalms and Hymns*	6
Hamilton (*Walter Kerr*), *a Sketch*, by H. P. LIDDON	76

𝔞𝔫𝔡 𝔞𝔱 𝔒𝔵𝔣𝔬𝔯𝔡 𝔞𝔫𝔡 𝔏𝔞𝔪𝔟𝔯𝔦𝔡𝔤𝔢

	PAGE
Help and Comfort for the Sick Poor	24
HERBERT (GEORGE), *Poems and Proverbs*	26, 88
HEYGATE (W. E.), *Allegories and Tales*	70
——— *The Good Shepherd*	31
Hidden Life of the Soul	17, 28
Historical Biographies, edited by M. CREIGHTON :—	
Simon de Montfort	83
The Black Prince	83
Sir Walter Ralegh	83
Historical Handbooks, edited by OSCAR BROWNING :—	
History of the English Institutions, by P. V. SMITH	80
——— *French Literature*, by C. BRIDGE	80
——— *the Roman Empire*, by A. M. CURTEIS	80
——— *Modern English Law*, by Sir R. K. WILSON	80
——— *The Reign of Lewis XI.*, by P. F. WILLERT	80
——— *England in the XIVth Century*, by C. H. PEARSON	81
HODGSON (CHR.), *Instructions for the Clergy, &c.*	33
HOLMES (R. R.), *Illuminated Edition of the Prayer Book*	3
Homer's Iliad, translated by J. G. CORDERY	86
HOOK (Dean), *Book of Family Prayer*	21
Hour of Prayer, with Preface by W. E. SCUDAMORE	21
HUTCHINGS (W. H.), *Mystery of the Temptation*	60
Hymnal, New Mitre, by W. J. HALL	6
Hymns and Poems for the Sick and Suffering, edited by T. V. FOSBERY	23
JACKSON (Bishop), *The Christian Character*	59
JAMES (Canon), *Christian Watchfulness*	30
——— *Comment upon the Collects*	5
——— *Spiritual Life*	30
JANUS, *The Pope and the Council*	46
JELF (Canon), *On the XXXIX Articles*	46
JONES (HARRY), *Priest and Parish*	36
JOYCE (J. W.), *The Civil Power in its Relations to the Church*	41
KAY (WILLIAM), *On the Psalms*	9
KEBLE (JOHN), *The Christian Year*	17, 23, 88
Keble College Sermons	54
KENNAWAY (C. E.), *Consolatio, or Comfort for the Afflicted*	25
KETTLEWELL (S.), *The Authorship of the " De Imitatione Christi"*	84
——— *A Catechism on Gospel History*	68
Keys to Christian Knowledge :—	
Key to the Four Gospels, by J. P. NORRIS	11
——— *Acts*, by J. P. NORRIS	11
——— *Holy Bible*, by J. H. BLUNT	15
——— *Prayer Book*, by J. H. BLUNT	4
——— *Church Catechism*, by J. H. BLUNT	65
——— *History (Ancient)*, edited by J. H. BLUNT	79
——— *(Modern)*, edited by J. H. BLUNT	79
KITCHENER (F. A.), *A Year's Botany*	85
LAUGHTON (J. K.), *At Home and Abroad*	87
LEAR (H. L. S.), *Christian Biographies*	73—76
LEATHES (STANLEY), *The Religion of the Christ*	61
——— *Witness of the Old Testament to Christ*	61
——— *St. Paul to Christ*	61
——— *St. John to Christ*	61

Index

	PAGE
LEE (WILLIAM), *Inspiration of Holy Scripture*	15
LEFROY (W.), *Pleadings for Christ*	62
Liber Precum Publicarum, by W. BRIGHT and P. G. MEDD	2
Library of Spiritual Works for English Catholics:—	
À KEMPIS, *Of the Imitation of Christ*	17
The Christian Year	17
SCUPOLI, *The Spiritual Combat*	17
S. FRANCIS DE SALES, *Devout Life*	17
———————*Spiritual Letters*	17
The Hidden Life of the Soul	17
LIDDON (H. P.), *Divinity of our Lord*	47
——————— *Elements of Religion*	47
——————— *University Sermons*	47
——————— *Walter Kerr Hamilton, In Memoriam*	76
——————— *Andrewes' Manual for the Sick*	24
Light of the Conscience	25
Litanies, Metrical and Prose, A Book of,	3
LOUISE DE FRANCE, *Life of*	75
LOWDER (C. F.), *Twenty-One Years in St. George's Mission*	33
Lycurgus, the Life of Alexander	82
LYTE (H. F.), *Miscellaneous Poems*	86
LYTTLETON (Lord), *Private Devotions for School-boys*	23
MACCOLL (M.), "*Damnatory Clauses*" *of the Athanasian Creed*	5
MANT (Bishop), *Ancient Hymns*	29
——————— *Happiness of the Blessed*	42
Manual of Private Devotions	22
Manuals of Religious Instruction, edited by J. P. NORRIS	66
MEDD (P. G.), *Household Prayer*	21
——————— *Parish Sermons*	63
——————— and BRIGHT (WILLIAM), *Liber Precum Publicarum*	2
——————— WALTON (H. B.), *Common Prayer, and Ordinal of* 1549	2
Meditations on the Life of our Lord, edited by T. T. CARTER	19
MELVILL (Canon), *Sermons*	56
——————— *Selections from Latter Sermons*	58
——————— *Sermons on Less Prominent Facts*	57
——————— *Lothbury Lectures*	59
MERCIER (A.), *Our Mother Church*	44
MEREWEATHER (J. D.), *Semele; or, the Spirit of Beauty*	72
MOBERLY (Bishop), *Plain Sermons*	55
——————— *Great Forty Days*	55
——————— *Sermons at Winchester College*	55
MOLYNEUX (R. E.), *The Reconciliation of Reason and Faith*	59
MONSELL (J. S. B.), *Parish Musings*	86
MOORE (C. R.), *The Elegies of Propertius*	86
——— (DANIEL), *Aids to Prayer*	21
——————— *Sermons on Special Occasions*	60
——————— *The Age and the Gospel*	60
MORGAN (A. M.), *Immanuel and other Poems*	86
MORRELL (M. A.), *Our Work for Christ*	24
MOZLEY (J. B.), *Lectures on the Miracles*	42
——————— *University and other Sermons*	53
——————— *Lectures on the Old Testament*	10
NEALE (J. M.), *The Virgin's Lamp*	22

and at 𝕺𝖝𝖋𝖔𝖗𝖉 and 𝕮𝖆𝖒𝖇𝖗𝖎𝖉𝖌𝖊

	PAGE
NEALE (J. M.), *History of the Holy Eastern Church* .	77
NEWMAN (J. H.), *Parochial and Plain Sermons* .	50
————— *Lectures on Justification* .	52
————— *Sermons on Subjects of the Day* .	52
————— *Fifteen University Sermons* .	52
NORRIS (J. P.), *Manuals of Religious Instruction* .	66
————— *Key to the Four Gospels* .	11
————— *Acts of the Apostles* .	11
————— *Rudiments of Theology* .	67
————— *Easy Lessons to Candidates for Confirmation* .	69
OMMANNEY (G. D. W.), *On the Athanasian Creed* .	4
OXENHAM (F. N.), *The Soul in its Probation* .	59
PARNELL (FRANK), *Ars Pastoria* .	33
Path of Holiness, edited by T. T. CARTER .	19
PEARSON (C. H.), *English History in the XIVth Century* .	81
PEPYS (Lady), *Morning Notes of Praise* .	30
————— *Quiet Moments* .	30
PERRAUD (Père), *Last Days of Père Gratry* .	76
Perreyve (Henri), by PÈRE GRATRY .	76
PHILLIMORE (Sir R.), *Ecclesiastical Judgments*, 1867-1875 .	40
————— (W. G. F.), and BLUNT (J. H.), *Book of Church Law* .	32
PHILPOTTS (M. C.), *The Hillford Confirmation* .	72
PIGOU (FRANCIS), *Faith and Practice* .	64
PLUMPTRE (E. P.), *Words of the Son of God* .	21
POLLOCK (J. S.), *Out of the Body* .	43
Prayer Book, American .	3
————— *Annotated*, by J. H. BLUNT .	2
————— *Illuminated*, by R. R. HOLMES .	3
————— *Interleaved*, by W. M. CAMPION and W. J. BEAMONT .	3
————— *Latin*, by W. BRIGHT and P. G. MEDD .	2
————— *of Edward VI., and Ordinal of* 1549 .	2
Prayers and Meditations for Holy Communion, by JOSEPHINE FLETCHER .	20
Prayers for the Sick and Dying .	25
PROBY (W. H. B.), *Ecclesiastes for English Readers* .	14
————— *Ten Canticles* .	14
Psalter, or Psalms of David .	5
PUSEY (E. B.), *Commentary on the Minor Prophets* .	9
————— *Lectures on Daniel the Prophet; with Notes* .	9
QUESNEL, *Devotional Commentary on St. Matthew's Gospel* .	14
QUIRINUS, *Letters from Rome on the Council* .	46
Reformation of the Church of England, by J. H. BLUNT .	79
Revival of Priestly Life in the Seventeenth Century in France .	75
RIDLEY (W. H.), *Bible Readings for Family Prayer* .	16
RIGG (A.) and GOOLDEN (W. T.), *Easy Introduction to Chemistry* .	85
Rivington's Devotional Series :—	
A KEMPIS, *Of the Imitation of Christ* .	25, 88
DE SALES, *Devout Life* .	25, 88
HERBERT (GEORGE), *Poems and Proverbs* .	26, 88
WILSON (Bishop), *On the Lord's Supper* .	26, 88
TAYLOR (JEREMY), *Holy Living* .	27, 88
————— *Dying* .	27, 88
CHILCOT (WILLIAM), *Evil Thoughts* .	28
The Christian Year .	23, 88
ROBERTS (JOHN), *English Nursery Rhymes translated into French* .	86

𝕴𝖆𝖙𝖊𝖗𝖑𝖔𝖔 𝕻𝖑𝖆𝖈𝖊, 𝕷𝖔𝖓𝖉𝖔𝖓

	PAGE
ROBERTS (WILLIAM), *Church Memorials and Characteristics*	78
ROMANOFF (H. C.), *Historical Narratives from the Russian*	82
——— *S. John Chrysostom's Liturgy*	46
——— *Rites and Customs of the Greco-Russian Church*	82
ROLLESTON (FRANCES), *Mazzaroth; or, the Constellations*	87
ROSSETTI (M. F.), *A Shadow of Dante*	85
SALES, S. FRANCIS DE, *Life*	75
——— *Spiritual Letters*	44
——— *Spirit*	28
——— *Devout Life*	17, 27, 88
SCUDAMORE (W. E.), *Notitia Eucharistica*	5
——— *Words to take with us*	20
SCUPOLI (LAURENCE), *Spiritual Combat*	17
Self-Renunciation, with an Introduction by T. T. CARTER	22
SHIPLEY (ORBY), *Ascetic Library*	29
SHUTTLEWORTH (Bishop), *Last Three Sermons preached at Oxford*	64
——— *Not Tradition but Scripture*	64
Sickness, Consoling Thoughts in, edited by HENRY BAILEY	24
——— *its Trials and Blessings*	24
Sick, Andrewes' Manual for the, edited by H. P. LIDDON	24
Sick Poor, Help and Comfort for	24
—— *and Dying, Prayers for*	24
—— *and Suffering, Hymns and Poems for*, edited by T. V. FOSBERY	23
SINCLAIR (Archdeacon), *Thirty-two Years of the English Church 1842-75*	40
SKENE (F. M. F.), *Life of Alexander Lycurgus*	82
SLADE (JAMES), *Twenty-one Prayers for the Sick*	31
SMITH (P. V.), *History of the English Institutions*	80
Soimême; A Story of a Wilful Life	70
Spiritual Guidance, with an Introduction by T. T. CARTER	22
Star of Childhood, edited by T. T. CARTER	19
STRACEY (W. J.), *Short Sermons on the Psalms*	62
STONE (S. J.), *Knight of Intercession*	85
SUTTON (F. H.), *Church Organs*	34
TAYLOR (JEREMY), *Holy Living*	27, 88
——— *Dying*	27, 88
Thirty-Nine Articles, by Canon JELF	46
——— *Questions illustrating*, by Dean BICKERSTETH	68
Treasury of Devotion, edited by T. T. CARTER	19
TRELAWNY (C. T. C), *Perranzabuloe, The Lost Church Found*	79
URLIN (R. DENNY), *John Wesley's Place in Church History*	77
VINCENT DE PAUL, *Life of S.*, edited by R. F. WILSON	77
Voices of Comfort, edited by T. V. FOSBERY	23
WALTON (H. B.), and MEDD (P. G.), *Common Prayer, and Ordinal of 1549*	2
Way of Life, edited by T. T. CARTER	19
WEBSTER (WILLIAM), *Syntax and Synonyms of the Greek Testament*	15
Wesley's Place in Church History, by R. DENNY URLIN	77
WILLERT (P. F.), *Reign of Lewis XI.*	80
WILLIAMS (ISAAC), *Devotional Commentary on the Gospel Narrative:—*	
Study of the Holy Gospels	12
Harmony of the Four Evangelists	12
Our Lord's Nativity	12

	PAGE
Williams' Devotional Commentary on the Gospel Narrative (continued):—	
Our Lord's Ministry (2nd Year)	12
———————— *(3rd Year)*	12
The Holy Week	12
Our Lord's Passion	12
——————— *Resurrection*	12
WILLIAMS (ISAAC), *Apocalypse*	13
———————————— *Beginning of the Book of Genesis*	14
———————————— *Characters of the Old Testament*	13
———————————— *Female Characters of Holy Scripture*	13
———————————— *Sermons on the Epistles and Gospels*	49
WILSON (Bishop), *On the Lord's Supper*	26, 88
———— (Sir R. K.), *Modern English Law*	80
———— (R. F.), *Life of S. Vincent de Paul*	77
WORDSWORTH (Bp. CHARLES), *Catechesis*	68
———————— (Bp. CHR.), *Commentary on the Holy Bible*	8
———————————————————— *Greek Testament*	8
———————————— *On the Inspiration of the Bible*	15
Words of the Son of God, by E. PLUMPTRE	21

London, Oxford, and Cambridge

www.ingramcontent.com/pod-product-compliance
Lightning Source LLC
Chambersburg PA
CBHW021203230426
43667CB00006B/536